THE MIRROR OF TIME

Recent Titles in
Contributions to the Study of Aging

THE MIRROR
OF
TIME

IMAGES OF AGING AND DYING

Joan M. Boyle and James E. Morriss

Foreword by Robert Kastenbaum

Contributions to the Study of Aging, Number 7

Greenwood Press
New York • Westport, Connecticut • London

Library of Congress Cataloging-in-Publication Data

Boyle, Joan M.
  The mirror of time.

  (Contributions to the study of aging, ISSN 0732-085X ;
no. 7)
  Bibliography: p.
  Includes index.
  1. Old age. 2. Death. I. Morriss, James E.
II. Title. III. Series.
HQ1061.B678 1987   305.2'6   86-33631
ISBN 0-313-25597-0 (lib. bdg. : alk. paper)

British Library Cataloguing in Publication Data is available.

Library of Congress Catalog Card Number: 86-33631
ISBN: 0-313-25597-0
ISSN: 0732-085X

First published in 1987

Greenwood Press, Inc.
88 Post Road West, Westport, Connecticut 06881

Printed in the United States of America

The paper used in this book complies with the
Permanent Paper Standard issued by the National
Information Standards Organization (Z39.48-1984).

10 9 8 7 6 5 4 3 2 1

To Didi

Dr. Parimal Das

With love and gratitude for
many years of wisdom, guidance,
and example

CONTENTS

FOREWORD

Why look into the mirror? Why court doubt and distress? A distinguished developmental psychologist in his seventh decade once told me politely but firmly, "I *am* aging! I *am* dying! Why should I have to think about it, too?" A fair question, perhaps you will agree. The answer may depend upon how we conceptualize the act of reflection. In one tradition, a positive, active, thriving person has neither the time nor inclination for reflection. This position is represented today by the so-called activity theory of aging. In its most naive form, this view assumes that keeping busy is the key to successful aging. The contrasting tradition finds value in the act of reflection *per se*. Socrates might be claimed as forefather of the belief that we live a truly human life only if it is an *examined* life. This approach is now represented in gerontology through such concepts as the life review, and the recent emphasis on reminiscence as a means of adaptive coping.

Tyranny is possible with both approaches. Relentless programs have been attempted to remotivate older people and distract them from considering the whys of existence. Keep busy, and don't think too much; play cards, or paint the fence. Advocates of a reflective approach have become increasingly aggressive in recent years. The medieval fantasy of angels and devils competing for the dying person's soul has been revived to some extent by expectations that the prospect of death should stimulate reflection and either acceptance or some other currently fashionable outcome.

Fortunately, a more sagacious spirit has informed *Mirror of Time: Images of Aging and Dying*. We are not obligated to stare into that mirror and confess to our own personal flaws, fears, and follies. Instead we are invited to explore the meanings of time, age, and death as embedded in a variety of historical contexts--and yet perhaps we learn even more about our own selves and our own time than could have been accomplished by a direct call to self-reflection. Is there perhaps something of myself in Descartes as he attempts to separate the subjective from the physical and impose the image of a clockwork universe? But isn't there also something of Augustine and Rousseau in my own flounderings with personal time? And do I feel myself only in the conquistador's infatuation with visions of an emergent future, or also in the Hopis' sense that past, present, and future are somehow part of a coherent whole? Does examination of the "beautiful death" tradition tell me something about my own underlying fantasies, and are these fantasies at odds with my share of Hume's skepticism? Each reader is likely to make a highly individual pattern of self- discoveries from the wealth of information presented.

Some books make their impact by imposing a view that readers cannot resist. This book offers a more subtle contribution. There can be a variety of conclusions drawn. One can come away from this book as either a friend or enemy of time. One can see contemporary Western society as the confused heir to outworn and contradictory traditions or as an incredibly rich and constantly changing mixture from which critical choices can still be made. From a methodological standpoint, one can judge that scientific and humanistic models of the universe are either on a courtship or collision course. Whatever the specific conclusions drawn, however, one is likely to come away from this book with a lively appreciation for the ways in which our lives have been influenced by ideas regarding time, age, and death. It even gives us something to think about as we play cards and paint the fence.

ROBERT KASTENBAUM

PREFACE

This book is about dreams and dreamers and the images, metaphors, and models through which they tried to gain control of time. Some sought control through intellectual understanding; some hoped for control through faith in a divine plan, or promise of salvation. Others looked to scientific progress as a source of control, while still others thought they could increase their control by accepting their limits as creatures of time in a self-conscious alliance with the time-bound universe.

This is a book about Promethean attempts to defeat time, to arrest aging, and to conquer death. There are stories of success and failure, tales of people with creative minds and strong wills, whose efforts to spin their dreams into the fabric of reality were sometimes fruitful and sometimes barren.

This is not a book of history, though it is historically structured. It is the unfolding of a tale about time, aging and dying in the lives of certain people who, like jewels in a setting, reflect in their philosophies not only themselves and their thoughts, but the tapestry of their culture as well. This account is about the human fear of time as well as the courage and insight of those who faced that fear. It describes the denial and dread of others who, in attempting to avoid it, turned inward on themselves.

One main thesis threads these events together. It is the connection between the dream of immortality, in all its multifaceted forms, and the search for timeless absolutes in the metaphors and models through which reality is viewed. The ancient Greeks sought a glimmer of immortality through a gods'-eye view of what, in their model, was seen as a universe of static, enduring forms. The Hebrews, not believing that such a view is possible for mortals, put their trust in faith. A just god, they believed, had a divine plan for his people. The Christians saw immortality in the defeat of death through resurrection. The Roman ideal of immortality was found in the metaphor of trumpeting fame. This idea of defeating time through achieving lasting glory extended into the Middle Ages. The concept of human progress, which originated in the seventeenth century, was carried forward in the metaphor of the machine and evolved into the model of mechanism. Through this model, which became the basis of modern science and medicine, many in the centuries that followed believed aging and death would be defeated.

In some ways our own century dreams more deeply than any before as it counts its technological successes that seem to guarantee that someday the irreversible arrow of time will at least be slowed down. The link between the wish for immortality and the search for absolutes is still here. It lives in the thriving hope that somehow, someday, the secrets of the cosmos will be whispered in the ears of mortals and time's grip will be loosened at last.

But today the belief in absolutes has been weakened, not only by philosophies that propose the adequacy of many models while pointing out their limits, too, but by quantum physics, which has overturned the Newtonian model with its simplistic, mechanistic explanation of reality.

We stand on the breaking edge of a new age where we are haunted by images of both terror and promise. Perhaps, by looking back at models that have guided humankind in the past, we can gain the courage and insight to proceed, recognizing that freedom can be found in the creative dreams of those who consciously assume the role of modelmaking, those who shape the future with their own hands.

ACKNOWLEDGMENTS

Our thanks to Stuart Spicker for his encouragement and evaluation of the original manuscript and to Dr. Parimal Das for her constant support and advice about the book. We are also indebted to Ann Marie Cook, Virginia R. Sperl and Barbara Levy for assistance in proofreading and editing suggestions and to Gail Ruber and Andrea White for their devoted attention to details in the final preparation of the manuscript. A special word of appreciation to the director, research librarians and staff of Dowling College Library for unfailing assistance during the course of this work. We are also indebted to our typist, Marie Miller, for her perseverance and to David Jansen whose technical assistance in preparation of the manuscript for publication was invaluable. We wish to acknowledge the Dick Fund of the Metropolitan Museum of Art in New York City for permission to use Brueghel's engraving *The Triumph of Time* and the Hopi Cooperative Arts and Crafts Guild and the Hopi Cultural Center Museum and Dawakema-Milland Lomakema, the artist, for permission to use the painting *Emergence*.

INTRODUCTION

We live in an era of vast changes, a churning riptide of social, political, and economic as well as philosophical transformations. On one side, these last decades of the twentieth century bring the most drastic and perilous phase of human development to date. On the other, signs of a new vision, shared on an extensive scale by a wide range of individuals and groups, seem to be emerging. But the problem that arises in anticipating the course of the future is that it has been difficult to understand adequately the nature and magnitude of the changes affecting the human community in our times.

The focus is on examining some major model shifts, transformations of entire conceptual systems, which have taken place in the history of Western consciousness. These changes are considered historically in order to lend perspective to the thesis that the model of time of a particular culture affects that culture's view of reality. The adequacies and inadequacies of pivotal historical models of time are explored in order to uncover the roots of attitudes, expectations, and assumptions about aging and dying which are embedded in present-day Western consciousness. The history of ideas in the West shows varied images of aging and dying in the form of rituals, arts, and popular practices. Within specific cultural contexts some of these images have coalesced into metaphors and have been extended into philosophical models, conceptual systems that attempt to explain reality as a whole. The models selected in this book are among those that have contributed significant new insights to the history of the philosophy of time. The purpose is to see cultural developments within the crucible of history in order to reflect on the way a culture's model of time affects its expectations and assumptions about aging and dying.

But this is not primarily a history of philosophical models of time, nor is it chiefly an investigation of the development of ideas on aging and dying. Rather, it is a metaphilosophical search, one that raises questions about the nature of a philosophical model in itself. It contains an implicit challenge to the assumption that a view from a neutral, objective vantage point can produce the truth. Since human knowledge is time-bound, a gods'-eye view of reality is not possible. Yet considering the futility of skepticism or radical relativism, the question remains: If the absolutist position is found suspect, what can take its place?

A new sense of reality seems to be slowly formulating among creative thinkers in science. It is an approach within which intuitive and rational processes are balanced, one in which casual experience and quantitative calculations are refocused within a definition of knowledge that puts in place the role of human imagination and personal values. The long-cherished mechanistic metaphors of Newtonian time, which have dominated Western thinking, have begun to reveal their inadequacies. A tentative hypothesis is offered, which is not a design for another model of reality or a new model of time. It is an alternative view of models themselves, the root metaphor view of philosophy that is a form of pluralism for which we are indebted, in large part, to the philosopher,

Stephen Pepper.

Those who are interested in following such a course of thought might be older persons, who are thinking through their roles in helping future generations live with greater human sensibility. The medical community and other professionals may wish to investigate the philosophical roots of models of aging and dying because they have been alerted to a new position in the creative construction of alternatives to present institutional inadequacies. The academic community, young and old, will be interested not only in the exploration of developing images and models of time, aging and dying, but will want to challenge the thesis and propose alternatives.

The approach taken here is to use the philosophical forum, not as a sparring ring for conflicting views, but as a meeting place for varied philosophical hypotheses. This work is an exploration of alternatives rather than a solution to the problems which have arisen in the sensitive areas of aging and dying.

IMAGES, METAPHORS, AND MODELS

The Unicorn's eye happened to fall upon Alice: he . . . stood looking at her with an air of the deepest disgust. "What is this?" . . . "This is a child!" . . . "I always thought they were fabulous monsters!" said the Unicorn. "Talk, child." Alice . . . began: "Do you know, I always thought Unicorns were fabulous monsters, too.". . . "Well, now that we have seen each other," said the Unicorn, "if you'll believe in me, I'll believe in you."

Lewis Carroll,
Through the Looking Glass

In the early 1970s, on a mesa in the American Southwest, the Hopi city of Oraibi lay dim in the quiet dawn. An elderly aunt, accompanied by a new mother, Lorinda Kay, carried an infant from the house for the naming ceremony. The child had been sheltered from light for the first twenty days of her life. Now, slowly, reverently, the older woman raised the infant toward the east, offering her to the sun god. She whispered a prayer begging the life-giving Sun to start this child on the Hopi way: "May you live always without sickness, travel along the Sun Trail to old age, and pass away in sleep without pain."[1]

The native American Hopi people had developed, over long generations, their own image of reality and the human person's relationship with nature. An image comprises a society's overall opinion or belief system that is more or less coherent and includes its memories, or commonsense mental attitudes toward the world.[2] Unlike a formal philosophical model, such an image provides a very broad picture of "the way things are." It is the people's way of selecting, classifying, and structuring reality, a kind of folk philosophy or worldview.[3]

Such an image of reality or folk philosophy is worked out gradually as a by-product of the practical concerns of life. The American philosopher, Mary Douglas, noted: "As a businessman, farmer or housewife, no one of us has time or inclination to work out a systematic metaphysics. Our view of the world is arrived at piecemeal, in response

to particular practical problems."[4] Another American philosopher,
Stephen C. Pepper, has called a people's view of the world the "material
of common sense" and pointed out that it is most often accepted without
much reflection as "self-evident."[5] Individuals of a particular culture,
for example, may be the last to recognize the assumptions that underlie
their images of aging and dying. One's own images are often hidden from
view, even when a society has a well-established formal tradition of
philosophical speculation as does the West. However, since aging and
dying always take place within a social and cultural context, one cannot
study them independently of the images, naive or sophisticated, through
which they are expressed.[6]

It is reasonable to believe that a culture's concept of time
influences attitudes toward aging and dying. In order to explore this
hypothesis it will be helpful to examine an unfamiliar culture to
sharpen perspectives on our own culture. A look at the native American
Hopi worldview follows. A sketch of their symbol system, that is, art
work, myths and ceremonies that played dominant roles in their daily
lives is necessary in order to contrast the Hopi's beliefs with those of
their sixteenth-century European conquerors. Subsequently we will
examine the way metaphors, which help shape the images of a culture,
evolve into models, or world hypotheses, that guide and direct behavior.
Finally, we will discuss the problem of understanding the nature and
limits of our own culture's world view.

TWO CULTURES MEET

The Hopi culture was at its peak when explorers sent by Francisco
Vasquez Coronado discovered them in 1540. The Spanish army arrived in
armor on horseback, carrying weapons that marked a culture well advanced
in the technology of sixteenth-century Europe. Given a choice to submit
or be destroyed, the Hopis, whose name means "peaceful people," responded
by simply drawing a line on the ground, using cornmeal, which is sacred
to the Hopis, indicating that the soldiers ought not to cross it. A
Franciscan friar, part of the Spanish army, is reported to have fretted
because so much time was being wasted in bothering to discuss surrender
with the Hopis.[7] Subsequently a loud cry of "Santiago" was given and the
Spanish soldiers rushed forward trampling the Hopis.[8]

Two cultures had met: one, the aggressor, conquerors of foreign
lands, seekers of fame and fortune; the other, followers of the Hopi way
of peace. Though repeatedly subjected to the rule of the white man
(*bahana*), the Hopis never submitted to foreign acculturation. Both the
religious and military zeal of the conquistadors were thwarted because
the Hopis were adamant in adherence to their own beliefs and rituals.
Just as the Spanish saw the Hopis as infidels to be converted and
subjugated, so the Hopis saw the ways of the white man as incompatible
with the Hopi image of the world. Even in the twentieth century this has
proven true. Don Talayesva, in his autobiography published in 1942,
wrote about his life in this traditional conservative community. He told
in one passage of the inability of the white missionaries to comprehend
the Hopi view of life or to grasp the principle of Hopi dedication to
their traditional way:

One day I visited Kalnimptewa, my father's old blind brother, and said, "Father, as I stood in my door I saw a missionary preaching to you from a Bible." "Yes," the old man answered. "He talked a great deal, but his words failed to touch me. He warned me that it would not be long before Jesus Christ would come down from the sky, say a few sharp words, and destroy all disbelievers. He said that my only chance to escape destruction was to confess and pray to his holy God. He urged me to hurry before it was too late, for a great flood was coming to Oraibi. I told him that I had prayed for rain all my life and nobody expected a flood in Oraibi . . . . "Now Talayesva, my son, you are a full-grown man, a herder, and a farmer who supports a family, and such work means a happy life. When our ceremonies come round, pray faithfully to our gods and increase the good life of your family, and in this way you will stay happy." I thanked him and went home feeling confident that I would never pay any serious attention to the Christians. Other gods may help some people, but my only chance for a good life is with the gods of my fathers.[9]

The Hopis never converted to Christianity and consistently showed passive resistance to what they saw as an alien way of life. In 1680 Hopi frustration with Western attempts to subjugate them reached a peak. For the first time in their history, the Hopis joined forces with other Pueblos and killed or drove out the Spanish, including the Franciscan missionaries, and destroyed their churches. In a final attempt to preserve their culture, the Hopis moved to the mesa and remained an isolated island of native people with their own way and culture.

The following scenario, in which two worlds meet, has been selected in order to provide a context in which to examine conflicting images of time. Such images are illustrated by two works of art. One, entitled *Emergence* (Fig. 1) is an aesthetic representation of the Hopi image of the universe.[10] The other is a sixteenth-century Western European engraving entitled "The Triumph of Time" (Fig. 2).[11] Each in its own way symbolically depicts its culture's image of time.

Images of Life and Death in the Hopi's Balanced Universe

The key to the Hopi view of the universe, as depicted in the painting *Emergence*, is founded in an ancient piece of folklore that describes the journey of the Hopi people from the underworld. Notice the dark figures on the bottom of the painting and the *Kachinas*, or dead ancestors, now gods, on the right. The Hopi people emerged from the lower world to this earthly world through the *Sipapu*, or earth navel, a hole believed to be located at the bottom of the Grand Canyon at the confluence of the Colorado and Little Colorado rivers. The fundamental belief of the Hopis was in a balanced division of space and time in the universe between the upper Earth world of the living and the lower world of their origins to which they returned when they died. The Sun, the principal Hopi symbol for life, represented here by an arc in the sky, rose from the eastern *kiva*, or home, traveled on its daily rounds, and descended into its western *kiva*. The Sun made its course underground

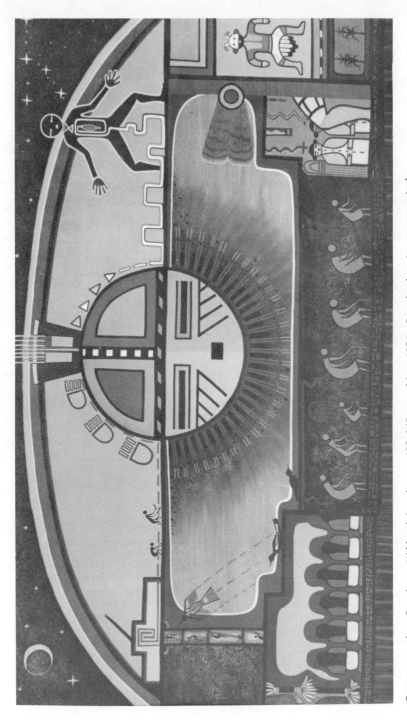

Emergence by Dawakema—Milland Lomakema. 48"x84" acrylic. 1974. Permission to use granted by the artist. In the Hopi Cultural Center Museum, Second Mesa, Arizona.

while it was night on earth, thus day and night were reversed in the two
worlds which operated, without discontinuity, as parts of a total
whole.

The cyclicalal alternation of day and night in the two worlds was a
symbol of balance and reciprocity. Thus   the universe as a whole was
seen as a harmonious system of correspondences.   So, too, was the
correspondence of summer and winter, youth and aging, life and death.
In the lower left corner of the painting the Hopi chiefs, with their
backs to us, have sent birds in search of the *Sipapu*, the symbolic womb
of rebirth.   By allowing a giant reed with a hollow inside to grow up,
the chiefs have provided a means of passage, like an umbilical cord,
connecting the two worlds.   This theme of the progressive cycle of
harmonious emergence and rebirth stood as the central metaphor in the
Hopi image of the universe.

Upon emerging into the Earth world, the Hopis met Massau, the
Creator and Father of Life.   He gave them a gift, a gourd filled with
water, a symbol of creativity and the source of growth for the Hopis'
chief crop, corn. But Massau was not only the Father of Life, he was at
the same time the Spirit of Death.   Earth, the Hopis believed, was
Massau's land, so people must always live in the presence of death.   In
the Earth world they must go through death in order to return to the
lower world where they belonged. Legend tells us that soon after coming
to this world a young Hopi boy, son of a village chief, fell sick and
died.   This was the first Hopi experience with death. They buried the
boy not far from the *Sipapu* and covered his grave with stones. Finally
a sorceress revealed to them that only the boy's *body* was beneath the
stones.   "He is not truly dead," she said, "for he lives on down
below."   Looking through the *Sipapu,* the boy's father saw for himself
that his son was happily playing with other children in the lower
world.   After realizing the continuity of the two worlds, the Hopis are
said to have no longer feared death.[12]

Ever after, when death came to the Hopis, it was seen as a kind of
birth.   The breath or life of the dead person, they believed, sought out
the *Sipapu* and thus found its way to the world below. Thus life and
death were not considered opposites: "Death was only a change in the
manner of existing."[13] Because time and space were divided between the
Earth world and the world below, the cycle of human life was continuous
for the Hopis. To die was not to become other than alive; it was to be
born into the only real life there is.[14]   Just as the infant was
presented to the life-giving Sun, so the body of a dead person was
placed in the grave in a squatting position facing the East. In the
Hopi ceremonies, their burial practices paralleled their birth
practices.   It was the Hopi view that this world, and the world of
spirits (or the underworld) were transformations of each other and
balanced one another.

Hopi Time and Aging

Time for the Hopis had a unique connotation. It was not the linear
time the West had inherited through Newton. Rather, time for the Hopis
was viewed as duration, what Benjamin Lee Whorf calls the "latering of

events."[15]   Hopi time was a storing up of change that held over into
later events.   Time was cumulative.   It gathered intensity and this
intensity was relative to the intensity felt by the group about the
event.   Frank Waters, who lived for three years with the Hopis, made the
point that, for them, the events of the past were embodied in the
present moment:

> I have been repeatedly annoyed and perplexed at the Hopis'
> complete disregard of dates and chronological sequence. They have
> related incidents which apparently occurred during their own memory
> but which, as I found out later, actually happened a century or
> more ago.   The importance of such events is not measured by their
> relative significance in historical time, but by the emotional
> intensity they created, as the hatred of the White Slave Church
> which impelled the destruction of Awatovi. Hopis at Oraibi still
> persistently point out great ruts scraped into the rock mesa top by
> the ends of huge logs. These logs . . . they had been forced to
> drag from the mountains nearly a hundred miles away for use as roof
> beams in the mission church. A casual visitor, looking vainly for
> the church, may learn with surprise that the ruts were made three
> centuries ago.[16]

Future for the Hopis, like the past, was ever present.
Expectations, desires, purposes and intentions that were striving
toward manifestation constituted the becoming of the world. The inner
and outer world were two aspects of one reality in the Hopi view.
There were no divisions between the subjective and the objective world,
only a reciprocal process in which both were each other.[17] According
to Whorf, the reciprocity of the manifesting or inner world of heart,
and the objective or manifest world was shown in the structure of Hopi
language, which he claims was timeless in the sense that it did not use
tenses the way many languages do. In the Hopi language the future was
spoken of, not as what has not yet come, but in the sense of what was
beginning to emerge.   This was the "expective" form that used a verb,
not a noun, to refer to the future.   Thus wishing, wanting and
intending actually brought events about.[18]   This was the key to the
Hopi folk philosophy.   Everyone in the community was responsible for
bringing about the future and for keeping the overall harmony of the
universe.   Only by maintaining this harmony and balance, and restoring
it when necessary, could the human race survive and prosper. Thus every
individual had a special responsibility which increased with age and
continued into the world beyond life.

According to the records of Castaneda, Indians on the American
continent were generally ruled by elders. One of the earliest known
paintings by a European artist, depicting the conquest of the
Southwest, showed natives led by an elderly man with a long white
beard.[19]   In the Hopi community the elders were considered a repository
of wisdom and tradition. Therefore, old people in this oral community
were charged with the task of reinforcing in the memories of the young
the only existing records of the past, Hopi legends. These stories
were repeated not entirely for entertainment, but to keep alive a sense
of their human continuity. Myth and fact were interwoven in long tales
displaying not just the events but the Hopi values, purposes and

priorities.

The elders were also charged with the task of keeping track of the seasons. Don Talayesva talked about the important business of old people as they watched the points of the horizon where the sun rose every day and thus charted the progress of the seasons:

> Old Talesemptewa, who was almost blind, would sit out on the housetop of the special Sun Clan house and watch the sun's progress toward its summer home. He untied a knot in a string for each day. When the sun rose at certain mesa peaks, he passed the word around that it was time to plant sweet corn . . . and on a certain date he would announce that it was too late for any more planting. The old people said that there were proper times for planting, harvesting and hunting and for ceremonies, weddings and many other activities. In order to know those dates it was necessary to keep close watch on the sun's movements.[20]

Key among the values of the Hopi system was respect for the aged and for the advice that they gave to the young. Don Talayesva recalled that as a young boy he and his peers valued the stories of the elders and took their advice:

> I began to pay more attention to the stories of the old people. . . . At night we were talked to sleep with true accounts of our ancestors. My father and grandfather were good storytellers and so were my great uncles. . . . My ceremonial father also answered many questions for me and gave me good advice. . . . Groups of boys and girls would go to the houses of the old people and beg for more stories. Sometimes we stayed in the *kiva* (ceremonial building where the men worked) in order to hear some blind old man recite the story of the Hopis from the beginning of the world up to the present and anticipate what would happen in the future. [21]

At the age of fifty Talayesva said he intended to do the same for his grandchildren.[22]

Life, then, for the Hopis was not an individual existence that ceased at death or an earthly existence that had a beginning, a middle and an end in time. Creation was repeated endlessly both in human intentions and in the world. Life had a continuity and death did not introduce discontinuity. Life took a fluid form as it flowed through, united and harmonized all things, the spirits of the dead, the living Hopi community, the animals and plants and the heavenly bodies. All objects shared in a web of relationships, a system of balance. In the Hopis' tenseless language, time disappeared and the all-at-onceness of the moving present was in harmony with the heart of the cosmos. Aging was seen as an accumulation of the ever-present past and the elderly were honored for their part in making the future come to be. Death, for the Hopis, was like stepping through the mirror of time. It was a rebirth into the underworld of their origin.

The *Triumph of Time* by Pieter Brueghel. Permission to use courtesy of the Metropolitan Museum of Art. Harris Brisbane Dick Fund, 1939. (39.94.7)

Sixteenth-Century Europeans: Conquering Time

It has been said that for Europeans of the Renaissance, time was "a great discovery."[23] It was not that the Western world was first taking conscious notice of time, but that it was discovering it anew, reinterpreting it as an antagonist that must be battled against, a marauder that must be defeated. Given all the self-confidence and optimism that this period exhibited, there was a paradoxical sense of defeat and pessimism. Their new sense of time was a double-edged sword that evoked, on one hand, an energetic and heroic response that vowed to challenge the ravages of time; and on the other hand, issued in a dark and gloomy pessimism, the knowledge that in the end time would triumph over human beings.

The sixteenth century was a period in which many people were becoming disillusioned with the Roman Church and its teachings. It was not only the time of the Protestant Reformation, but a period in which some were beginning to question the promise of a life beyond the grave. A negative attitude toward aging was present in the literature of this period in which depressing physical aspects of aging were often accentuated.

Pieter Brueghel's (c. 1525-1569) *The Triumph of Time* (Fig. 2) is an engraving that provides a typical representation of the new image of time:

> Time . . . became more and more intimately related with Death, and it was from the image of Time, that about the last years of the fifteenth century, the representations of death began to borrow the characteristic hourglass. . . . Time in turn could be shown as a procurer of Death whom he provides with victims or as an iron-toothed demon standing in the midst of ruins.[24]

Brueghel's engraving is a reinterpretation of a familiar classical figure of Time, but this classical figure had different characteristics from what became known in the Renaissance as Father Time. Edwin Panofsky has discussed the difference between the old and the new figure of Time. The ancient figure was a young man shown in the presence of symbols of time's precarious balance, or else it was represented in symbols of eternal and inexhaustible creativity and infinite fertility. The Renaissance produced the new image of Time in symbols of decay and decadence.[25]

Brueghel's *The Triumph of Time* is a moral allegory with Father Time as its centerpiece. Typical of his appearance throughout Renaissance and Baroque art, Time is an old man, a personification of earthly time backed by a globe and surrounded by the signs of the zodiac. The figure, in the process of devouring an infant, symbolizes relentless time that devours everything in its path. Father Time is poised in a chariot in ceaseless motion headed by two horses: one light and marked with a symbol of the sun, one dark with a symbol of the moon, both referring to the rhythms of day and night. [26] A master of allegorical landscapes, Brueghel pictured far off in the background on the right all the symbols of life. It is spring, the dancers celebrate, performing the fertility rites around the Maypole. Lovers walk hand in hand, and birds sweep the pleasant sky. The productive fields, the quiet town buildings and the church are all signs of stability and an almost beguilingly peaceful existence. This, for Brueghel, is the security of an ordered universe where a Divine Plan is being carried out in time and in the lives of ordinary people.

But most prominently in the foreground is the sinister side of time, represented in the destructive power of autumn storms leaving leafless limbs showing starkly against the threatening sky and a ship listing on the shore. The crushing weight of time stands triumphant, symbolized by the clock set in the tree. It is a weight-driven clock and has no face or hands, but a poised hammer stands ready to strike the passing hour.[27] Timepieces of all kinds including the hourglass had become associated with the idea of death and aging just as the mirror, in the Middle Ages, had been associated with old age and dying.[28] Time's victory over all things material is center stage as the chariot crushes the symbols of daily life, household items, work implements and pieces of clothing. Also ground under the wheels are the symbols of luxury and war--a crown, a strongbox, a soldier's helmet, swords and spears. Even musical instruments and books, symbols of art, are crushed and lost in the rush of inevitable devouring time. At the end of the procession are two prominent figures: one is Death, a skeleton loosely wrapped in a winding sheet and carrying a scythe; the other is Fame, a young child riding an elephant, symbol of the exotic, sounding a trumpet, announcing the temporal accomplishments possible for humankind.[29]

Brueghel's picture can be taken as a kind of paradigm that showed the paradoxical state of the sixteenth century person in relation to his universe. During this period there was an overwhelming sense of optimism, self-confidence and love of life represented in the immense vitality of reaching out to explore the world and conquer nature. But on the other hand there was deep pessimism, the first stirrings of a new alienation, founded in the new perspective on time. The Spanish armies as they met the Hopis represented the late Renaissance person's greater emphasis on the things of this world. A new realism and sense of practicality developed, not only in individual life-styles, but also in their representation in the arts. Both placed a more profound faith than ever before in the immediacies of concrete experience. The Renaissance view was that the physical environment was an objective entity to be controlled and subjugated to the needs of human beings. For the scientist, there was an unprecedented yearning to experience immediate concrete facts through the vehicle of mathematical calculation. These facts about the world were believed to correspond to the laws of nature.

The next century focused on Descartes' conviction that once these laws were understood, control of nature would be entirely possible. To the merchant, numbers were applied to business matters. There was the necessity for accuracy in measure, exactitude in calculations, and careful counting of hours to insure greater productivity. Pride, plunder and pursuit of fame governed the acts of the explorer sent by the monarch in the name of God and kingdom. For all three, scientist, merchant and explorer, linear historical time took on a new value. The world now was seen as a treasure unto itself. Life was to be lived for its own sake as much as for the next world. Associated with this new image of the world, a seemingly unquenchable thirst for fame served to focus the energy and optimism of the Renaissance. The poem, part of Brueghel's engraving, describes:

Fame which alone survives all things,
Follows behind, riding on a Gaetulian bull
Filling the world with the sounds of the trumpet.[30]

The Renaissance age's return to the classics, so zealously pursued by the Humanists, reignited the universal Roman ideal of seeking glory at all costs. As Rome itself had stood as a symbol of timelessness, so the arts were seen as a means of transcending time. Now, a preoccupation with the extension of human life through the search for fame was one of the fundamental urges that impelled its aspirants to invention, exploration and expansion of power—fueled by a new consciousness of time as a source of pressure. An increase in the tempo of life would be coupled with a deep realization of the frailty of the human condition, of the brevity of the human life span. Time would pursue the pursuer of glory.

Opposing Images

No wonder the Hopi image and the Western European image were incompatible, indeed, antithetical. Unlike the Hopi view of the universe, which stressed harmony and reciprocity of the Earth World and the Spirit World below, the sixteenth-century discoverer of time would come to focus on the reality of the physical universe which would come, within a century, to be seen metaphorically, and even literally, as a clockwork universe.

Hopi belief that expectations or intentions brought about reality was confronted with a contrary view in which the inner and outer world were seen as distinct. In the following century, Descartes' mind-body dualism would further increase the separation of inner and outer reality. For the Hopis, events of the past and events of the future were ever present and the time of life and the time of death merely transformations of each other. Time for the Renaissance European was seen as the time of history, divisible into segments of the past, the present and the future. Time, in this more quantitatively oriented image, could be measured and counted because it progressed at a uniform and standard pace with a beginning, a middle and an end.[31] Unlike the Hopi oral culture in which creation was being repeated endlessly (as long as rituals, ceremonies and myths were attended to carefully), the Western European came to have a deep regard for quantification and chronology: written history, accounting and record keeping.

Whereas the Hopis were inextricably tied by their faith in the legend of emergence to their traditional home near the Earth's navel, the Europeans were driven by their lust for gold and their military zeal for subjugation and conversion of the infidels across the seas to new worlds where wealth and fame acted as lures. But it would be the metaphors for time that would divide the two images most profoundly. The Hopi metaphor of ever-present time, a creative unity, and the

European metaphor of fleeting time, a destroyer, had each cast its shadow on their images of aging and dying. Growing older for the Hopis meant more serious responsibilities in leadership and in preserving and teaching the tradition, as well as projecting a vision of life for the generations to come. Growing old for the European meant watching the clock and seeing in the mirror the price that is paid for being creatures of time.

FROM METAPHORS TO MODELS

Stephen Pepper in his theory of root metaphor has pointed out that philosophical systems in their earliest stages are founded in the material of common sense; that is, in the images and metaphors of a culture. "Every philosophical theory," he says, "is a far-flung metaphor."[32]

But what is the nature of metaphor and of philosophical metaphors in particular? Metaphors may be thought of as literary devices that add aesthetic vividness and impact to poetry or prose. But metaphor in philosophy may be distinguished from metaphor in poetry, because its role is different. In a philosophical setting metaphors act primarily as explanatory rather than aesthetic devices; that is, they function to clarify concepts and provide insight into philosophical models.[33] Philosophical language, itself, is formed in the restless sea of metaphor, though in time the metaphors tend to become faded and hidden from view. The familiar verb "to be," for example, originated in a metaphor. It comes from the Sanskrit word *bhu*, to grow, and our words "am" and "is" come from the Sanskrit *asmi*, "to breathe." The American philosopher Susanne Langer believes that all abstract words were once metaphors but, like ancient coins, their original images have been worn away with use.[34] Both science and philosophy are disciplines that deal in abstract ideas and both are, therefore, dependent on the generative power of metaphor.

Colin Turbayne in *The Myth of Metaphors* explains that metaphors have two specific characteristics that make them appropriate for use by scientists and philosophers. First, they make use of sort-crossing, which is applying one sort of thing to something very different from itself. Second, metaphors call on imagination, requiring the user to fuse the two different sorts, "making believe" there is only one sense.[35] The clock was a metaphor that had been used to describe the way time triumphs over human life. The metaphor of the mechanical timepiece was widely used in European art and literature to represent the sixteenth-century image of time. This metaphor also came to govern, in a broad way, the image of aging and dying that prevailed in the general public consciousness.

Thinkers who lead a society in formulating philosophical tenets, consciously or unconsciously, are influenced by vague images they have inherited from their culture. Descartes, father of mechanistic philosophy, was entranced by automata of all kinds, especially the clock and the mechanical garden fountains that were so fashionable in the sixteenth century. Therefore, the machine became his metaphor. Philosophers do not merely inherit the common images of their society;

they sort out, from their personal and social experience, the insights they wish to use and then enter into the task of selecting only certain characteristics of the metaphor to act as categories in a broad philosophical system. They then apply them to the world as a whole. In this way metaphors evolve into models. Descartes' metaphor became the root metaphor for the seventeenth century's model of the universe, a model that has largely survived until the present. In this model, the clock-machine and the cosmos were seen to have similar characteristics. They were both interpreted as having parts that, when fitted together, functioned as a whole. The Renaissance person knew a machine was governed by the laws of mechanics, which were extended metaphorically to fit the laws of nature. Thus seventeenth-century thinkers came to see the entire universe as a giant clockwork. The refinement of the model consisted of testing the metaphor for its capacity to be generalized into guiding concepts of a "world hypothesis." The exponents of the clockwork model of the universe increasingly sought empirical evidence to bolster that interpretation. Soon they came to believe that their conclusions were incontestable.

The Hopi image of the universe was based entirely on myth, with its metaphor of the life-giving sun and its concept of time and space as a continuous and harmonious flow between the world of the living and world of the dead. The Hopis made no attempt to confirm empirically the validity of their view--it was simply taken for granted that the experience of the past bore out its truth.[36] In this way the Hopis' view remained an image, provocative and highly aesthetic in nature, but was not expanded into a philosophical hypothesis in Pepper's sense.

World Hypotheses

If we follow Pepper's line of reasoning, world hypotheses can be defined as conceptual systems rooted in common sense images or metaphors that have been extended, by a process of refinement and modification, to describe the world. For example, the clockwork universe metaphor was applied to the world as a whole, but not all metaphors can be used so broadly. William Harvey's (1578-1657) metaphor of the heart as a pump is meant to be a limited one, used only to describe one organ in the body. Today we have the artificial heart as witness to the success of his metaphor. A successful world hypothesis is one in which the root metaphor is used more broadly and its categories make the world more comprehensible. The vigorous growth of modern science, and particularly of medicine, since the seventeenth century, bears witness to the success of the mechanistic model. Descartes' followers reveled in the mileage they derived from their metaphor. In using imagination, in "making believe" that the world is a machine, the philosopher and scientist must act as if it were mechanistic. This "as if" allows the distance needed to keep the theory from being taken as literally true. To think of the world "as if" it were a machine maintains the hypothetical nature of the system and keeps the user conscious of the metaphorical character of his categories.[37]

It is difficult, however, to be alert to the fact that a selected metaphor has become too strained, or to be aware that one has been taken advantage of by the attractiveness of one's metaphor. Descartes himself fell into the trap of reifying his machine metaphor. At first he saw the human body as if it were a machine; later he took his own metaphor literally. Once one assumes that one set of categories is suitable to describe the world the way it really is, access to varied models is lost. The Hopis and their Renaissance counterparts had not retained the capacity to take the other's model seriously. This is because they were each totally convinced that their image of the world was the true one, that their way was the only way to see reality. Therefore, the Hopis were treated by their conquerors as, at best, a naive and helpless people, and at worst as infidels, good only for the gold they might give to their masters. The Hopis, steeped in their traditional ways, could not see the value of the material and technical progress of the white men, or they simply considered it secondary to the preservation of their way. This is not at all uncommon, since people tend to be blinded by their own convictions. The physicist Erwin Schrodinger has told us that the naive physicist takes a biological organism as a clockwork. He claims that if this scientist has learned his physics well, especially its statistical foundations, he can use his metaphor to advantage. But this is so only if he is conscious of using it as a metaphor; that is, in Schrödinger's words, if he takes the metaphor "with a big grain of salt."[38] Turbayne underscores this, speaking about philosophical models: "A metaphor which is used for purposes of . . . explanation may become a model; and when it does, there are definite disadvantages to . . . taking it literally."[39]

Taking a model literally means, he continues, that there is a claim that the world really is that way. This, he insists, is not a useful way to approach the world or to approach knowledge of the world because "it minimizes the possibility of employing other models to illustrate the facts in question."[40] Pepper reminds us that using philosophical metaphors is like putting on glasses. The lens acts as a filter, coloring our vision of the world.[41]

STEPPING OUTSIDE THE MODEL

Social institutions are deeply impregnated with metaphors that are simply taken for granted. In addition, the beliefs and values of ordinary people are saturated with metaphorical biases that mold attitudes, assumptions and expectations. Our language, as well as the way it is used, helps to shape our views. One may wonder what difference it would have made had "organism," rather than "mechanism," become the basic metaphor of Western science, or had tenses been absent in the structure of European languages as they were in the Hopi language. It seems evident that the language we use, and the metaphors at the root of our social institutions and workaday world, influence our thinking and behavior. Consider the medical professional who has been trained to view the body as a machine, as opposed to one whose training has given emphasis to the psychosocial aspect of patient care. Or consider the contrasting, if not conflicting, metaphors of the employer who says to his employee, "I thought I told you to have this job knocked out by the end of the day," and the employee replies, "I'm putting the finishing touches on it now." A different approach to the same work is implied by a metaphor from prize fighting and a metaphor from art.

The ordinary person inherits metaphorical biases and linguistic structures, images of the world and even philosophical models. These are perpetuated through generations that are often habituated to them and unaware of their advantages and disadvantages, their strengths and limitations. Turbayne has noted that, to most ordinary viewers, metaphors are not apparent; there is only the face of literal truth. Even for the initiated, the metaphors at the heart of their culture's way of thinking are frequently invisible. The more the metaphorical system is used, the more convinced its users tend to become that it is a "true" description of the world as it really is. We invent our metaphors and, in turn, they invent us:

> When the world began
> God, they said, created man.
> Conversely dancing round the sod,
> Man, they said, created God.
> Be careful that your words don't do
> Something of the same to you.[42]

The question, then, is how can we escape this prison of our own making? How can we critically evaluate the advantages and limits of a system of thought that we have inherited and that so completely immerses us? Can the committed user of a philosophical model ever have the objectivity to see it from an uncommitted perspective? Could a conquistador ever take a *Kachina* (masked god) seriously, or a Hopi abandon his concept of balance for the European's goal of conquering nature? Michael Polanyi, a contemporary philosopher known for his study of knowledge and the imagination said:

> A hostile audience may in fact deliberately refuse to entertain novel conceptions . . . because their members fear that, once they have accepted this framework they will be led to conclusions which they . . . rightly or wrongly . . . abhor. Proponents of a new system can convince their audience only by first winning their intellectual sympathy for a doctrine they have not yet grasped. Those who listen sympathetically will discover for themselves what they would otherwise never have understood.[43]

Plato believed philosophy could provide the universal and absolute perspective, the ultimate truth, a kind of gods'-eye view. Modern philosophers are less sanguine about this possibility. They believe that there can be many legitimate frameworks and novel conceptions of the world, in fact, many models of reality. Metaphors and models have the capacity to dominate us only to the extent that we are unconscious of them. Therefore, it is necessary to step outside one's own model to see it more objectively. One way of doing this is to explore the root metaphors and categories of philosophical models that are not our own. Pepper said, "Once one has the keys of the root metaphors and categories in his pocket, he is . . . able to unlock the doors of the cognitive closets of other cultures and times."[44] One can also return home and see with a critical eye, perhaps for the first time, what is in one's own cultural closet.

It is not easy to cast off the spectacles through which we are accustomed to view the world, or look in unfamiliar mirrors that appear at first to distort our vision of reality, and see there some possible glimmer of truth. Perhaps it is a Promethean quest to attempt to attain such a tolerant or inclusive point of view, but we can begin to move in this direction by at least reminding ourselves of the multiplicity of spectacles and mirrors that have shaped human perspectives. In the end, though we may find ourselves paradoxically trapped in our own models, we may be better able to understand and accept their inherent limitations. If we can be convinced that first we must offer "intellectual sympathy" for the doctrines we either disagree with or have not yet grasped, perhaps we would discover for ourselves what we would otherwise have never understood.

We have seen, in sharp focus, two contrasting worldviews collide: that of the Hopis and their European counterparts. We examined the images and metaphors of each regarding time and suggested that one's concept of time may influence attitudes and assumptions regarding aging and dying. We saw how metaphors, which lie at the root of our science, social institutions and philosophies, influence our thinking and thereby evolve into models and world hypotheses which structure our attitudes and shape our behaviors. We noted that our images and metaphors, as well as the models within which we operate, are often hidden from view. We see them not for what they are but " the way things are," as literal truth. In order to examine the biases our own culture has inherited we must step outside our own model. This, perhaps, can best be done by first recognizing the nature of images, metaphors and models and then sympathetically, but critically, evaluating them.

The chapters that follow examine some of the predominant metaphors and models of time in Western culture, as well as images of aging and dying. The purpose is to expose the roots of twentieth century attitudes and assumptions regarding the elderly and dying. In the final chapter we will look at some of the new images that seem to be emerging, images which may eventually change our metaphors and models and alter our beliefs and values.

THE GODS'-EYE VIEW

Time is a child playing checkers. Kingship is in the hands of a child.

Heraclitus

Who oversees the passage of time? What power drives events? Do humans have a place in determining these events, or are they mere pawns in a grand game of chess? Can man grasp a picture of the universe as a whole? What is the meaning of aging and dying? These are the questions regarding time and man's place in the cosmos that were first addressed by poets and embodied in the myths that were passed down for centuries in song and verse.

This chapter will look at the answers given to these questions by two ancient Greek poets, Homer and Hesiod, and by two great philosophers of the Golden Age of Greece, Plato and Aristotle. It will also trace the evolution of some of the earliest recorded thoughts about time, aging and dying and show in the development of these thoughts the origins of Western philosophy. The chapter is called "The Gods'-Eye View," not in the sense that it is a view from the eye of some personal god who is watching events, but in the sense that the ancient philosophers believed it was possible for man to have a perfectly objective and neutral point of view from which absolute truth was accessible.[1]

The Greek poets, Homer and Hesiod, as well as Plato and Aristotle, looked into the mirror of time and saw the image of an eternal scheme that governed all events. The early poets saw the eternal scheme as *fate*, the unavoidable destiny of all beings. Plato saw it as the principle of rational order and Aristotle pictured a Divine Mind (*Nous*), which was the first cause and prime mover. For Plato and Aristotle it would be impossible to describe, or even think about, the system of the universe as a whole without positing an ideal observation point from which the rational human soul could comprehend eternal truths. As the philosophy of the Golden Age of Greece developed in the fifth century B.C., it was the belief in the possibility of a gods'-eye view that supplied the reason not to despair. This Greek image of order and a larger controlling force, which could be comprehended by human rationality, made it easier to live in the face of time with its prospects of aging and dying.

HOMER: TIME IS FLEETING, FATE IS INEVITABLE

The Homeric poems, the *Iliad* and the *Odyssey*, are thought to have originated as a part of the oral tradition, before the beginnings of Greek literacy--around the end of the eighth century B.C. The myths from Homer's epics held and nourished the minds and imaginations of generations of Greeks. They were recited to the community, memorized by its members, and passed orally down through the ages.These Homeric poems provided, through thought and language, a means by which traditions could be transmitted. They passed down images of the way in which the good life was to be lived and the honor of the community upheld. For hundreds of years Athenian youths committed to memory vast quantities of Homeric verse, which contained the symbols and values of Greek culture. The constant recitals of these stories at banquets, family rituals, in the theatre and in other public performances urged emulation of Homer's courageous, larger-than-life heroes. This also encouraged loyalty and identification with the ideals praised in the myths; it fostered imitation and conformity rather than originality or critical thought.

Two interwoven themes that pervaded Homer's epic poems influenced Greek consciousness and affected later models of time, aging and dying. These themes involved, on one hand, an awareness that the passage of time is ineluctable and human life transitory and, on the other hand, the related theme of Fate, a profound sense of destiny. The picture of early Greek life drawn by Homer is a constant reminder of these themes. The gods were immortal, not subject to dread old age and death, but humans were creatures of time, and therefore, aging and dying were their lot. This awareness of human finitude was accompanied by the often-repeated lesson written into the mythological accounts of events in the lives of the heroes: one cannot counter fate or hold back life's unavoidable end. A famous scene near the end of Homer's *Iliad* illustrates this awareness. Achilles, who was leading the battle against Troy, had killed Hector and all the other noble sons of Priam, the king of Troy. In a scene of unparalleled pathos the old king, endangering his own life, goes alone to the enemy camp to ask Achilles for his son's body:

> With solemn pace through various rooms he went,
> And found Achilles in his inner tent: . . .
> Thus stood th' attendants stupid with surprise:
> All mute, yet seem'd to question with their eyes: . . .
> "Ah think thou favour'd of the powers divine!
> Think of thy father's age, and pity mine!
> In me, that father's reverend image trace,
> Those silver hairs, that venerable face; . . .
> No comfort to my griefs, no hopes remain,
> The best, the bravest of my sons are slain! . . .
> Suppliant my children's murderer to implore,
> And kiss those hands yet reeking with their gore!" . . .
> Satiate at length with unavailing woes,
> From the high throne divine Achilles rose; . . .
> "Alas! what weight of anguish hast thou known,

Unhappy prince! thus guardless and alone
To pass through foes, and thus undaunted face
The man whose fury has destroy'd thy race!..."[2]

This scene, one of the most celebrated episodes of the *Iliad*, was subsequently depicted by artists in myriad vase paintings, sculptures and other art forms. The event provides an example of the tragic note that sounds throughout Homer's epics and anticipated the great dramatists of the fifth century B.C. Life's precious value was contrasted with the knowledge of fate's grimness and the inevitability of death. For the Greeks, this was the paradox of human existence in the face of time: one could know of one's mortality, but this knowledge gave no power either to hold back time or make its passing easier. "Our bitterest sorrow is that we have consciousness of much and control of nothing."[3]

Even the concept of afterlife, anticipated by the Greeks, offered little relief. Life beyond death would be in Hades, the abode of the dead. This form of existence was believed to be inferior to life, and therefore, life's true value lay in the living present and not "beyond the Styx," the river across which souls were ferried at death.

The Homeric view of man presented no concept of a unified soul as would be developed in later Greek thought. The "psyche" or soul, was merely a life force, which remained in man while he was alive. When he died, he went to Hades, becoming a ghost or bloodless replica of the human. The psyche was never thought of as consciousness or mental life, nor did it play any part in the emotions or feelings. Thoughts and feelings were loosely attributed, not to the life force or psyche, but to the "phrenes," associated with organs of the chest or midriff, and to the heart and "thymos," mysterious in its nature but somehow connected with breath. At death it was believed that the psyche would leave the body and exist as a shadow of the former person. Thus, Achilles claims he would rather be a slave on earth than a king in Hades.

Not only was the concept of soul undeveloped in Homeric times, but the concept of individuality, as a characteristic of the human person, was also lacking. The concept of self-consciousness, according to many modern scholars, appeared rather late in the development of language.[4] One author has recently suggested that self-consciousness was only beginning to emerge in Homeric times and was largely absent from the *Iliad*.[5] Human existence was generally depicted as anonymous and impersonal in the epics. Man was a thinglike cipher, a checker in the game of the gods. Man's fate, "*moira*," was determined by the will of the gods. The Fates, in both Greek and Roman mythology, were pictured as three goddesses who controlled human life and destiny. The first, Clotho, spun the threads of life, the second, Lachesis, determined its length, and the third, Atropos, cut it off.

Actions and events in the *Iliad* were directed, not by the conscious will of humans, but rather by the voices of the gods. Homer's account of fate involved a sense in which the gods were sometimes whimsical or capricious. It was the gods who started the quarrels among men that led to war. One god made Achilles promise not to go into battle, another urged him to go. It was the goddess Athene who told Achilles to kill Hector. Then the same goddess appeared to Hector as his dearest friend.

But when Hector challenged Achilles and demanded another spear from his friend Athene, he turned to find no one there. When, toward the end of the war, Achilles reminds Agamemnon of how he robbed him of his mistress, Agamemnon declared that it was Zeus, not he, who was the cause of this act. Achilles fully accepted this explanation, for he knew the gods had their ways and he also was obedient to the gods. Zeus, the supreme deity of the ancient Greeks, had in the words of Achilles:

> Two urns by Jove's high throne have ever stood,
> The source of evil one, and one of good;
> From thence the cup of mortal man he fills,
> Blessings to these, to those distributes ills;[6]

The gods in Homer were amoral. They had no need to reward goodness or punish evil by the gifts they gave. Man's behavior was not related to the good or evil things he was given. The gods needed no reasons to act as they did. They were not moral agents. This fact deepened the sense of helplessness in Homer's human characters, who could, in the end, neither resist nor override the higher powers. Any denial of the power of the Fates or the gifts of Zeus was considered "hubris," a form of excessive pride leading to insubordination, which attempted arrogantly to avoid or change the course of destiny dictated by the gods.

Warnings about hubris and its dreadful consequences echoed in the ears of men and were reinforced in their memories from childhood. One such warning rang in the opening lines of the *Iliad*, which condemned the excessive wrath of Achilles and the arrogance of King Agamemnon. Their acts of hubris brought ruin upon themselves and their armies:

> Achilles' wrath, to Greece the direful spring
> Of woes unnumber'd, heavenly Goddess, sing! . . .
> The king of men his revered priest defied,
> And, for the king's offence, the people died.
> For [the priest] sought with costly gifts to gain
> His captive daughter from the victor's chain . . .
> The Greeks in shouts their joint assent declare,
> The priest to reverence, and release the fair. . . .
> Not so [Agamemnon]; he, with kingly pride,
> Repuls'd the sacred sire, and thus replied: . . .
> "Mine is thy daughter, priest, and shall remain;
> And prayers, and tears, and bribes, shall plead in vain; . . .
> Hence then! to Argos shall the maid retire,
> Far from her native soil, and weeping sire."
> The trembling priest along the shore return'd,
> And in the anguish of a father mourn'd.[7]

Homer's hearers are reminded that hubris will come to naught. Paradoxically, however, the great characters in Homer's poetry were almost envied and admired for their boldness in spite of the fate that awaited them. In this story of human and divine interaction, the tension, implicit in the paradox, was screwed to its tightest point. While humans remained mindful of the inevitability of their fate, they also felt an overwhelming sense of helplessness, which drove them to a resistence against the gods that they knew, would prove futile in the end.

The Homeric Sense of Time

It should be noted that Homer's themes of transitoriness and fate were spelled out in the lived experiences of the stories and were not defined or analyzed as abstract theories. Homer had no abstract conception of time and destiny, nor did he speak of time as a continuum. Mythology was his vehicle. Just as children's fairytales begin with a provoking "Once upon a time . . ," so myths treated time nontheoretically and nonanalytically, without need of precision or sense of history. Nor was there any attempt in Homer's poems to reflect philosophically on questions such as the origin of the universe.

The time of the myths was primordial time. As with the Hopi, the past and present merged in a kind of eternal present. The spell of the myth made immediate the happenings of the past and thus, through its oral tradition, helped determine human behavior. Characteristic of early Greek thought was its view of cosmic time as cyclical and harmonious. The cosmos was conceived of as an ongoing process without beginning or end. Time was seen as eternal and repetitive as night and day or the change of the seasons. The Greeks, however, always saw the course of human affairs in contrast to the larger backdrop of cosmic time, which in its harmony showed up the pathetic nature of the human condition. The tenuousness and finitude of man stood out starkly against the permanent and eternal nature of the cosmos. Man must suffer corruption and dissolution whereas the course of nature would continue eternally. For the early Greeks the only progress for humans was found in returning to the past, by taking the myths seriously. Like a cosmic circular pattern, the memorized repetitions of the stories of the heroes renewed Greek values and made them come alive again and again in the hearts of the listeners.

HESIOD: MOVING TOWARD INDIVIDUATION AND PHILOSOPHY

Hesiod, a second and lesser poet than Homer in the opinion of most critics, is generally dated about a generation later. Although both poets depicted fate as the inevitable course of human destiny and did so through myths, there was between these two poets a distinct transition in both form and intention. Three general shifts took place that distinguish in profoundly important ways Hesiod's works from Homer's. First, there was a sign of more individuation in Hesiod's characters, which was to be carried on by the lyric poets of the seventh and sixth centuries. Second, as in Homer's poetry, Hesiod retained the form of the myth, but his intention shifted. He related myths for the purpose of teaching morality. Third, in keeping with the latter point, his stories about particular characters moved toward more universal and abstract themes. For example, Hesiod showed a deep concern with exploring the overall order of the universe, and thus he moved in the direction of philosophy.

In Hesiod's *Theogeny* there is a myth of creation in which, out of Chaos (a confused and shapeless mass), earth, sea and air were formed. After animals were created by the gods, Hesiod tells us that a nobler animal was wanted, so Prometheus (one of the Titans, who inhabited the earth before man) took some earth, mixed it with water and made man in the image of the gods. He gave him an upright stature so that, unlike the other animals whose faces turned downward toward the earth, man could raise his head to the heavens and gaze upon the stars.

Subsequently, Hesiod described Epimetheus, the brother of Prometheus, as having the office of providing all the animals of the earth with a means of survival. He gave some courage, others claws, some swiftness, others protective shells. However, when Epimetheus (his name means *after*thought) came to humans, he had no gifts left to give. Therefore, Prometheus (his name means *fore*thought) provided a means for survival. With the aid of the goddess Athene he went up to the heavens to light his torch on the chariot of the sun, bringing the gift of fire to earth. Fire enabled human beings to forge weapons for defense, to make tools for cultivating the soil, and to keep themselves warm. This was the beginning of "techne," the art of making what is needed to support human survival.[8]

The legend of Prometheus underscored a fundamental paradox: the human race, on one hand, knew of its mortality and vulnerability, but still stretched up to the heavens to seek the means of self-preservation. Humankind, with a profound awareness of its own finitude, would in the future even attempt to reach beyond itself and catch hold of the dream to extend life and to defeat death. Zeus punished Prometheus for stealing fire from the gods and punished man for accepting the gift. Hesiod tells us that the order was given that the first woman, Pandora, be created. Through her curiosity, she came to open a jar filled with all sorts of evils for hapless man. Among these were old age, misery and death. Telling the tale with bitter relish, Hesiod explains that all ills were brought to earth by "the woman." The tribes of men lived remote from ills but "the woman" took off the lid of the jar containing countless plagues, which now wander among men who in misery grow old and die.[9] He pointed out the moral of the story: accursed old age and death were the will of the gods, and man's proper role in the face of these ills was one of humility and submission. Something was left lying at the bottom of Pandora's jar, which did not escape when she opened the lid. It was blessed hope.

The symbolic forms of both art and philosophy were built on the ground of myth. Homer had already moved in the direction of drama by imposing conscious form on the content of the myths. Hesiod, also using mythical elements, applied rational speculation to his stories, thus his works stand as a bridge connecting myth with the beginnings of philosophy. This can be seen in Hesiod's famous "Myth of the Ages" in his book, *Works and Days*. This didactic poem, in spite of its title, did not trace the ages of the world. Rather, it used metaphorical elements to picture separate ages in the moral life of men and, connected with these, were different experiences of aging and dying. Four ages, named after metals, were probably based on accounts not original with Hesiod. However, he modified the traditional theme to give the image of four unconnected periods in which, starting from Chronos, there was the birth of mortals, who in time drifted from acceptance of their fate, refusing to worship the gods. This was followed by continued excesses that resulted in degeneration and finally premature old age, anonymity and violent death. The last race, the Iron Race, was the generation of Hesiod himself. He was probably describing the Dorians who, with iron weapons, destroyed the Mycenaean strongholds, taking the land for themselves. This race was typified by some good and some evil, and Hesiod predicted they would be destroyed by Zeus as soon as infants at their birth had gray hair on their temples. This strange prediction of Hesiod's indicated that in the Iron Race it would come to pass that infants would be born old and childhood would not exist.[10]

Two messages are found in the "Myth of the Ages." There is a warning against lack of moderation, especially all excesses associated with the individual stages of human life. In addition, the orderliness of the temporal cycle, both of the seasons and of man's stages of development, is seen as tied to the moral order. Hesiod used myths related to time to teach morality. Human justice was conceived of against the background of the temporal order of the universe. It was man's role to accept his place in that order. *Works and Days* is an explanation of the dire effects of human disorders and their relationship to human time, aging and dying. By assigning to the person responsibility for his own acts, Hesiod shows injustice stemming from flaws in human character. The capacity for justice, he pointed out, marks the difference between man and beast.

Thus, a complex cosmology with humans as responsible creatures emerged from the ground of mythological tradition, and this required a new way of seeing time. A necessary adjunct to Hesiod's sense of justice was the need to use a spatialized metaphor for time. In Homer, primordial time of the myths had not separated past, present, or future, but had focused on a kind of eternal present wherein the past infused all immediate events and thus nothing was new. In Hesiod, however, there was the beginning of a partial shift to spatial succession of time. The future was associated with events in the present: for example, committing violence begat a punishment at some future time.[11] Or, Zeus was wrathful and laid bitter penalty upon those who wronged orphaned children or reproached an aged parent.[12]

There is also a new concept of Zeus, who was depicted by Hesiod as neither violent nor capricious, but as a possessor of moral integrity. According to consistent moral principles, Hesiod's Zeus punished injustice and rewarded good deeds. This new view of the gods as moral had its counterpart in a new concept of men as responsible for living a moral life in accordance with the rules decreed by divine authority. With this new sense of divine laws and of time as a succession from past to future came a shift of attention from primordial time to everyday problems of living. This emphasis is quite different from that found in the god-centered poems of earlier times. Discussion turned from the ageless past to the secular present. It can, then, be concluded that the dimension of humanness, and an awareness of human existence in time slowly evolved hand in hand with a concern for the overall order of the cosmos. Yet it should be said that the discovery of the human dimension, as gradual and ambiguous as it was in the early poems, was by no means the emergence of anything near full-blown subjectivity. Greek art, for example, similar to the art of the East, did not capitalize on individuals or on their personalities; it mainly bypassed these elements of the self. For the most part, the Greeks saw the human person as an object in the natural order of the cosmos, and Hesiod saw awareness of the human person as separate from nature, though destined for harmony with it. Humans were responsible under external laws of society and the cosmic order of the universe but were still capable of violating these laws.

Writings about heroes and heroic events, prior to Hesiod, were in the form of genealogies; they were merely lists and not historical in the sense that they did not reveal the events of the past as they are connected to the present. Hesiod attempted a rational reconstruction that pointed out the origin of present disorder in the events of the past, and thus his writing moved in the direction of the historical. Hesiod's *Theogeny* was also a concentrated effort to discern the origin of the temporal world, human vicissitudes and the birth of the gods, all in the light of an overall cosmology, a larger order that governed individual events. Hesiod thus foreshadowed the abstract and universal principles of order and justice in Greek philosophy. Later philosophers' thoughts were deeply colored by their familiarity with Hesiod's poetry.

From Oral to Written Literacy

During the next four hundred years, in the time leading up to Plato's birth (427 B.C.), we find another transition of great significance taking place. It is the gradual shift, within the Greek community, from oral tradition to written literacy. In order to appreciate the dramatic changes that the Greek alphabet brought to the Western world, it is important to understand the nature of two distinctly different communication environments: the oral tradition, which had existed for millennia, and literacy in the written word, which appeared in ancient Greece and spread throughout the Western world.

In an oral society the spoken word is always in the present. It commands attention. One can turn away from the written word, but sound fills auditory space and is not boxed in like writing on a page. It is dynamic, always in flux, creating its own dimensions moment by moment. The auditory makes present the absent thing. Writing annuls this magic by making present the absent sound. Spoken words tend to be warm, spontaneous and subjective, and are never isolated from the body that produces them. Oral communication is face to face. The written word is cold, abstract, objective, timeless and more durable than its author. In the oral cultures of the past, the spoken word was transmitted from generation to generation. Thus, the elderly had an exalted place because they were the storehouse of memory, knowledge and experience. Writing gave the young access to knowledge without actual experience. Writing also relieved the young of the laborious task of memorization, which was itself an enormous feat. Even today, where oral cultures still exist, anthropologists have been astonished by the accuracy with which volumes of material are committed to memory. In order to be remembered, oral communication had to be felt deeply. Words were charged with emotion, and familiar themes were repeated. Rhythm and rhyme were employed as aids, and even melodies from the lyre or flute often accompanied the memorization and recitation of epics.

The Greek alphabet, which was introduced around 700 B.C. and finally standardized in 403 B.C., when Plato was a young man, was to have a profound effect on individuation, critical thinking, concepts of time and attitudes toward aging and dying. According to Eric Havelock, the Greek alphabet "changed somewhat the content of the human mind."[13]

Though writing in various forms, such as Egyptian hieroglyphics and

Phoenician and Semitic syllabaries, had existed for thousands of years, it was not until the invention of the Greek alphabet that symbols (letters) made sounds visually recognizable without ambiguity. Those early writing systems had not been available to the populous at large: they required the skills of scribes to read and interpret meanings. The Greek alphabet, by limiting the number of letters and indexing linguistic units on a one-to-one basis, took a great leap beyond any writing system previously developed. Only with the Greek alphabet was it possible for everyone, commoner and king alike, to read and understand the meaning of what they were reading. For the first time in history, young minds could be liberated from the thoughts and emotions of the group. The oral community had kept people together; writing encouraged independence. The reader wants to be alone. Writing brought a sense of detachment and a critical attitude that was not possible in an oral community. The written word is abstract, objective and timeless. It is an object for contemplation 'and reflection. The written word can be read and re-read for centuries, engaging the reader in a great conversation with all the poets, philosophers and writers of the present and the past.

PLATO: TIME MIRRORS ETERNITY

Theory (*theoria*, derived from the Greek verb "to view") was the name given to the spectators at the Greek games because they looked at the game as distant viewers. Theory refers to viewing ideas in a public way rather than as private thoughts. The shift from myth to philosophy involves an emphasis on theory, the move from particular stories about particular events to a more universal viewpoint. Heraclitus (about 500 B.C.), who was from Ephesus, a settlement in what is today western Turkey, gave full voice to pre-Socratic Greek conceptions of time using terms that were more philosophical than those of the earlier writers. His influence on Plato was profound; therefore, a brief review of some of his main themes is necessary.

Themes of Heraclitus

Heraclitus saw time as the sign of ordered change in a dynamic world. Just as Homer had concentrated on the transitoriness of life and the rule of fate, so Heraclitus focused on the pervasiveness of change: "It is not possible to step in the same river twice."[14] However, he insisted that hidden beneath the appearances of change, a divine rhythm of law, which he called Logos, guided the universe. Although humans are frequently sleepwalkers, without vision, they can awaken to a recognition of the unchanging law, which binds diversity and dynamicity into a continuity. Heraclitus selected fire, a symbol of dynamic change, as his metaphor for this diversity within unity. "This ordered universe, which is the same for all,. . . was . . . and is and shall ever be living fire."[15] The heavenly fires, the sun, moon and stars, traditionally referred to the realm of the gods. The hearth fires, which were kept perpetually burning in Greek homes, signified the presence of ancestors who were considered to be gods.

Heraclitus saw the universe, permeated by change, like a circle without beginning or end, but it was a universe where, in the flux, a balance existed between opposites. "God is day-night, winter-summer, war-peace, satiety-famine."[16] Youth was balanced by age, life was balanced by death, and all humans came to learn this basic fact. Persons "are born, they are willing to live and accept their fate (death) and they leave behind children who will experience the same."[17] It was a human being's capacity to observe and understand this flux that enabled him to grasp the pervasive nature of the law, which gave the whole world its unity, a harmony at first hidden but available to those who searched it out. Within the soul was a measure of the same divine unity, which was the guide of flux; and the search the soul conducted opened the way to a vision of the logos which, in turn, revealed the meaning of the ordered universe.

Heraclitus was perhaps the first to use "soul" in a way that envisioned it as possessing a sort of dignity of its own. This dignity was not unlike the divine law that guided the universe. He did not compare the soul to parts of the body as Homer had done. Nevertheless, soul was still not used to refer to a unique individual; rather, it implied an impersonal entity that was collectively shared with others.

The passage of time was a theme throughout Heraclitus' writings, now known as *The Fragments*. Thus, change in the form of aging and dying was a locus of attention. He believed that in recognizing the harmony of opposites and the tension implicit in them, humans could recognize what was right. "We would not know the name of Right, if these things [the opposites] did not exist."[18] So aging and dying, as part of the ever-changing universe, were a means to a vision of the oneness of the world: "And what is in us is the same thing: living and dead, awake and asleep, as well as young and old, for the latter [of each pair] having changed becomes the former, and this again having changed becomes the latter."[19] Here we see Heraclitus' conviction that instead of accepting time as master of his fate, man could, by reasoning, use time to understand change as part of the game of life. Only in this sense can we read that: "Time is a child playing draughts [checkers]; kingship is in the hands of a child."[20]

Time: The Moving Image of Eternity

In the "Timaeus," Plato hypothesized a universe of two radically different but related realms. The first realm was that of time, the world in which we live; the second was that of timeless or static eternity from which, he believed, time in our world was derived. Time is a mirror of timeless eternity, "the moving (changing) image of eternity."[21] Just as a mirror does not tell lies but is not the object mirrored, so time is not eternity but is a means of reflecting eternity. Because of its orderly succession, time appeals to reason and reveals the universal order of the cosmos. Plato looked into the mirror of time, the realm of change, and saw eternity, the realm of the unchanging.[22]

Some have represented Plato's idea of time as pure illusion, but this goes too far. Plato held that time was an important means of showing or mirroring the eternal principles of Nature, which he, like Heraclitus, referred to as *Logos*, a term he used interchangeably with "Reason." In postulating this transcendent order and connecting it with both Reason itself and with man's reason, Plato took a new direction and a new giant step in the world of philosophy. It is clear that he saw the realm of time as lesser in value than the realm of eternity in that he believed that time, in its uniform flow, mimicked imperfectly eternal truth. Nevertheless, it is the sight of the sun and the seeming revolution of the years that have "given us our conception of time and the power of inquiring about the nature of the universe and from this source we have derived philosophy from which no greater good ever was or will be given by gods to mortal men."[23] Without our experience of the passing of time, Plato believed, we could not partake in an understanding of the "absolutely unerring courses of God."[24]

At the heart of Plato's thought was the Greek insight that Nature was alive and that Reason, the Logos, was steering all things from within. Nature was neither supernatural nor material but a systematic whole pictured by Plato in the metaphor of an organism. He used myths to express this vision. The "Timaeus" was such a myth, "a likely story," but its overall meaning coincided with Plato's general philosophical aim which was to lead his reader, step by step, into the insight that Reason is the best way for humans. The Universe was seen as the product of Reason that sought to realize itself. At the heart of the cosmos an intelligence was at work. This was the key to Plato's comprehensive vision of Nature. His aim was to show how the transcendent order (eternity) is related to and integrated with the order of time. Eternity and time were an organic whole having a purpose, *telos*, which is the principle of teleology. Every part of the system has its purpose and is made to work harmoniously toward an overall end.

At the heart of Plato's thought was the power he attributed to the human soul to comprehend that overall order of the cosmos from an impersonal, timeless vantage point. To understand this assumption of a gods'-eye view, we must consider Plato's meaning for soul. As we have seen, the word *psyche* or soul accumulated many varied meanings in the centuries before Plato. The original sense of psyche, for the early poets, did not imply human consciousness or even possession of senses. The function of the term was to describe life shared by all living things in common. Homer's sense of psyche continued to evolve in the hands of the Orphic religion and the early Pythagoreans prior to Plato. For them, psyche was supremely important in that it had a permanent individuality and was consequently immortal. As a matter of fact, it was seen as a spark of divinity or a god in exile.

In Plato, the translation for *psyche* as "soul" was an unfortunate one. A better translation would be "reason," "mind," or "intelligence." Plato identified *psyche* with personal intelligence and character. He consequently gave the governance of one's life to the person himself, and this theme took a central place in his philosophy. For Plato, the soul steered the person from within, and though it was the author of change, the soul itself was unchanging. Using his metaphorical method, Plato pictured the soul, or reason, as a charioteer who drove two steeds, one good and beautiful, one wanton and ugly. The driver was the controlling force who directed the steeds, compelling them to the goal, and thus the three became one unit.[25]

The Transcendent Order of Forms

Plato believed that the greatest accomplishment of the soul was to comprehend the Forms. We will explore Plato's concept of the Forms in order to have a context within which we can speak of his images of aging and dying. The Platonic term Forms is misleading in English because it does not connote today's meaning of the word. Form had a specific meaning in Plato's writing and referred to the ordering principle by which the world was constituted. This is not the totality of laws that science and scholarship have found, but the principle of all laws, the Logos or Intelligence itself. Plato assumed that if we could have any knowledge at all, it was because permanence and order were already there. He believed that through reason we could partake of this Logos, or Intelligence, and attain a kind of absolute truth or gods'-eye view. This is described in his metaphor of the cave.[26]

Plato pictured humans in their ignorance as being chained in a dark cavernous chamber where they could see only the shadows of objects thrown by firelight on the cave wall in front of them. The prisoners, he said, would believe reality was nothing but the shadows that danced before them. If one of the prisoners were set free and led out of the cave into the sunlight, once his eyes became adjusted to the radiance, true forms would be revealed to him, and the prisoner would realize the limitations of his former state and know that without having had this vision of the true Forms, no one could act with wisdom. The shadows in the prisoners' cave, Plato said, corresponded to what was revealed on earth through the sense of sight. The ascent to the light stood for the upward journey of the soul to the region of the intelligible. Therefore, the soul was like an eye that must be directed toward the light. The soul was the instrument of rational investigation of the Forms that existed outside the human mind but for which the mind had a natural affinity. Therefore, the soul was akin to the Forms and, like them, was imperishable. Reason, Plato believed, had some kind of life after death, but what kind was not clear. As to any proof for survival of individual human consciousness after death, Plato argued for it, but knew his arguments were inconclusive. Clearly, though, it was his conviction that every man had the duty of tending the soul. Happiness lay in perfecting this rational aspect of human existence. For Plato it was an obligation to grasp the overall meaning of the cosmos found in the Forms. This could be done by human beings, who, living the rational life, could read the intellectual principle in the changes that are part of their existence in time. Thus they could manage their conduct in keeping with those principles. In this regard we see the mirror of time as an indispensable instrument. The destiny of rational creatures was to come to know the eternal truths. The soul's power to comprehend the transcendent order of Forms stands between and unites the things of time with eternity's unchanging laws. It is the undying soul that makes humans what they are. The soul is superior to the body as eternity is superior to time.

Growing Old in Wisdom

The Greek image of aging and dying was generally pessimistic. The Greeks saw youth and early manhood as the prime of life and looked upon the years of old age as, at best, anticlimactic, if not loathsome. This view is derived from what was almost a prevailing philosophy in Greece in the literature of the seventh century. For example, Mimnermus, a poet of that century, sang of youth as menaced by the twin dooms of old age and death, and of the two he thought old age was likely the worst.[27]

> Youth is always dear to me;
> Old age is a load that lies
> More heavily on the head
> Than the rocks of Etna.[28]

It was acceptable in ancient Greece to reach old age, but not to linger there. The last years of very old age, especially in case of infirmity, ought to be brief; thus, at this stage death was a preferred event.

Plato's thinking reached a middle ground between pessimism and optimism, recognizing the decline in power of mind and body in old age, but at the same time, reflecting on some compensating gains in growing old. As a person matured, Plato believed, it may have been possible that their education could continue, culminating in a conversion process, not unlike that described in the myth of the cave, where "the soul is able to endure the contemplation of essence and the brightest region of being."[29] The dialectical process used by Plato in his "Dialogues" reflected the process Socrates used. It was a conversation between friends, designed to advance from vague opinions, commonly accepted by the man in the street, to refined definitions and confirmed insights to which one was willing to commit one's beliefs.

Plato thought young people often pursued studies disconnectedly as children do, but an older man, he said, would not share this craze. Those that entered into training as dialecticians could become more reasonable and moderate. Older men were excellent candidates for dialectical training because an orderly and stable nature was needed to use it well, and because one must bring one's experience to bear and shed the light of reason on unwarranted assumptions, thus enabling oneself to come to a new insight and be converted to the truth. When discoveries or new insights were made by a person who was sincere about the process, these discoveries became more than intellectual truths, they became a way of life. Yet young people in learning the intellectual skills of the dialectic, and lacking proper wisdom, often misused them as a form of sport, employing them contentiously. Thus at the age of fifty, Plato thought, one was ready for the study of philosophy which would prepare him to put his wisdom into practice by holding important social posts.

> At the age of fifty those who have survived the tests and proved themselves altogether the best in every task and forms of knowledge must be brought to the last goal. We shall require them to turn upward the vision of their goals and fix their gaze on that which sheds light on all and when they have beheld the good itself they shall use it as a pattern for the right ordering of the state and the citizens themselves throughout the remainder of their lives, each in his turn, devoting the greater part of their time to the study of philosophy, but when the turn comes for each, toiling in the service of the state and holding office for the city's sake, regarding the task as not as a fine thing but a necessity.[30]

These guardians of the state (philosopher-kings) would be honored by public memorials when they died and would depart to the Islands of the Blessed.[31] Plato believed that older people were more likely to be able to have a single aim and purpose in life, rather than the young who had yet to view the form of the good and had yet to grasp the order of the cosmos. Older women, too, endowed with requisite qualities, should receive the same training and be given the same opportunities as men.[32] Thus old age might entail the highest stages of rational development, at least for *ideal* aged persons, in that they would be able to use their knowledge of worldly things to discriminate right from wrong, both for themselves in their private lives, and for others, by holding of public office. But even the average elderly person could also progress to a unique form of wisdom and insight. This was illustrated by Plato at the beginning of the "Republic," as he wrote about the conversation between Socrates and the aged Cephalus. Plato described Socrates' manner as respectful toward Cephalus though the old man was no dialectician. Socrates, as the conversation continued, described himself as filled with admiration for the old man's words. Plato also claimed to enjoy talking with the very aged.

One important refinement of the Greek view of aging was Plato's denial that the decline of physical pleasures in later years was necessarily a loss. Cephalus claimed:

> for my part, as the satisfactions of the body decay, in the same measure my desire for the pleasures of good talk and my delight in them increase. . . . For in very truth there comes to old age a great tranquility . . . fierce tensions of the passions and desires relax . . . we are rid of many mad masters.[33]

In addition Plato claimed through the old man that if we were temperate and moderate, old age would be only somewhat burdensome--but if moderation were lacking, life would be hard for both young and old. In conclusion, Cephalus spoke of a review of life that goes on in the last years before death. This was a call to justice that entailed a consideration of one's past deeds and an attempt, through truthtelling and paying one's debts, to right the wrongs of the past. "When a man begins to realize he is going to die, he is filled with apprehensions and concerns about matters that before did not occur to him."[34] He reviews his life with a vision he could not have had before. "And apart from that the man himself 'either from the weakness of old age or possibly as being now nearer to the things beyond has a somewhat clearer view of them."[35] When he was conscious of having settled matters, Sweet Hope, the nurse of old age as Pindar called her, attended him. Here we see Cephalus struggling in his elder years with philosophical questions of a very practical kind. He questioned attainment of his happiness, spoke about the relationship of wealth and comfort to that life goal, and pondered questions of an ethical and religious nature.[36] Thus, experience was seen as adding to character development, which was traditionally viewed by the Greeks in four virtues: temperance, courage, justice and wisdom.

The general idea seemed to have existed among the Greeks that certain intellectual qualities (prudence, discretion and mature judgment) were the natural heritage of old age and that the old had a duty to

advise the young and to help them gain these qualities. It had been from
the tongue of Nestor, one of the heroes at Troy who was distinguished for
his great age and wisdom, that "words sweet as honey" flowed.[37]

Nevertheless, Plato did not claim old age could bring a complete
reversal of life's habits of virtue or vice. For example, one who had
not valued friendship during his life would be lonely in his later years:
"Old age is wretched to the fool, a man of no friends. Time discovers
him in trials of age at the end of his days destitute of companions and
children."[38]   The old person must also count on good health to make the
quality of his life worthwhile.   Exercise, massage and outdoor life,
Plato said, should be continued into old age. In spite of the short
average life expectancy at that time, once one reached maturity, the
chances of living long improved exponentially. Many great figures lived
until a ripe old age, including Gorgias, who died at one hundred,
Sophocles at ninety and Plato at eighty-two.

Plato compared an elderly survivor, Herodicus, to an elderly
carpenter-craftsman who preferred a fine quality of life to length of
years alone. Herodicus, the survivor, was an invalid who constantly
struggled by means of a strict regimen of gymnastics and medicine to stay
alive, but whose life was miserable for himself and everyone around him
because of the way he had to live. He persevered to "a doting old age"
in spite of the poor quality of his life. On the other hand, the
carpenter-craftsman, who was in bad health, made the decision to stop
doctoring because he believed a life preoccupied with illness and neglect
of his occupation was not worth living. He went back to his active life
and customary work, figuring he would either regain his health or die and
be free of his troubles.[39]   Plato's point was that without health, old
age was a burden.

To keep in perspective the optimistic picture of old age that Plato
painted in the scene with Cephalus, we might reflect on the note of
ambiguity that hangs over much of Plato's comments in other passages
about long life. His attitude matched the ambivalence that was never far
from the surface in the Greek dread of death, which was thought of as
"the most terrible of all things."[40] Plato's mood was less idealistic
when in his elder years he wrote in the "Laws" about the wine cup which
Dionysius bestowed on advancing years, as a sacrament and a pastime, a
comfortable medicine against the "dryness of old age" to renew youth and
"melt the harsh mood." A cup of wine would bring "forgetfulness of our
heaviness as iron is melted in the furnace and is so made more
tractable."[41]

The sharp contrast with the optimism of the Cephalus scene in the
"Republic," can be best understood, if it is kept in mind that the
"Republic," as a whole, aimed at explicating an ideal state of affairs,
almost a utopia, which Plato himself was not sure would come about. In
contrast, the "Laws" was a carefully thought out form of constitution or
legal code that Plato thought necessary if Hellenic civilization was to
survive.   In the "Laws" he appeals to lawmakers to design rules to punish
those who did not respect the elderly. He had also lost a good bit of
his youthful idealism, noting that children ought to minister to their
parents in three ways: with their property, with their person and with
their soul.[42] Those who would lift impious hands against parents would

receive penalties and even stripes for neglecting them. In some cases it
was recommended that they be put to death for violent acts against their
seniors. All through the "Laws" Plato shows deep concern about the
problems of older people and attempts to point out practical ways to care
for them when they suffer or are in misery. The implication that
disrespect existed and required correction lifts the veil of idealism
about the supposed picture of universal respect for old age in the Greek
community of the fifth century.[43] Plato wrote the "Laws" as an elderly
man, at a time when he not only thought about aging but was realistically
experiencing it.

Practicing Death Daily

The life and thought of Socrates deeply influenced Plato's ideas.
It is believed that Plato was so affected by Socrates' death that it
influenced the whole direction of his philosophical effort. In the
"Phaedo," Plato described Socrates' courage and serenity as he discussed
the nature of death in the last hours before he drank the hemlock. In
order to cope with death rationally, Socrates had advised a method of
self-education by means of which dying could be put into proper
perspective. He pointed out that all those who followed the agonizing
path of philosophy would search out insights that would illuminate their
way. Socrates made an interesting connection between death and truth--he
suggested that philosophers constantly pursue dying because they are in
search of truth. This connection is found again in Plato's belief that
the body was subject to death, but the soul was undying. With this
doctrine Plato stepped out of the mainstream of Greek tradition that
emphasized the immense imbalance between gods and men, one eternal and
undying, the other temporal and subject to death. In this doctrine
afterlife became something far greater than an unattractive form of
existence in Hades.

Plato's "Phaedo" explained that if at its release the soul were pure
and did not carry with it contamination from the body, it was because of
the regular practice it had engaged in throughout life. The practice
that freed it from the body was the daily practice of death.[44] This
notion of practicing death refers to a kind of preparation for life
separate from the body. Death was like a play for which philosophers
rehearsed daily in order to be prepared for release.[45] There was a sense
here that philosophy was a way to keep the soul pure and prepare it for a
life after death: "If a man has trained himself through his life to live
in a state as close as possible to death, would it not be ridiculous for
him to be distressed when death comes to him?"[46]

Death was a basic and immensely important theme in Plato's system.
He saw death as a release from the prison of the body, a means of
dispensing with the mirror which could only give a reflected or imperfect
copy of eternal truths. By seeking truth one could see beyond death,
aging, and all the changes of life wrought by time, to the "Form of the
Good." Thereby one could keep his eyes lit by the fire of rationality.
While in the realm of time, one should prepare everyday by being aware of
the limitations of time, and thus, by keeping one's eye, not on that
mirror, but on the things of eternity reflected in it.

The inspiring insight that stood at the heart of Plato's metaphysic and his overarching theories about the cosmos was the transitoriness of the things of time against the stability of the World of Forms with the former only a stage in an ascent to the latter. A second insight was Plato's belief in the regenerative power of philosophy. The philosopher was the one who died best because he shared the view, from the universal vantage point, of the comprehensive rational order of being. This was what put the process of aging and dying into perspective.

Though Plato argued for immortality in the "Phaedo" and "Phaedrus," he admitted that rational grounds for this belief were not successfully established. Perhaps it remained only a hope. Many scholars believe Socrates' agnostic position, taken at the end of the "Apology," represented Plato's real view. Here Socrates claimed that fear of death was but ignorance because no one knows what death entails: "to be afraid of death is only another form of thinking that one is wise when one is not; it is to think that one knows what one does not know. No one knows with regard to death whether it is not really the greatest blessing . . . but people dread it."[47]

Socrates viewed death as one of two things. It was either total annihilation, in which the soul has no consciousness but only dreamless sleep, or it was migration to a better place where the great heroes abide: "How much would one of you give to meet Orpheus . . . Hesiod and Homer? I am willing to die--ten times over, if this account were true."[48]

Plato, influenced by belief in the soul's release and return to its divine status, always tended to treat the mind as the immortal part of the soul. He pointed out in the "Phaedrus" that there is a possibility that souls would migrate after death through repeated incarnations.[49] The soul, or *psyche*, thus came to be regarded as independent of the body in a way quite different from the older Homeric sense, in which it outlasted the body as a mere shadow of the person. Plato spoke of a pre-existence and a transmigration after death, which was in keeping with the Greek tradition of cyclical time, suggesting a repeated passage from life to death and back to life again. Some souls, Plato said, eager to reach the heights of eternal bliss, fall or are sucked down, and the charioteer is powerless to control the steeds. For all that toil, they still lose the full vision of truth and are deceived by appearances. Subsequently the soul must pass through a series of incarnations for as long as ten thousand years to regain the high place, but this long period could be shortened, Plato said, if in three successive incarnations one could live as a philosopher.[50]

Evidently Plato's concepts of the soul, time, aging and dying were the result of his comprehensive vision of Nature as a two-level cosmos, an orderly system that integrated time and eternity. For Plato, the human soul stood between the temporal and eternal realms and was capable of participating in both. Though man's thirst for knowledge and real happiness would never be quenched in this world by wisdom and knowledge, which as reserved for the gods, intelligence, he believed, existed at the heart of things. Plato believed that with consistent striving, not in spite of aging and death, but *through* them, human beings could achieve eternal destiny. By passing through the realm of time, the soul, in contemplating the "Good," could spring open the hinge of the oyster shell of a body it is enclosed in and reach the heights of rational bliss.[51]

ARISTOTLE: OLD AGE, COLD AND DRY

Aristotle's (384-322 B.C) aims and interests as a philosopher were different from those of his teacher Plato; therefore, his theories of aging and dying took a different direction. In addition to his interest in cosmology and metaphysics and his exploration of the origin of the universe and the nature of the soul, Aristotle wrote treatises on such topics as physiology, biology and physics. Since one of his great concerns was with the principles that govern the natural world, his investigations dealt with the physiological as well as the philosophical aspects of aging and dying.[52] His physiological theories were aligned with the Hippocratic school of ancient medicine.

During Aristotle's time there were basically three schools of medicine in Greece: the temple school that maintained its magico-religious origins and conducted healings in the temples of Aesculapius, the philosophical school, which remained basically theoretical; and the Hippocratic school of rational medicine whose physicians, while retaining the dialectical skills of the philosopher, concentrated on the practical aspects of medical care. Hippocratic doctors were mainly practitioners, craftsmen, deeply convinced that nature was a healing force in itself. Thus they concentrated more on the health of the body's natural systems than on the nature of disease. They believed in the treatment of the whole body, not part of it.

The Hippocratic school based its model of medicine on a scheme of four "humors" or fluids--blood, phelgm, choler (yellow bile) and melanchol (black bile). These determined not only the organism's state of health, but its disposition as well. The ages of human life were, therefore, divided into four humoral categories: childhood was seen as hot and moist; youth was hot and dry; adulthood was cold and dry; and old age was cold and moist. Aristotle concurred with the humoral theory. However, he insisted that old age was not cold and moist but cold and dry, a state more like death than life. "We must remember that an animal is by nature humid and warm, and to live is to be of such a constitution, while old age is dry and cold, and so is a corpse."[53] This hypothesis about aging as cold and dry is illustrated in Aristotle's picture of youth and old age from "Rhetoric" where he contrasted two profiles: one of youth and one of a man in old age, and balanced them with the profile of a man in his prime of life.

Aristotle pointed out three general areas of comparison between the behavior of the young and the old: the first had to do with passions, the second with self-evaluation, and the third with relationships with others. Young men, he said, are quick to anger; they are generally given to strong passions that are over quickly, to self-gratification, especially regarding sex, and are egotistical, loving honor and superiority. Old men, past their prime, are chilly, neither loving warmly nor hating bitterly; their anger comes in fits, but is feeble. Some people see them as having much self-control in sensual matters, but

Aristotle believed their sensual passions had flagged. In his view old men talk too much about the past and live on memories rather than on hope for the future. The young are the opposite--they are overly optimistic about the future, trusting, and even reckless in their over confidence and lack of fear. As a result the young are vulnerable to disappointment because they underestimate their limits and think themselves equal to great accomplishments. Old men, on the contrary, are timid and, having made many mistakes, think life as a whole is bad business. Their pessimism and suspicion mark them as cynics. They grow stingy and small-minded because life has humbled them. Feeling sure about nothing, the old are often cowardly and always anticipate danger. Their desires are minimal. Often they seek only what will barely keep them alive.

In contrast, Aristotle believed, young men are outgoing and fond of friends whom they often fail to value enough. Living more by feeling than reason, and overdoing everything, they love heroism and applause. They wrong others they never mean to hurt, and they feel pity out of kindness. But, most of all, young people love laughing and good times. By comparison, elderly men seek their own personal gain rather than friends. Living more by reason than feeling, they look for what is useful rather than noble. When they wrong others, they intend to injure them and, instead of laughing a lot, they are querulous and mean tempered.

Aristotle's view of aging was pessimistic at best. It stood in sharp contrast to Plato's optimistic profile of Cephalus. This is not surprising, since Aristotle's practical and realistic approach to life differed basically from Plato's idealistic views, especially those expressed in the "Republic." Aristotle thought that mid-life was the time of greatest physical and mental strength as well as a time of emotional balance. Men in their prime have neither excess nor lack of passion. Rather they display moderation: "To put it generally, all the valuable qualities that youth and age divide between them are united in the prime of life, while all their excesses or defects are replaced by moderation and fitness."[54] Aristotle claimed that the body was at its most perfect point between thirty and thirty-five and the mind at about forty-nine. Aristotle was about forty-nine years old when he wrote this.

At first glance these profiles of youth and age might seem mere stereotypes because they are so stark in their delineation of extremes of behavior. Nevertheless, in the light of Aristotle's larger works, this picture can fall into place especially when taken in the context of his notions of time, his concept of the soul and his theory of moderation.

Time: A Physical Definition

In following his prime motivation, to understand the principles of the natural world, Aristotle studied the functions of time. His central thesis about time and motion has influenced the thoughts and writings of philosophers and scientists ever since. That thesis, simply stated, was that time is nothing more than the measure of change.

A very pivotal question occurred to Aristotle in his reflections on time. It was the simple but profound question: Is there time, if human consciousness is not present? Is there measurement without a measurer?

In "On the Senses" he answered this question from a psychological point of view. He claimed that time would not exist apart from consciousness. The soul was thus tied to time as a necessary perceiver of continuity. The "true perceiving subject" could unify separate instants by perceiving change in its own state of self-awareness.[55] Here Aristotle was on the verge of seeing that time is not dependent on physical change primarily (the time of things), but on the intelligent subject for whom the experience of time is not merely outward, but inward as well (the time of persons). By making this connection between self-awareness and time, Aristotle was on the brink of discovering subjective time, time that requires the self-awareness of the human person. However, this line of thought was not compatible with the model that Aristotle was developing, therefore, he abandoned it in favor of the time of physical bodies.

Time for Aristotle involved the traditional Greek cyclical model of the uniform revolution of the heavenly bodies acting as a standard by which all change could be measured and numbered precisely. In his attempt to explain the time of natural physical bodies on earth, Aristotle introduced the metaphor of time as a line. The "now" was seen as a point on a line and successively discriminated linear points accounted for change or movement "as to before and after." Aristotle's physical model of linear time proved immensely useful to future scientists and was broadly adopted through the centuries that followed. Nevertheless, though the physical interpretation of linear spatialized time would become a very valuable instrument for the West as a whole, as with every metaphor, it would prove to have its limits. The scientist is concerned with using the concept of time to understand change, but this using of time would lead to its reification as a commodity. Time would become abstracted and lose its connection with the human experience of change.

Hans Georg Gadamer pointed out how human it is to see time in terms of its usefulness:

> It is surely a fundamental human attitude rather than a mere consequence of Greek ontology to regard time as something to be used, counted and measured. This use of time implies the ability to conceive it *in abstracto*, i.e., as "empty" and that is what Aristotle has in mind when he speaks of the "feeling of time" as characteristic of men.[56]

But Gadamer also remarks on the limitations of this concept: "But, it must be admitted that this is a very one-sided way of experiencing time: it is seen as being at a man's disposal, as 'empty' time, a homogeneous expanse stretching before him into a distance as if specially smoothed out for his benefit."[57] Time, seen apart from human experience, became the objective counting of moments and years that are uniform and devoid of human content or interpretation. In connection with our concern for time, aging and dying, it is crucial to see how Aristotle pictured time as related to change.

Nature, Growth and Decay

Like Plato, Aristotle believed in the principle of the intrinsic directedness of Nature. Every step of the natural process of growth was controlled by the character of the whole. But Aristotle's "internal teleology" differed from Plato's "external teleology" because Aristotle believed that the forms were not external but internal. He argued that individual substances have a form within them that in its beginning, exists only potentially. As a sculptor works his clay, eventually form works in the substance until it takes shape and realizes itself or becomes actual.[58] For example, one might have the form of a good lyrist, but the potential for the accomplishment of the perfect performance on the lyre must be developed before an actual performance can be given. Aristotle saw the perfect actuality of the form of man in terms of his rational powers. But this development of the form of an object or person from potential excellence to actual fulfillment must take place over a period of time. The metaphor used by Aristotle is that of "growth" which takes place "'in the complete life' for one swallow does not make a summer nor does one day . . . make a man blessed and happy."[59] Aristotle concluded that time works for man in the sense that it enables him to develop good habits of life; therefore, "Time is a good discoverer or partner in such a work."[60]

Aristotle, then, conceived form as an active force working within natural limits to reach the fulfillment of its purpose. It was the metaphor of growth that Aristotle used to describe the form, coming into actuality. Moving from potentiality to actuality the form reached its "most perfect point," *entelechy*, the best realization of its purpose, not the "final point." For example, Aristotle considered the soul as the form of the body, because it had the potential to bring the body to its intended and best point, rational living, the peak of human capacity.

By his use of the concept of the rational soul as the perfect form of the body, Aristotle showed that human nature had a basic tendency toward rationality and an affinity for ordered thinking. It was the rational "psyche" that enabled one to reach his highest peak of accomplishment, the activity of thought.[61] Growth toward actuality in humans did not necessarily go on to the end of one's life, but until the peak or prime of life, when the person had attained the highest fulfillment of his nature. This explains Aristotle's view that the peak of physical development was in the thirties and mental development near fifty and why he anticipated progressive physical decline after that age.

Time, therefore, was a "good discoverer" of growth. But time was also the cause of decay. Things in time, Aristotle said, are wasted by it.

A thing, then, will be affected by time, just as we are accustomed to say that time wastes things away, and that all things grow old through time and that there is oblivion owing to the lapse of time, but we do not say the same of . . . becoming young and fair. For time is, by its nature, the cause rather of decay since it is the number of change and change removes what is.[62]

Time is the condition of destruction, and since at this period there was no concept of time as progress, there was a feeling of drudgery in what was seen as an infinitely repeatable cycle. Once one reached the age of prime, physically and mentally, time became a countdown toward death.

The Way of Moderation

The picture of an overall harmony and balance in the universe was another central theme in Aristotle's thought. He applied it to human conduct in the "doctrine of the mean," or "the middle way," which was seen as the universal principle of the good life. Observance of the mean made it possible for persons to reach a perfect point. This rational course steered men between too much or too little of anything. This notion of the "mean" was the old Greek idea of moderation, *sophrosyne*. *The Iliad*, for example, focused on the consequences of excessive wrath or immoderate pride. Again, Euripides centered the whole play, *Medea*, on a condemnation of lack of moderation found in fifth-century values in Athens: "Life, is changed and the laws of it o'ertrod./ Man hath forgotten God. . . ."[63] What the Greeks admired all along, and what showed up here in Aristotle as nothing new, was a self-imposed discipline that balanced reason and desire without dismissing the passions. Humans that follow the mean, then, live by order and restraint; and the opposite representes excess and extremes in human conduct.

Old Age: Past the Prime of Life

The profiles of aging and youth in "Rhetoric" can only be understood within the context of the doctrine of the mean, which was the centerpiece of Aristotle's ethical thought.[64] In fact, set in the middle of a discussion of human character, emotions and moral qualities, these profiles can be interpreted as Aristotle's way of illustrating the theme of the middle way. Therefore, the old man described in the passage in the "Rhetoric" was not the ideal aged person but an extreme. The man in his prime had all the valuable qualities of both youth and old age but was free from the extremes of either. Nevertheless, it was not merely to illustrate his doctrine of the mean that Aristotle drew this grim picture of the plight of the elderly. We must go beyond these profiles to see Aristotle's ideas about old age within the perspective of his philosophy of time, the measuring of change without reference to the person who experienced it. Aristotle saw time in youth as growth toward a point of potential physical and mental perfection. It implied the reaching of as perfect a point as one's habits and circumstances would allow, which would be followed by inevitable decline and death.

Aristotle described time in old age as the condition of inevitable destruction. Later life was the period when old people withdrew, losing their idealistic views and becoming difficult company for others. In all this he offered little advice on how to grow old gracefully. He suggested that one simply accept in stride the decline that ensues after the prime of life. Old age and death were a natural part of the orderly coming-to-be and passing-away of the things of time. Whatever was born, grew and reached maturity, died and decayed. Aristotle irretrievably connected aging and dying, for aging was a form of dying. In fact he expressed his admiration for Nature's ability to arrange for this orderliness of events. In one passage he spoke of Nature's wisdom in having old people's teeth decay and fall out when they were no longer needed because of the imminence of death.[65] Acceptance of old age was in keeping with the Greek tradition, which, though it had a tolerance for the old, at the same time expressed an extraordinary dread of the enfeeblement of growing old. The Greeks "were interested in obtaining a long life, if they might retain good health and activity. Long life without these blessings possessed no charm."[66]

There is evidence that Socrates, when given the opportunity to escape death, may have hesitated to prolong his days, lest he be forced to pay the price by having to endure the frailties of old age. Xenephon, in his report of Socrates' trial, suggested that the seventy-year-old philosopher had come to the conclusion that death was more desirable for him than life. Xenephon had Socrates say: "Now if my years are prolonged, I know that the frailties of old age will inevitably be realized. . . . Perhaps God in his kindness is taking my part and securing me the opportunity of ending my life not only in season but also in the way that is easiest."[67]

Aristotle described growing old painlessly as desirable, "for a man has not his happiness, if he grows old . . . quickly or . . . painfully".[68] He believed proper aging could be assured only by a good constitution and good luck. Aristotle emphasized the importance of health, mentioning, as Plato had, the invalid Herodicus and commenting that Herodicus' life was such a struggle that it seemed too much for a human to bear, since "he had to abstain from everything, or nearly everything, that men do."[69] For the Greek health was defined as balance or harmony achieved by proper diet, exercise, recreation and clear thinking. The ideal was *kalos kagathos*, the beautiful and brilliant, harmony of mind and body. Excellence in a young man was having a body that was both beautiful and fit to endure the exertion of the races. In a man of prime excellence was fitness for the exertion of warfare. For the elderly it was in maintaining enough strength to manage a life free of those decrepit deformities that caused pain to himself and to others. In general it can be said that the Greeks were imbued with the idea that aging was as ineluctable as Fate's decrees and that ideally this fact was to be lived with, not avoided.[70]

Courageous Death: The Ultimate Gods'-Eye View

Aristotle's attitude toward death was colored by his views on immortality. He believed that reason, as one part of the soul, was immortal, but he was indefinite when it came to telling clearly what he meant by this theory or spelling out how reason *is* immortal. Earlier in his career he gave intimations of agreement with his teacher, Plato, on pre-existence and transmigration of the soul after death, but as his analytic and empiricist tendencies developed in the mature years of his philosophical career, he withdrew these views and explicitly denied migration of the soul.[71] In place of these views Aristotle expressed real doubts about survival of the soul after death: "We must examine whether any form . . . exists afterwards."[72]

Toward the end of his life he made an important distinction in order to clarify his position on the immortality of reason--he distinguished "passive reason" from "active reason." He taught that passive reason merely received knowledge, but active reason was a cause of knowledge. Using the metaphor of light, he explained that in the presence of active reason, knowledge became possible just as in the presence of light potential colors become visible. What stands out is that Aristotle argued that this active reason was separable from the body. In fact, he believed that only when it was separated from the body did active reason have its true nature, which was "immortal and eternal."[73] Here Aristotle clearly stated that at death, mind escaped the body and attained perfection: "When mind is set free from its present conditions it appears as just what it is and nothing more . . . immortal and eternal."[74]

There have been bitter debates about what Aristotle meant when he talked about the immortality of reason. Whether he held that the individual consciousness continued or that the spark of the divine in humans became one with the eternal prime mover, is not known. What we are sure of is that he believed that "something divine present in man" allowed the person to enter into the activity of reason, which was superior in worth because it aimed at "no end beyond itself."[75] "That which is proper to each thing is by nature best and most pleasant for each thing; for man, therefore, the life according to reason is best and pleasantest, since reason more than anything else *is* man."[76]

Aristotle's first priority was not to strive for knowledge regarding the form reason would take after death. His first concern was that we "strain every nerve to live in accord with the best thing in us."[77] Though he viewed time as destructive and aging as a miserable state of decline, he consoled himself and advised us to take consolation from the fact that mind did not decay. Strength came from the vision of the cosmos as a whole. He claimed the solution to the fear of dying and the general destructiveness of time was to be found in rational courage, realistic acknowledgment of the limits of the body and a faith in divine, eternal and indestructible Nature and man's ability to know Nature's purpose. This was the ultimate gods'-eye view."

In the final analysis, Aristotle advised control of the fear of death by a rational acceptance of the inevitable. Yet the same sense of finality and even pessimism, with which the Greek tradition resounded, rings in his own words when he insists that death is "the most terrible of all things, for it is the end and nothing is . . . any longer either good or bad for the dead."[78]

For the ancient Greeks, the forces that controlled human destiny loomed large on the horizon of their cosmos. The mirror of time reflected either a capricious fate or an eternal scheme, which, though rational, was still unavoidable. If Plato or Aristotle were alive today, they might be shocked to find that some two thousand years later their thoughts and ideas are not only discussed, but that these ideas have deeply influenced the images, metaphors and models that emerged through many centuries. The same philosophical questions raised by the ancient Greeks still exist today. At the heart of human destiny stands the perennial figure of time. Aging and dying are still played by the rules and kingship is in the hands of time.

IMAGES OF IMMORTALITY: JEWISH AND EARLY CHRISTIAN CONCEPTS OF TIME, AGING AND DEATH

For a thousand years in thy sight are but as yesterday.
Psalm 90

The roots of Western culture were richly nourished by the Judeo-Christian heritage, which provided images and metaphors that helped shape the models that emerged in the following centuries. Implicit in the Jewish heritage was a unique concept of time, which fostered solid respect for the elderly, the "blessed fathers" and implied specific attitudes toward death. With the emergence of Christianity a new image of immortality took hold that engendered attitudes toward both aging and death that were different from those of the Greeks and Hebrews.

MAY YOU LIVE TO BE 120

In contrast to Greek pessimism and preoccupation with the unavoidable consequences of time, the Jewish tradition, from its ancient beginnings, reverberated with the consistent ring of "le Chaim," the optimistic theme celebrating life. On festive occasions Jews greet one another with the blessing: "May you live to be 120." This wish refers to Genesis, where both aging and death are put into perspective by the word of God. On one hand, God warns that humans, made of flesh, must die. "Then the Lord said, 'My spirit shall not abide in man forever, for he is flesh.'" On the other hand, God makes a promise: "but his days shall be a hundred and twenty years" (Gen. 6:3).[1]

Again, in the closing lines of *Deuteronomy* (34:7), the Bible states that Moses, the towering hero who led the Jews out of captivity in Egypt in the thirteenth century B.C.E. after being shown the Promised Land by God, died at the age of 120 and, far from being decrepit, "his eye was not dim nor his natural force abated."[2] Jews believed traditionally that long years were a blessing from God and a reward for holiness; hence, morality and length of life were tied together. Nevertheless, the chronological counting of years was considered less important than honesty and wisdom: "Honorable age is not that which stands in length of time nor is it measured by numbers of years. Wisdom is grey hair unto

men and unspotted life is of old age" (Wisd. of Sol.4 :8-9). There is
within the Hebrew tradition a deep conviction that emphasizes the
qualitative more than the quantitative interpretation of time.
Therefore, we will consider the attitude of Israel toward both aging and
dying within the context of this unique interpretation of time.

The Biblical View of Time

Hebrew concentration on time was a perfect contrast to Greek
preoccupation with space. Both related the determination of time to the
heavenly spheres. Greeks called the luminaries "bodies" and determined
time by their positions in the heavens. Hebrews referred to these
illuminations as "lights, bright and warm." Using the irregular phases
of the moon to orient themselves temporally, they focused on the rhythmic
alteration of light and dark, not the apparent circular movement of the
sun. Thus, the quantitative and spatial emphasis of the Greeks can be
contrasted to a qualitative and operational interpretation of the
Hebrews.

While time for the Greeks was interpreted within the context of a
standard, the eternal circular motion of the heavenly bodies, time for
the Hebrews was not primarily concerned with duration or extent of time,
nor its measurement. Rather it was related to the flow or rhythm of time
which had an interior relationship to human life and God. Therefore, the
functions of the heavenly luminaries were mainly revelatory in character;
first they told of God's power, glory and goodness, then they marked out
the holy seasons of the priestly year; and only then did they date
secular time.[3]

Time for the Hebrews was seen as relative to the actions of both God
and mankind; it was understood in terms of events and defined by
circumstances. Time periods were spoken of, for example, as "in the days
of King Solomon" or "in the reign of Tiberius." Rather than using the
metaphors of time cycles or time lines, the Hebrews preferred the
metaphor of rhythm as in the beating of a pulse, a biological rhythm, or
their customary round dances. The shortest unit of time for the Hebrews
was not a point or even a duration, but a beat *(regha)*, like a heartbeat,
but with the connotation of anticipation as in a sudden unexpected event.
This sense of time was, therefore, identified with human action and
experience.[4]

The Hebrew sense of consciousness is also important here. As space
was a container that held the universe together for the Greeks, so time
did that for the Hebrews. Consciousness served to unify the experiences
of the past and to anticipate the future; therefore, it was a
consolidating and unifying force within the people. In viewing the events
of life from inside, people formed their identity and their world.
Consciousness discerned meaning in events. Therefore, Israel could see
the meaning of its exiles, defeats and victories and in them could
discern Israel's character before God. The Hebrews also believed that
it is God's consciousness of himself that is his divine identity: "It is
clear what meaning God's consciousness must have had for the Hebrews; the
life of man encompasses a small part of the history of existence, the
life of a people a greater part, the life of humanity a still greater

part, but the life of God encompasses everything."[5]

This sense of world consciousness, which was all-embracing, could be contrasted with the gods'-eye view of the Greeks in which humans could comprehend timeless truth; the way things *are*, being itself. The Israelites, however, made no such claims. A more correct view for them would be that only the transcendent God could have such a view. It is the difference between being divine and being a limited human, a condition that humans ought to accept. To raise oneself up to the level of knowing what God knows would be the greatest sin of all: "Know that the Lord is God! It is he that made us, and we are his; we are his people, and the sheep of his pasture" (Ps. 100:3).

For the Jews the passing of time, aging and death were the lot of all things created, but the Lord was eternal in all his actions and pronouncements. "The grass withers, the flower fades; but the word of our God will stand for ever" (Is. 40:8). The Jews saw past, present and future as a historical unity. Whereas the Greeks, essentially ahistorical in their approach, considered the functions of time (seeing its units as uniform), the Jews viewed time, or more properly, we should speak of "times" from the point of view of the consciousness of the people interpreting events that happened past and present. Thus they evaluated them in relation to the future and to God. "My times are in thy hand" (Is. 31:15).

The solidarity of the Jewish nation was retained in this common consciousness and in the memory of what God had done for its people. This consciousness of the people of Israel was a historical consciousness. To select one example, Jacob, the divinely inspired patriarch of the Jewish people, called his sons to his bedside near the time of his death, saying: "Gather yourselves together, that I may tell you that which shall befall you in the days to come" (Gen. 49:1-33). Jacob offered his blessing; but not just his blessing, he offered God's blessing and promises of God's protection. He offered predictions, historical descriptions of the future of Israel. He spoke for God and predicted that the people of Israel would continue in his sons. The blessing of the father was on the head of his sons: "All these are the twelve tribes of Israel; . . . he blessed them, blessing each with the blessing suitable to him" (Gen. 49:28). There was a powerful sense of unique destiny felt by every generation of Jews. The Bible expressed it in its description of Israel as a chosen people.

The Jewish Nation and Time

Judaism was one of the primary shaping forces in Western culture. The name "Hebrew" ("ibhri") referred to the people who descended from Abraham, whose ancestor was Eber or Heber (Gen. 10:21). After their sojourn in Egypt, these people reconquered Palestine and finally settled there, forming the first Hebrew state in the eleventh century B.C.E. under King Saul. However, in 933 the Northern tribes revolted, splitting the state into two kingdoms, Israel in the North and Judah in the South. After a few centuries, both kingdoms were driven into exile by enemy invaders, but it was mainly the descendents of Judah that returned in 538 B.C.E. and reestablished the Palestinian state. After that they were known as "Jehudins" ("Yehudim") which later became "Jews."

Adonai was an ancient desert god, gradually accepted by the Semitic tribes as the national God of the People of Israel and eventually as the one God of all.[6] The backbone of the Nation consisted of the relationship between God and the Chosen People of Israel. The main emphasis, then, was on the communal aspect of Jewish existence. The individual Jew had significance mainly as a member of the holy nation, and the actions of that individual were important only insofar as they affected the nation for good or evil. This was a religion of action in that it focused on a people seen as fashioning, with clean hands and a pure heart, a world according to God's will.

This theology had its own interpretation of history. For example, the prophets such as Isaiah, Jeremiah, Ezekiel and Daniel customarily reminded the Jews of their allegiance to Adonai by appealing to their memory of the deliverance from exile and cruel slavery in Egypt and their ancestors' settlement in the promised land of Canaan. These events signaled the providence of Adonai, in his care of the people of Israel. About the ninth century B.C.E., the story of these actions of God and the people was written in a long narrative going back to the creation of the world, through the lives of the progenitors of the Israelites, the patriarchs, Abraham, Isaac and Jacob, unfolding the events of the long sojourn in Egypt to the conquest of the promised land. The influence of this story, which became part of sacred scripture, was profound. It molded the Jewish concept of time as "the field in which God manifested his power and his providence in their behalf."[7]

The history of the events in the lives of the people of Israel was interpreted teleologically, that is, as revealing divine purposes. Just as Plato and Aristotle had their form of teleology, as a universe embodying the eternal purpose of a cosmic order, so the Jews believed in an historical teleology--that the temporal process gradually unfolded a plan that was set out by God, beginning with creation. The destiny of Israel was the main concern of that plan. For the Jews, the mirror of time reflected the face of God in that it showed a divine plan in progress. Thus, the Jews are said to be the "builders of time."[8] They built a history of a people. In no way did they think speculatively concerning time; rather "time is grasped in terms of purpose, will and decision."[9] The transcendent Lord of time revealed himself in the events of time. In this sense time had a life of its own; it is "charged with substance."[10] Each day was the day of the Lord, and each generation had within it the generations before and after. The son had the father within him, as all humans had God within, and all this was played out in the course of time. To the Israelites, the repetitive cycle of nature was of less significance than the unique events of history. Unlike other peoples whose deities were connected with places and things, the Jewish God was the God of events. What was sacred was the consciousness of the people that brought together the memories of the past with the events of the present and carved out the future in the light of both.

It was a basic tenet of Jewish tradition that the God of Israel, on certain momentous occasions, entered into a formal covenant with the Jewish people as a whole.[11] "Then God said to Noah and to his sons with him, 'Behold, I establish my covenant with you and your descendents after you'" (Gen. 9:8-9). When Abraham was ninety-nine, the Lord appeared to him and said, "I am God Almighty; walk before me, and be blameless. And I will make my covenant between me and you and will multiply you exceedingly" (Gen. 17:1-2). Again, Moses was called up to the top of Mount Sinai, in the middle of the desert, on the way out of Egypt where he met and talked with God who said:

> You have seen what I did to the Egyptians, and how I bore you on eagles' wings and brought you to myself. Now therefore, if you will obey my voice and keep my covenant, you shall be my own possession among all peoples; . . . and you shall be to me a kingdom of priests and a holy nation.(Ex. 19: 4-6)

Then God gave the Jews the Ten Commandments, and they pledged to serve him and no other god. The covenant sets up the unique historical relationship between God and people of Israel. The people were sent by God to advance into history and to engage actively in directing it toward a goal: "Biblical man, plunged into the flow of history, discerned its direction."[12]

Unlike the Greeks, the Jews believed in a final catharsis, an end point of time. Though there may be failures on the way, Jewish insight was one of consistent hope, both in God and in humankind. That hope represented the optimistic view that time would come to fruition when God's plan was complete and harmony was restored to all nations. The day would come when an enduring age of uninterrupted peace would reign among all men. But all this must take place through the effort and faithfulness of man. This is the antithesis of Greek deterministic thought. The Jews believed that history challenged the People of God. God acted for Israel, so Israel must act for God. But no divine plan could dictate or even forsee the future as it would in an order based on Fate. The reason was that in Jewish thought, the community was granted a freedom that was so radical that it was capable of jeopardizing the whole plan of God. Human freedom, for the Jew, was radical in the sense that one could choose to renounce one's relationship with the Divinity. Nevertheless, in the Jewish view, freedom was conditional in that mankind still relied on God for the creation and sustenance of life. God in his freedom, it was believed, could destroy the world at any time. God's freedom was unconditional; human freedom was conditional. Both God's and man's freedom were radical in that either could hypothetically abandon the other. But the Jews were theologically optimistic. They believed that, though wickedness would exist and that individuals would sin, in the end evil would not prevail:

> This notion of freedom, as terrifying as it is, is essential to the ways of the Hebrew God. The possibility of choice must be present and this choice between cooperation or resistance is what creates a genuine dilemma for God. We are able to alter the course of affairs even against God's will.[13]

The Bible is full of examples of deviance, rebelliousness and refractoriness: "Remember and do not forget how you provoked the Lord your God to wrath in the wilderness; from the day you came out of the land of Egypt, . . . you have been rebellious against the Lord" (Deut. 9:7).

In the Jewish scripture the sinner was seen as stiffnecked, that is, as having the capacity to lose contact with God and to abandon the consciousness that can see through events to discern in them the will of God. Freedom represented "the divine watershed" in that it could lead to the fulfillment or destruction of God's creation. God's decision: "Let us make man . . . [and] . . . let them have dominion . . . over all the earth" (Gen. 1:26) was a risk, because all creation could come to naught in human hands. By retaining this notion of human freedom, the strict and terrible logic of the Jewish theologians depicted a God who in the evolution of relationships implied by the Sinai covenant, pushed man not to a logical choice, but to one of the heart: to retain one's freedom while choosing to serve the one God. This was the paradox at the core of the Jewish notion of the person. The essence of Jewish ethics was found in the paradoxical combination of self-assertion and self-resignation that made for voluntary moral conduct as well as compliance to the law. Thus the *Torah* (fourth century B.C.E.) put the law in the form of a set of principles, routine laws and binding customs that people could live by. Even after being scattered all over the world, Jews could be united by the keeping of the law and traditions. Herein lay the power of the law to unite: its aims transcended the individual. Judaism's central emphasis was upon the destiny of mankind and, within mankind, of the Jewish people in this world.

The individual may try, like some Jewish philosophers, to rationalize the law but cannot change it. The Bible did not offer reasons or explanations about the nature of things, and, even where the origin of the universe was considered, it was no metaphysical treatise. Rather than searching out the "why" of things as the Greeks did, the Bible reflected on "what" was the relationship between God and man, and what was man to do on earth, given this relationship. The history of events was uneven and changing and covered many eras. Metaphysics, such as the Greeks had, would be seen by the Hebrew as futile rationalization, which implied a gods'-eye view that the they believed to be impossible for human beings. In its stead they tried to render meaningful the immediate experience of man in the light of the spiritual history of the people, and waited in patience for the will of God. "For a thousand years in thy sight are but as yesterday when it is past, or as a watch in the night. Thou dost sweep men away; they are like a dream, like grass which is renewed in the morning . . . in the evening it fades and withers . . . . So teach us to number our days, that we may get a heart of wisdom" (Ps. 90:4-6, 12).

This humble and patient submission, which was required of the People of Israel, stands in stark contrast to the view of the Greeks, who held that the cosmic order could, through the proper use of reason, be comprehended not as it seems but as it is. The Jews believed that the rational approach was futile, not because there was no order, but because only God could encompass it, and the relationship of God and man involved far more than reason alone; it involved faith. For Plato the guide was philosophy, by which humans could contemplate "all time and all existence" (*Rep.* VI, 486a) since philosophy was the gift and guide "than which no greater gift has ever been bestowed by the gods." For the Jew, God was that guide. "This is God, our God for ever and ever. He will be our guide for ever" (Ps. 48:14).

Blessed Fathers

In the consciousness of biblical writers, this earthly life, in spite of its inevitable flaws and pains, was essentially good. Therefore, length of days was a blessing: "He who dwells in the shelter of the Most High, who abides in the shadow of the Almighty . . . . With long life I will satisfy him, and show him my salvation" (Ps. 91: 1,16). Abraham was promised long years for faithfulness: "You shall go to your fathers in peace; you shall be buried in a good old age" (Gen. 15:15).

If God is the God of life, the one that neither ages nor dies, perhaps in longevity one could find wisdom and become more like God. Perhaps in enduring suffering without having to understand why the innocent are afflicted, one becomes closer to God. The problem of suffering was poignantly raised in the *book of Job.* Here Job, the righteous man, was afflicted, and he poured out his laments before his family and friends and before God, who finally responded in a majestic and sweeping demonstration of his mighty power over the puniness of man. Appearing in a whirlwind, the Lord asked Job, "Who do you think you are? Who is this that darkens counsel?" Then God presented a list of questions that were unanswerable: "Where were you when I laid the foundations of the earth?" "Who laid the cornerstone thereof? . . . Who shut in the sea with doors? Hast thou commanded the morning . . . and caused the dayspring to know his place?" (Job 38:4-12).

The poet here drew attention to the fact that in the presence of Adonai one ought not ask questions, for the Lord was both the questioner and the answerer as well. It was not for humans to ask why they suffer, because in the Jewish view, that was tantamount to asking if there is a God and if that God is good. These were the unaskable questions for the person of faith, the equivalent of Greek hubris, a demand that the inscrutable ways of the deity be laid out before humans. These were the philosopher's questions that seek an understanding of the cosmic plan. In the face of this powerful response from God, Job submitted, not because he understood why he suffered, but because he saw the power of God and recalled that he already believed: "I know that thou canst do all things, and that no purpose of thine can be thwarted" (Job 42:2). He questioned who he was in relation to God: "Who is he that hides counsel without knowledge?" He recognized his own limits: "Therefore I have uttered what I did not understand, things too wonderful for me . . . therefore I despise myself, and repent in dust and ashes" (Job 42:3,6). After this reconciliation the Lord gave Job twice as much as he had lost in his calamities: "And after this Job lived a hundred and forty years, and saw his sons, and his sons' sons, four generations. And Job died, an old man, and full of days" (Job 42:16-17).

As the movements of the heavens revealed the power of God, so did long years. The story of Job indicated that old age was not attained by gaining control over nature, nor was it up to humans to attain it by their efforts. Rather it was a reward for humble submission to the power of God. In the Jewish way of seeing things, the number of man's days was in divine hands. It was up to God to give or to take life.

The fifth chapter of Genesis told of people who lived to extreme ages. At 130 years Adam begot a son and then lived until the age of 930 years. His son lived 912 years after begetting a son at the age of 105. But in Genesis 6, a divine decree fixed 120 as the span of human life, and in accord with this we have the popular greeting: "May you live to be a hundred and twenty." Clearly the extremes of old age here described have more symbolic than literal meaning. The emphasis in Jewish thought, less on longevity than on faithfulness, is more on the continuity of the People of Israel than on continued years of any individual.

As Plato and Aristotle, in their approach to old age and death, ultimately looked for the continuity of existence in the life of reason and its continuation, they retreated from history. They were trapped with a quantitative approach to time that necessitated, at least for Plato, an escape in the form of the afterlife he envisioned. The alternative was the stark realism of the Greek model of dreaded death. The notion of qualitative time, however, caused the Jews to find their salvation within history itself. The verb in the greeting "May you *live* to be 120" does not mean may you "survive" or "last," but may you have a qualitative life.

As a religion of action, Judaism professed to consist of nothing more or less than a particular people who lived their lives retaining the quality of Jewish insight. This life was the field wherein the action of God was carried on through the faith and deeds of the people. The quality of this insight and its conversion into action rested on the person's yielding from within, making room for Adonai's presence in this life, taking on God's vision by seeing, in the transparency of events of time, the will of God. For when: "The words of the *Torah* enter and find the chambers of the heart unoccupied, they make their home in that person."[14]

The Jewish religion was not a matter of ceremonial rites but was seen by many as a passion of the heart that lures one to living justly and compassionately. What God asked was not that his people should attain power in life but that they ought to renew again and again, as Job did, their sense of the limits of human existence and their conviction that history begins from within.[15] This living with the constant unfolding of the plan of God, in a freedom tempered by faith, was encompassed within the larger picture of the promised continuity of the people of Israel. Hope never vanished, in spite of holocausts, for if it did, God would vanish. This hope was not that suffering, aging, or death would be removed, but that the continuance in faith of the Judaic community, as it formed itself in terms of particular lives and circumstances, would not be overcome. This was the covenant, a commitment on the part of God and a commitment on the part of the nation: God would preserve Israel and vindicate the enemies that attempted to thwart the plan, and the people would remember the past and work out the future. The scandal of life was not that individuals grew old and died, but that the wicked sometimes gained ascendency in thwarting God's plan. Yet the spirit of Judaism was always to return from the desert of suffering to tell the tale of God's providence. Israelites must do more than continue to exist; they must return from the sufferings of life with the vision that these hardships were integrated into God's deepest intentions. A longer life, then, far from avoiding or putting off death, afforded a person a further chance to enhance the quality of one's engagement with the affairs of God and to see the way of the Lord.

What one did with allotted time and the terrifying gift of human freedom, rather than length of years alone, brought respect:

> Happy is the man who finds wisdom, ... She is more precious than jewels, and nothing you desire can compare with her. Long life is in her right hand; in her left hand are riches and honor . . . . She is a tree of life to those who lay hold of her; those who hold her fast are called happy. (Prov. 3:13-18)

Length of days in the Jewish view was valuable only insofar as wisdom grew in the individual and enhanced the quality of life of the community. Older people were seen as blessed and deserving of respect. The term "fathers" or "elders" appeared in the Bible and *Talmud* as a synonym for "judges," "leaders," or "sages." The Jewish image of leadership and rule was associated with old age. Nevertheless, the *book of Job* also stressed that there might have been young people who were wiser than elders, as with Elihu who recognized: "I am young in years, and you are aged; . . . therefore I was timid . . . to declare my opinion to you. . . . Let many years teach wisdom. But it is the spirit in man, the breath of the Almighty, that makes him understand. It is not the [old] men that are wise." The *Talmud* told of a man appointed at eighteen as the head of the Sanhedrin, the supreme council of the Jewish people, who suddenly became grey as a sign of his fitness for office. In the *Talmud* the learned were always aged, regardless of their years (Qiddushin, 33a).

It was clear that chronological age in itself was not idealized by the Hebrews. The most definitive statement about the burden and dependency of old age was found in Ecclesiastes 12:1-7 in which old age was spoken of as "the calamitous days" in which a person had no pleasures, the senses being dulled and death being inevitable. The *Talmud*, the collected literature of centuries and the compendium of Jewish law, including oral law, which governed every detail of daily routine, recognized that for some individuals, to be old was to be *yashish*, substantial, mature and wise, but for others it was to be *zaken*, shrunken and weak, or *hashish*, unproductive and fruitless.[16] Another Talmudic definition marked the beginning of old age at sixty, grand old age at seventy, reborn strength at eighty, stooped shoulders at ninety and uselessness and death at one hundred (Abot. Chapt 5, Parag 27).

Quality of life from youth to aging was stressed by the elderly rabbis in the *Talmud*, who claimed the secret of longevity was found in a range of conduct, from a mere formal obedience to ritual law to a higher level of moral behavior. Maimonides, a physician, philosopher and Talmudic scholar of the twelfth century, tied intellectual and spiritual discipline to good health habits as a means of reaching good old age. After quoting many dietary prescriptions from the *Talmud*, he concluded that if one lives wisely, he will not be in need of a physician but will enjoy normal health all his life except for unusual circumstances such as pestilence or drought.

Death: A Turn Toward Life

The God of the Jews was the living God, the divine creator who in living forever, transcended all things. But men and women differed radically from God in the fact that they were finite creatures who were slated to die. In the biblical sense there was no "why" to this absolute difference between humans and the divine, one deathless and the other fated for death, but this is not to say that the Bible did not reflect on death; neither did this intimate that all biblical reflections on the subject were without pessimism. There was a dark side and a light side to the Jewish attitude toward dying. These attitudes and the overarching themes that persist in Judaic history regarding death will be put into perspective; but because attitudes toward death were deeply affected by attitudes toward afterlife, it will be important also to take into account the Jewish view of existence after death.

In any discussion of death in the Jewish tradition, it must be kept in mind that there was very little attention paid to the concept of death or to the significance of human finitude in Jewish scripture itself. Although there were stories about deaths, there was little motivation for abstract speculation on the subject of death or survival after death because the Bible's overriding concern was for life or, more correctly, for the concrete process of living. Scripture, as a whole, was "enormously busy with life."[17]

This preoccupation with life does not mean that the Bible was absorbed with quantity of years, as such. Rather its concern was with the source of life, God, and the continuation of the creative process, which was the life of the Chosen People. Whereas the Greeks generally had a pessimistic approach to both death and afterlife, the Hebrews ideally placed these two experiences in a larger and more optimistic context, not the context of the overall plan of God's creation alone, but in the context of the earthly continuation of the life of the whole nation. When we look at the Judaic account of the dying actions of Abraham for an example, we find that the writer is absorbed, not so much with the personal elements of an individual leader's demise, as dramatic a scene as it is; rather he seems preoccupied with the great leader's dying words, which are directed almost exclusively to providing for the continuation of his line through his sons. The 145 year-old patriarch urged his servant to swear by Adonai that he would obtain a wife for his son, Isaac, from the land of Abraham's birth, saying: "The Lord, the God of heaven, . . . who spoke to me and swore to me, 'To your descendents I will give this land,' he will send his angel before you, and you shall take a wife for my son from there" (Gen. 24:1-9). The old man obviously saw the meaning of his life in terms of the fulfillment of the promise he had received from God. He was an actor in the continuing process of purposeful historical development and would be remembered only insofar as his accomplishments would be continued in history through his offspring and their offspring. This theme resounded through Jewish tradition, providing the springboard for Israel's response to the experience of death.

Again, when the dying Jacob (or Israel as he was called) was told that his son Joseph and his two grandsons had come to see him, he made a

Now the eyes of Israel were dim for age, ... So Joseph brought them near him; and he kissed them and embraced them and . . . said, "Behold, I am about to die: but God will be with you, and will bring you again to the land of your fathers." (Gen. 48: 10-21)

The old man was the visionary and as he keenly experienced his own limitations, he put into focus for future generations the promises of Adonai, reminding them of their part in the covenant. In like fashion, Moses, when he was dying, invoked the blessings of God on the descendents of Jacob: "The eternal God is your dwelling place, . . . Israel dwelt in safety, the fountain of Jacob alone, in the land of grain and wine; yea, his heavens drop down dew." (Deut. 33: 27-28). These are the words by which the great old man of Jewish history in his dying vision drew his progeny into a shared and universal destiny with "creative words which were able to shape the future" and give it a meaning and hope that would preserve the days to come as an open choice for the generations that endure.[18] This is the sense of death out of which springs life, for enduring involves more than a single individual's longevity.

Life after death, then, for the Jews took a social form, the endurance of the Chosen People in this life, not in spite of the deaths of the generations gone, but *through* their deaths. In the passing on of life they pass on not just physical, but spiritual life to their progeny. Death, instead of bringing discontinuity into history, brought continuity: "Even though I walk through the valley of the shadow of death, I fear no evil" (Ps. 23:4).

The Dark Side of Death

In order to give proper perspective to this sense of death, we must first consider the dark side of death in the Jewish outlook. There are some passages in scripture that can be read as doleful and pessimistic; for example, Job spoke of death as the "king of terrors" that drives human beings out of the world (Job 18:14,18). Jeremiah spoke of a grim reaper: "The dead bodies of men shall fall as dung upon the open field, like sheaves after the reaper, and none shall gather them" (Jer.9:22). The grave as the common lot of both men and beasts is reflected on in the later Ecclesiastes: "For the fate of the sons of men and the fate of beasts is the same; as one dies so dies the other . . . man has no advantage over the beast; . . . All go to one place; all are from the dust, and all turn to dust again" (3:19-20). The followers of Adonai, in an effort to establish the supremacy of their God, were particularly ardent to suppress the elements of the cult of the dead that existed among their people. The cult of the dead was a primitive cult that proposed a significant form of afterlife for the dead, and these beliefs and the practices associated with them were condemned (Deut. 14:1 ff; 18:11; Lev.19:27ff, 31:20,27). In an attempt to negate the very basis of these mortuary cults, the Jews present a picture of human nature that represents death as an absolute that began when God condemned Adam's sin with the words, "Dust thou art and unto dust thou shalt return" (Gen. 3:19).[19] There was a idea prevalent in Judaism, which was born out in rabbinic thought, that death constituted a punishment for sinfulness. "Surely there is not a righteous man on earth who does good and never sins" (Eccles. 7:20). And "Even Moses and Aaron died through their sins as it is said 'Because you believe not in me.' Hence had you believed in me, your time would not have come to depart" (Shab. 55a).

The Person in the Bible

In order to grasp fully the Jewish view of death, it is necessary to review the way the human person was construed in that tradition. Genesis 1 and Genesis 2 gave two accounts of the creation of the first human. The first described God as creating humans in his own image: "So God created man in his own image, in the image of God he created him; male and female he created them" (Gen. 1:27). The second said he formed man from the dust of the ground: "and breathed into his nostrils the breath of life" (Gen. 2:7). In direct contrast to the Greek dualism, which saw the soul as the antithesis of the body, one mortal and the other immortal, the Jew viewed the person as a psychophysical unity, the breath of whose body was his life. "Man's personality is always identified with the animated body; hence it is always conceived of as an indivisible organism functioning as an integrated whole."[20] Although the Hebrew word *nephesh* is frequently translated as "soul," it in no way makes reference to an immortal soul. This idea is directly contrary to the Jewish notion. Rather, *nephesh* would be better translated as "living person" or "self." The word "self" is the nearest English concept to the Hebrew term.[21] In addition, it should be remembered that the emphasis in early Judaism was always on the person as a member of the community. Personality and identity were terms associated not so much with the individual person, but with the People. Thus at death the personality and identity were not discontinued as long as the People continued. Mankind, even if made in the image of God, was, in fact, mortal, and when the *ruach,* the "life-breath" is taken away, the person is no more: "The years of our life are threescore and ten, or even by reason of strength fourscore; yet their span is but toil and trouble; they are soon gone, and we fly away" (Ps. 90:5-6, 9-10).[22]

Realm of the Dead: Focus on Life

But the Jew could not admit of total extinction; therefore, there was a realm of the dead, called "Sheol," conceived of variously as a land of thick darkness, an awful pit, or a walled city covered with dust.[23] The psalmist cried out, "For my soul is full of troubles, and my life draws near to Sheol" (Ps. 88:3).[24] At death, the psychophysical organism was obliterated and whatever remained (this is not explained further) descended to Sheol. To make the bleakness of the prospect of Sheol even more uninviting, it was believed to be cut off from everyone, even God. As the "dismissed among the dead" the psalmist was among "Those whom thou dost remember no more, for they are cut off from your hand" (Ps. 88:5). This negative existence was the common fate of all and was, therefore, not tied to reward and punishment nor to a continuation of life. "Sheol is not a consequence to life, but a contrast to life."[25] The negative character of this realm of the dead sharply contrasted the positive state of life in the world. Isaiah said: "For Sheol cannot thank thee, death cannot praise thee; those who go down to the pit cannot hope for thy faithfulness. The living, he thanks thee as I do this day" (Isa. 38:18-19). But this dark picture could serve the living who, by viewing it,

might be turned back to life. The vision of a spiritual vacuum, where
Adonai no longer exerted any influence, could have the impact of turning
attention to the fact that those who envisioned it were still alive and
the blessings of God were conferred on the kingdom of the people of God
on earth.[26] For one who was a servant of the Lord there were trust,
humility and resignation, mingled with hope that though death could not
be avoided, it brought the possibility of a positive act of
relinquishment that involved turning life over to others who could move
into the future. This hope was exactly contrary to the bitter grimness of
Aristotle, who in a weak attempt to connect wisdom with old age and
reason with death could not undo the terrible feeling of defeat that
accompanied the necessity of dying because, he believed, "Death is the
most terrible of all things" (Ethics, 115a 11).

The Jews, then, took a realistic look at death, seeing it as natural
and inevitable, but not as evil, because faith in God and hope in his
plan always took priority. They infused death with meaning. Evil entered
only when human beings could not see through the events of life, its dark
side as well as its light side, and therefore could not discern therein
the goodness of God. A successful death was tied to one's satisfaction
with life. "To die satisfied with life belongs to man's nature as
created being."[27] As a creature, one neither authored his own life nor
expected it to be immortal; death was merely a frontier, not an enemy.
The implication is that the desire for immortality is a revolt against
our status as creatures of God. When one has lived creatively, there is
no need to cling further to life or harbor expectations of its
continuation. Thus, "Abraham breathed his last and died in good old age,
an old man and full of years, and was gathered to his people" (Gen.
25:8). This was not the death that is a burden, but a victorious
relinquishment of a man full of years. The holy progenitor was, in the
Jewish view, "gathered to his people" and thus continued as part of the
family, his merits living on in those that followed. The same phrase,
"gathered to his people," was used of Jacob and of Aaron at their deaths,
and Moses was told by God he would lie with his fathers when he died.

Individualism within Common Purpose

A gradual refinement was to occur in this Jewish view of Israel as a
corporate personality, and a realignment would take place in the
relationship between God and humankind. The subsequent shift in Jewish
thought placed more emphasis on individuality and personal responsibility
for one's acts. National defeats, exile and considerable suffering were
experienced by the people, especially around the sixth century, B.C.E.
The scattering of the people, and finally the overthrow of the Jewish
national state by the Romans in 70 C.E., called for more complex
theological explanations of God's justice and rewards for faithfulness.
The older notion that God rewards with length of years and prosperity
became a challenging belief indeed. But more important, the very concept
of God as just, good and all-powerful demanded the promise of justice for
individual men and women, if not in this life, then in the next. In the
fifth century B.C.E., Ezekiel had prophesied the removal of the broken
nation, Israel, and its restoration as the holy land, by using vivid
imagery that suggested physical resurrection: "Behold I will open your
graves, and raise you from your graves, O my people; and I will bring you

home into the land of Israel" (37:12). Three centuries later there is evidence of a general acceptance of both resurrection of the dead and final judgment in Judaic thought. The book of Daniel, in approximately the second century B.C.E., offered a prime piece of evidence of this: "And many of them who sleep in the dust of the earth shall awake, some to everlasting life, and some to shame and everlasting contempt" (12:12).

Judgment was considered in the Jewish tradition to be universal collective judgment of the people. By 70 C.E., when the hope for remaining a nation was shattered, judgment became viewed as personal but maintained the theme of God's final vindication of his people. "Judgment meant, for the Hebrew of this age, God's ultimate assertion of his sovereignty over his creatures."[28] One famous rabbi, Johanan ben Zakkai, made a grand statement of faith on his deathbed. He attested to his conviction in personal resurrection and placed the notion of judgment in a truly Jewish perspective by maintaining that resurrection and judgment were not only within God's power, but ultimately proclaimed his justice and goodness:

> The ones who were born are to die and the ones who have died are to be brought to life again and the ones who are brought to life are to be summoned to Judgment and understand that he is God, he is the maker, he is the Creator, he is the discerner, he is the judge. . . . blessed is he in whose presence is neither guile nor forgetfulness, nor respect of persons, nor taking of bribes, for all is his. And know that everything is done according to the reckoning.[29]

Later on, under the influence of Greek thought, another strange concept appeared in addition to resurrection. It is immortality of soul. The Jews had come a long distance from their original vision of faith in the continuation of the nation, the person as a psychophysical unity and the shadowy pit of Sheol. Yet one element did remain: the motivation behind these theological revisions was the faith in God as a just God. In addition there was little emphasis on making resurrection and immortality of soul dogmas. The emphasis for Jewish thought was on right behavior rather than on belief in dogma.[30] It was also well known that in spite of the incursion of teachings about resurrection, judgment and immortality of soul, the insistence on the major theme of social responsibility was still given heavy stress in Jewish thought.

What can be sifted out of all these changing ideas were four general points. First, Jewish theologians had, over generations, been flexible in their teachings and often adapted theological ideas to the needs and circumstances of the people, for example, in David, where the doctrine of Adonai was significantly adjusted to meet the realities of Israel's political situation of exile.[31] Second, Jewish tradition looked mortality in the face and did not try to gloss over it. From the beginning the theme of death as absolute was found in the Bible, and later the rabbis placed much stress on the natural aspect of death in the *Talmud*. Third, paramount was the overshadowing belief in God as the God of both justice and mercy, who was faithful to the needs of his people. Jewishness rested on the notion that, though a strict taskmaster at times, God was a good God, the world he created was a good world. Lastly, there was always and remains until today a Jewish reluctance to erect a dogmatic structure of rewards and punishments or to give detailed explanations of the concepts of death and afterlife because these matters are best left in God's hands. If one were to ask the rabbi the question: "Is there life after death?" he might answer, "Is God a good God?"

THE EARLY CHRISTIAN CHURCH: DEATH AND RESURRECTION

Early writings of the Christian Church, like Hebrew scriptures, claimed to be based on events that occurred at a particular time and place in history. The three synoptic Gospels that began the New Testament consisted of a collection of reports that were circulated orally among believers for twenty or thirty years before they were recorded by the evangelists Matthew, Mark and Luke. These Gospels described the life of Jesus of Nazareth as a human being born in Bethlehem during the reign of emperor Augustus: "In those days a decree went out from Caesar Augustus that all the world should be enrolled. . . . Joseph also went up from Galilee, . . . to the city of David, which is called Bethlehem . . . with Mary his betrothed, who was with child. . . . And she gave birth to her first-born son (Luke 2:1-7). Matthew opened the New Testament announcing it as "The book of the genealogy of Jesus Christ, the son of David, the son of Abraham" (Matt. 1:1). Then he traced the genealogy of Jesus, step by step, all the way back to Abraham. It seemed obvious that Matthew used this method to underscore not only the Jewishness of Jesus, but his humanness as well.

The synoptic writers made it abundantly clear that the historical Jesus was subject to all the limitations of a creature of time. He possessed no exemptions from the common human experiences of being born as a helpless infant or having to die. Jesus' words and deeds did not contain direct discussion of death; in fact, Jesus' teachings revealed almost no mention of the concept of death. There are a few minor allusions to a place of comdemnation where the damned gnashed their teeth and where both body and soul were destroyed, but these probably reflected assumptions generally held at this time in Jewish tradition.[32]

On one occasion Jesus was questioned on the subject of the manner of existence humans had after resurrection, but in typical Jewish fashion he gave the "Is God a good God?" response. On this occasion the Sadducees, who did not accept the notion of resurrection that was taught by some Jewish sects, attempted to trip up Jesus by asking a question that was impossible to answer. If a man were required by Mosaic law, they asked, to marry his brother's widow, if they are without offspring and one woman is married seven times and each time her husband died, "In the resurrection whose wife will she be? For the seven had her as wife" (Mk. 12:18-22). Instead of fielding the question directly, Jesus claimed his questioners were ignorant of scripture, because the dead neither marry nor are given in marriage. But as far as the dead being raised was concerned, Jesus told them that God was the God of the living, therefore, they, too should focus on life. It was better to get on with the business of living than to speculate and dispute what is beyond them. Faith in the living God should suffice as the answer to questions about afterlife: "Have you not read in the book of Moses, in the passage about the bush, how God said to him, 'I am the God of Abraham, and the God of Isaac, and the God of Jacob'? He is not God of the dead but of the living" (Mark

12:26-27). Moses was involved in the life of the Chosen People, and this was Jesus' concern as well; therefore, disputations and speculations on the meaning of death, resurrection and judgment were simply not important to him. As a result there was no definitive statement about any of these concepts in the synoptic Gospels as there was none in the Judaic scripture. The synoptic Gospels, which report Jesus' words and activities, were written out of a Judaic intellectual concept in which the person was presumed to be a psychophysical unity and where the emphasis was on history and the salvation of the Chosen People. In these writings death was pictured not as an evil or as the opposite of life, but as the natural resolution of human living. In short, there was no enlargement on the traditional Jewish interpretation of death as it stood before the incursion of new ideas of resurrection and judgment.

Jesus' Death

The fact that Jesus did not give formal definitions or enter into elaborate discussions on the nature of death did not mean he was not engaged with it. Indeed Jesus, who was to die at a relatively young age, saw death as a real experience, "his" death, and in no way did he hide his fear when it came time for that death, which was both violent and seemingly ill-timed. Unlike Socrates, Jesus was abandoned by his disciples in his hour of need, and unlike Socrates (who seemed to indicate that, as a philosopher, he welcomed death), Jesus made it clear that he would prefer to avert it, especially in the agonizing form in which he foresaw it:

> And he said to them, "My soul is very sorrowful even to death; remain here and watch." And going a little farther, he fell on the ground and prayed that, if it were possible, the hour might pass from him. And he said, "Abba, Father, all things are possible to thee; remove this cup from me; yet not what I will, but what thou wilt." (Mk. 14:34-6).

Jesus showed dread in the face of oncoming torture and suffering. Only in the will of God did he find some small comfort. The complete absence of any reference to resurrection or afterlife here indicates that the emphasis was on life as a gift to be taken or given by God in this world, not in the next.

It was not always easy to distinguish the original form of Jesus' teaching in the synoptic Gospels, since they were written from oral reports that were, of necessity, interpretations. Yet it seems clear that Jesus was received by disciples who regarded him as the Messiah who would accomplish God's purpose on earth.[33] There was some note of urgency in his message even from the beginning of his mission in Galilee when Mark reported Jesus as urging, "The time is fulfilled, and the Kingdom of God is at hand; repent" (1:15). It is believed that the followers of Jesus were convinced that the order in Palestine, which was under Roman rule with a puppet Jewish dynasty in command, would be brought to an end. Adonai would vindicate his People in some manner. Whether that would amount to the overthrow of the Roman rule in Judaea, with the reestablishment of the independence of the Jewish nation as its result, or whether it meant that God would do away with the existing order of the universe and recreate it with a heavenly Jerusalem at its center was vague in the minds of those who listened to Jesus.[34] But it is clear that these followers saw him as the Messiah and expected that the new order would come about within their lifetimes: "They will see the Son of man coming on the clouds of heaven with power and great glory; . . . Truly, I say to you, this generation will not pass away till all these things take place" (Matt. 24:30, 34).

The disciples not only held this belief during the life of Jesus, but also after his crucifixion, when they looked forward to his second coming. However, as time passed, the delay of this coming forced the infant Christian community to adjust its sights to see the divine purposes as extended into time and made manifest through many future ages. This had a profound effect on the Christian philosophy of time as well as on the organization of the Christian church. Though the new order expected by the early Christians was associated with reports of the resurrection of Jesus Christ from the dead, it was the disciples' belief in vindication at the second coming and their faith in immortality that would grow with the spread of Christianity.

The Jewish Christians had to struggle with serious problems resulting from the lack of clear concepts in Jesus' sayings as well as their own unfulfilled expectations about the timing connected with the justification of God's ends in the institution of a new order. It would fall to the lot of two sophisticated theologians to interpret these events and surmount potential inconsistencies. One was St. Paul, a convert to Christianity and contemporary of Jesus (though he never saw Jesus in person), and the other was St. John, one of the evangelists.

St. Paul: A New Image of Immortality

During the first several decades after Jesus' death and before the synoptic Gospels were written, Paul's writings, unlike later Gospels, did not consist of a general overview of events in Jesus' life, but were exclusively about his death and resurrection. The Jewish Christians from Jerusalem and the synoptic Gospel authors, spoke about the glorious return of the Messiah. But Paul's writings had a completely different character. Paul traveled to Rome and Athens visiting small Christian communities and carrying out the mission on which Jesus had sent his disciples: to baptize all nations and to do what Jesus had done, preaching to the people the message of repentance, love and forgiveness.

Resurrection was clearly defined by Paul as a kind of "bodily" existence given by God as a reward to the righteous dead:

Star differs from star in glory. So is it with the resurrection of the dead. . . . It is sown in weakness, it is raised in power. It is sown in a physical body; it is raised a spiritual body. . . . Just as we have borne the image of the man of dust, we shall also bear the image of the man of heaven (1 Cor. 15:41-49).

For the Pauline, Christian life must be transformed in order to be continued, and the transformation was not into a continued historical life but into a different kind of life. The resurrected person by faith gave up his natural body and took on a new body, a spiritual one. In Paul's words: "Death is sentenced to death."[35] With the otherworldliness of a mystic, Paul continued: "Lo! I tell you a mystery. We shall not all sleep, but we shall all be changed, in a moment, in the twinkling of an eye. . . . For the trumpet will sound, and the dead will be raised imperishable. . . . this mortal nature must put on immortality" (1 Cor. 15:51-53). But this was not the immortality of the Greek model, an automatic continuance of the soul; it was resurrection by the power of God's hand. The victory over death was complete: "Death was swallowed up in victory. O death, where is thy sting? O grave, where is thy victory?" (1 Cor. 14:41-35). But nowhere in Paul's further writings is there any additional intimation about the form of the resurrected life, no explanation of the new form the resurrected body would take.

Contrary to Jewish tradition, Paul saw death as a discontinuation of life, its transformation through faith into a state of resurrection. Death, depicted by Paul, was therefore not so much the opposite of physical life, as the enemy of the spiritual body: "The last enemy to be destroyed is death" (1 Cor. 15:26). Nevertheless, there was no Greek pessimism here, because resurrection removed death's sting and God was clearly the victor. Paul, in raising the subject of resurrection of the dead to his listeners in Athens (Acts 17:32) was mocked because the Greek mentality admitted of immortality of soul but not resurrection. Paul distinguished between natural man and spiritual or "pneumatic" man. Natural man remained within the limits of humanness, whereas spiritual man received the spirit of God and became aware that he was the recipient of divine life. Spiritual man arose out of natural man, but only through a sudden break with the past, a rebirth or conversion such as Paul himself experienced on the way to Damascus. "Pneumatic" referred to breath. As human beings were first created of the breath of God, so now man was reborn by a sudden gift of God. According to Paul this is clear evidence that God intervenes in the history of the person's life.

Paul often spoke to an audience that understood Greek vocabulary better than Jewish terms. Therefore, he did make some concessions to his listeners' way of seeing the world. One example was the juxtaposition of the terms "spiritual" and "natural," an opposition that was not in the Jewish style of thinking. Nevertheless, he did not turn to Greek metaphysics or psychology in describing the resurrected state. Paradoxically, though the notion of resurrection was completely outside the pale of the original Jewish tradition, Paul maintained the Jewish outlook in the description he gave to the resurrected state in three ways. First, he saw no division between body and soul in his doctrine of spiritual or " pneumatic" man. The life of God was a gift that made the natural person into a spiritual person. But this is not the life of the Platonic "psyche" which dwelled within the body. "Pneumatic" man is a totality that included the body. His proof is that Jesus rose. Second, Paul carefully distinguished the individual as subordinate to the community as did the tradition of the people of God: "For by one Spirit we were all baptized into one body" (1 Cor. 12:13). Third, in typically Jewish fashion, Paul saw no escape from death, which must come first before resurrection. He viewed death as a necessary preparation for a better existence, yet he did step outside the usual Jewish perspective in insisting that the transformed life was outside earthly history. In fact he described the struggle between life and death as taking on cosmic proportions: "Creation waits with eager longing; . . . because the creature itself will be set free from its bondage to decay and obtain the glorious liberty of the children of God. We know that the whole creation has been groaning in travail together until now" (Rom. 8:19, 21, 22).

It is clear from Paul's own words that his teachings, especially regarding the universality of the Church, had not come through the apostles of the Jerusalem church. He claimed they came directly "through a revelation of Jesus Christ" (Gal. 1:12-12). Since Paul had never met Jesus, these revelations must have been of mystical origin, and they could, therefore, contain ideas that were not held by the Jerusalem church and those who had personally known the historical Jesus. Paul said, "For I would have you know, brethren, that the gospel which was preached by me is not man's gospel. For I did not receive it from man, nor was I taught it, but it came through a revelation of Jesus Christ" (Gal. 1:11-12). Not everyone appreciated Paul's claims to direct revelation: "Paul's letters reveal a deep and serious conflict between himself and the leaders of the mother church of Jerusalem. From their point of view, Paul's interpretation was not only a travesty of the true faith, of which they were the guardians, but it also had dangerous possibilities."[36] His teaching that Christ was the savior of the Gentiles, as well as of the Jews, ran counter to the tradition of a superior spiritual status for the Chosen People. A serious conflict ensued between Paul and the church in Jerusalem, and a considerable body of evidence exists indicating that there was a temporary eclipse of Paul's reputation.[37]

But time and the world would have its way with the Jews and the Jewish Christians of Jerusalem. In A.D. 66 a nationalist rebellion arose against Rome, and after four years of fighting, the city of Jerusalem fell. An arch, which still stands today, was erected by the Romans, containing reliefs and vessels from the destroyed Temple. The infant Gentile churches were to experience the obliteration of the mother church and would be left with the loss of this original source of authority. In the meantime, Paul's writings and teachings had spread significantly to the Church outside Jerusalem. In addition, Paul's influence remained in that he had proposed for the Church a universal character. Mark, one of the evangelists, would actively confirm this notion by making the Second Coming dependent on preaching the Gospel to all nations. Paul's vision was that the Church as a unified society would grow in its universal character as the Mystical Body of Christ. Thus Jesus Christ would be as the head; the Holy Spirit would be as the soul; and it would include a diverse body such as prophets, healers and incorporated members from all nations (Rom. 12:4-8, 1 Cor. 12:12-31, Eph. 4:11-16). With the Jewish theme of community still in the forefront, Paul's universalist Church tied his notion of resurrection to the Second Coming of Christ and proposed both a general resurrection and a general judgment of all mankind.

Time: God's Face in the Mirror

Henceforth, far from repudiating the Judaic scripture, Christian theologians gradually evolved the definition of the Church as the rightful heir not only to God's covenant, but also to the promises God had made to Israel. The notion that the Jews lost the covenant and that the Christians had inherited it became a basic tenet of Christianity. Paul had spoken of Jewish sacred literature as the "Old Testament" claiming that the past "was glorious," but what happened with the coming of Jesus was not only glorious, but was revealed in "plain speech." Jesus had spoken of the chalice at The Last Supper as the "cup of the new testament:" "This cup is the new covenant in my blood" (1 Cor. 11:25). He had made his disciples "competent to be ministers of the new covenant" (2 Cor. 3:6). Thereupon, as the Christian church developed sacred writings beyond the Jewish scriptures, it used these terms in making the distinction between the Jewish and Christian sacred writings calling them the Old Testament and New Testament. The former led up to and culminated in the latter; therefore, time was divided by the birth of Christ, but it was also united to the entire flow of history. That one event would stand out in the Christian cumulative memory as the single most pivotal event in the entire history of the world. Both Christians and Jews knew the important role time played in their history and the tremendous symbolic significance the calendar played in the conscious life of the people, especially the calendar of religious celebrations. Therefore, the Christians began in the sixth century A.D. to count each year after the birth of Christ as *Anno Domini*, "the year of the Lord," *A.D.* thus giving witness to the new age that was unfolding.[38] In the eighteenth century the practice of counting backwards prior to Christ's birth came into being; B.C. stood for "before Christ." Today, the Jews use the Christian dating system in their secular lives but retain the Jewish calendar in their religious ritual because they know, as they knew in the past, that their collective memories and the consciousness of their Jewish history has kept them together:

> The soul of Israel, its religion and its customs, is anchored in its time. Replacing its national-religious time by the time of others . . . is suicidal . . . for a distinct and independent people. Every people has its own time . . . in which its history and holidays are embedded. . . . Every people that has tried to separate itself from its time has disappeared and is no longer remembered among the living. . . . We have to decide once and for all--either ours or theirs, a Jewish calendar or a Christian calendar. It is impossible to have a common way between these two times.[39]

In these two dating systems we see a symbolic witness to the complete split that gradually took place between Jewish and Christian traditions. There are four elements that bear witness to this split, paralleling the four points made earlier. First, the focus of the Jewish community on itself as the Chosen People proved restrictive as the Christians developed a universal church. Varied backgrounds, both linguistic and philosophical, converged to form a singularly different development in Christian theology than had existed in the Jewish tradition. Second, both Christians and Jews took death seriously, seeing it as a part of human travail, but the Christians de-emphasized the importance of death, if only indirectly, by their focus on resurrection and afterlife. Paul seems to see death as almost desirable:

> For me to live is Christ, and to die is gain. If it is to be life in the flesh, that means fruitful labor for me. Yet which I shall choose I cannot tell. I am hard pressed between the two. My desire

is to depart and be with Christ, for that is far better. (Phil. 1:21-23)[40]

Matthew underscores what would become a theme in the Christian church: "Look not to this world but the next... Do not lay up for yourselves treasures on earth, where moth and rust consume...but lay up for yourselves treasures in heaven" (6:19-20).[41]

Third, the notion of God as a good God is paramount in both traditions, but in the Christian Church this teaching took the form of Jesus as Savior. Paul saw Jesus' crucifixion as part of a Divine Plan set by God to rescue mankind from a state of spiritual perdition due to original sin. This notion that a Savior bought back mankind, redeeming it with a huge ransom, was an interpretation that prevailed but which was basically contrary to the Jewish and Jerusalem-Christian belief in Jesus as the judge and vindicator of the elect. Lastly, Jewish and Christian traditions contrasted sharply in that the Jews were reluctant to construct a system of dogmas related to reward and punishments or to define death and afterlife in a philosophical manner. Christian tradition would, on the other hand, develop an elaborate system to explain death, judgment, heaven and hell, which they referred to as "the four last things."

REFLECTIONS FROM THE MIDDLE AGES

In the mirror of his own death each man would discover the secret of his individuality.

                                        Philippe Aries

The Middle Ages were permeated by a Christian interpretation of time, yet there existed the full spectrum of views from an optimistic otherworldliness to a lurking cloud of pessimism. During one part of this period there appeared an unbounded confidence in the resurrected life; at others a widespread preoccupation with damnation, accompanied by highly emotional representations of final judgment, dreaded death and gruesome old age. Finally, as the Middle Ages moved on to the early Renaissance, a new kind of hope appeared. It was the dream of preventing disease, premature aging and early death. The story reveals a consistent battle as religious faith and human self-confidence pitted themselves against nagging despair.

GREEK INFLUENCE ON CHRISTIAN THEOLOGY: STRANGE BEDFELLOWS

As the early days of Christianity evolved into the beginnings of the Middle Ages, Jewish and Christian models became more widely split. A tradition of philosopher-theologians emerged that had profound effects on the thinking of generations that followed. It was a new marriage between Christian faith and Greek rationalism. This chapter will present three major representative figures, selected because of their pervasive influence. All were Latin philosophers and theologians, who brought Neoplatonic and Aristotelian ways of reasoning into Christian thought. The first of these is Boethius. Boethius (A.D.480-542) lived just prior to the sacking and evacuation of Rome in 546, which has been thought of as the dividing line between ancient and medieval cultures in Italy. He is considered an eminent founder of the Middle Ages, the last Western thinker to whom the works of Plato and Aristotle were familiar in Greek and to whom ancient thought was, in all its fullness, still familiar.

Boethius' works were read by those who brought about the revival of

classical thought in the eleventh century, and thus his influence on the
Middle Ages can scarcely be exaggerated. By his example he set in motion
a profoundly important dynamic among Christian theologians: coupling
faith with philosophy. It was his conviction that human reason should be
used to understand and explain the dogmas of Christianity and that reason
could support and strengthen church authority. Thus he imported a Greek
theme into Judeo-Christian thought. Two concepts defined by Boethius
that have become classical in Christian theology are the definition of
God's eternal existence and the concept of the human person. Boethius'
notion of the eternity of God is reminiscent of Plato's idea of eternity,
which meant not that eternal things exist for an infinitely long time,
but that eternity exists as the opposite of time. For Plato, even though
the mirror of time reflects eternity, eternity not only transcends time
(Tim. 37c-38c) but is considered the opposite of time in the sense of
change. For Boethius the eternal existence of God, simply stated, is the
total, simultaneous and perfect possession of unending (unendable)
life.[1] God alone is strictly eternal in the sense of transcending time,
but the physical world, though it does not transcend time, is a
reflection of God's perfection. Thus Christian theologians came to view
God's all-powerful and omniscient reflection in the mirror of time, and
with it came the promise of immortality in the form of resurrection.

The other concept that Boethius contributed to Christianity is the
first formal philosophical definition of person. His interpretation
again rang with Greek overtones. He saw man as an individual substance
that was naturally rational.[2] It has been pointed out that this
definition is not only valid for medieval Christianity and its
theological and philosophical tradition, but "it still determines modern
thinking to a great extent."[3]

The concept of person which was based on Boethius' definition,
variously modified, came to have significant effect on the development of
Christian dogma regarding death, judgment and resurrection. This is
because it focused on several characteristics of human existence: the
person was seen as a spiritual being that is unique and independent in
the sense of having an identity of his own. In conjunction with this,
the person was considered valuable, in himself, as an individual.[4] The
difference between God and humankind, Boethius pointed out, is that God's
divine intelligence can view all things from an eternal perspective,
while human reason can only see from a temporal point of view. In the
Boethian tradition Christian theology came to place a great emphasis on
the freedom and dignity of the individual human person. Man was seen as
responsible for shaping his own destiny in this world, which Christians
believe leads to the next:

> God's freely uttered word addressed to men as precept and promise at
> once, calls man and his responsive liberty to be partaker of his own
> living reality. The unique and individual person stands free to
> select or reject his own salvation and, "This is a freedom which can
> be exercised by none but itself."[5]

This notion of individual freedom within the scope of God's creation
would characterize Christian thought for centuries to come.

A second philosopher and theologian who played a key part in the transition from classical antiquity to the Middle Ages was St. Augustine, who was born in northern Africa (A.D. 354-430) and became a bishop of the Christian Church in A.D. 395 Augustine's great goal was to integrate biblical and Greek cultural inheritances into a single intellectual system, and his success can be measured by the fact that his work dominated Western thought until the thirteenth century. During Augustine's lifetime Rome adopted Christianity as the official state religion. He also lived through innumerable upheavals, political, military and social, which led to the decline of the Roman Empire. In fact it was the sack of Rome by the Visigoths in 410 A.D.that led Augustine to write his monumental *City of God*. Prior to this time the Roman Empire, which had been regarded as eternal since the time of Virgil, was popularly viewed by Christians as an essential instrument in working out God's plan on earth. Now Augustine was motivated to reevaluate and downplay the role of secular institutions in the plan of God.

In Platonic dualistic fashion, Augustine's *City of God* drew a very sharp distinction between the eternity of God and the temporality of man. Augustine saw the city of God as consisting of souls who, because of their unselfish lives and faithfulness to spiritual disciplines, were the elect of heaven destined for eternal glory. He believed that it takes a combination of Divine grace and human effort to achieve the rewards of heavenly bliss. On the other hand, he spoke of the city of this world which is made up of those souls who, because they are devoted not to the things of God, but to the things of time, are destined for the torments of hell. He believed that man's essential nature was found in his ability to use his will for good or evil. Thus Augustine interpreted original sin as the sin of pride:

> Our first parents fell into open disobedience because already they were secretly corrupted; for the evil act would never have been done had not an evil will preceded it. And what is the origin of our evil will but pride? "For pride is the beginning of sin . . ." the craving for undue exaltation . . . when the soul abandons Him to whom it ought to cleave as its end, and becomes a kind of end to itself.[6]

Against this Promethean sin, reminiscent of Greek hubris, Augustine advises temperance, *sophrosyne* as the Greeks called it, "which bridles carnal lusts and prevents them from winning the consent of the spirit to wicked deeds."[7]

Augustine followed Neoplatonic tradition in that he had interest in the physical world only insofar as it concerned the kingdom of God. Order in the cosmos expressed Divine rationality at work in all natural happenings. Behind the order of the world there is the creator and sovereign ruler, God, who stands outside of time, and all things are witness to his almighty presence. It is in the context of this model that Augustine explains time, aging and dying. To human eyes, suffering, aging and dying may seem like disorders, but to Augustine this is only because of short vision and limited perspective, which are the lot of all finite creatures. Miseries associated with human mortality are, in the Christian view, miniscule compared to paradise. Men can accept human limitations only within a larger spiritual perspective.

Augustine not only saw no inconsistency between Neoplatonism and Christianity and no need to disentangle the two, but he thought Neoplatonic philosophy had actually served to prepare the way for the Gospel. In fact, in one place in *The City of God* he claimed that he found distinctive Christian doctrine in the teachings of the followers of Plato. What they were missing, he thought, was belief in the incarnation and the Gospel account of the life of Jesus Christ.[8] Later, however, he came to see a greater gulf between them. Augustine did not agree with Plato on one main point: cyclical time. He argued for a linear model wherein events were not repeated but happened only once and therefore could be meaningful as acts that can lead to specific outcomes as the death of Christ had led to salvation for the human race.

Like the Greeks, Augustine claimed humans have immortal souls and corruptible bodies, and except for sin, the first man and woman would not have been subject to death at all.[9] Like the Jews, he believed that this corruption was connected with punishment. "For the corruptible body, presseth down the soul. The word 'corruptible' is added to show that the soul is burdened . . . by the body such as it has become as a consequence of sin."[10] With Paul, Augustine claimed life on earth is a warfare against forces that would bar souls from salvation. The heavenly kingdom, he believed, is the one goal for all: "In that final peace . . . our nature shall enjoy a sound immortality and incorruption. . . . God shall rule the man, and the soul shall rule the body with sweetness and felicity of a life which is done with bondage."[11] On the other hand, Augustine warned, doom awaits those who make their city in the earthly kingdom. A first death of the body will overcome them, then a second death which will never end, but remain a continual process of dying from which there is no relief. "They who do not belong to this city of God shall inherit eternal misery, . . . called the second death, because the soul shall then be separated from God, its life . . . and the body . . . subjected to eternal pains. This second death shall be more severe, because no death shall terminate it."[12] In keeping with his doctrine of immortality of soul, deathlessness coupled with the fires of hell await the sinner: Carse remarks on this point:

> When immortality is introduced death itself ceases to be a punishment; it is rather that the death of the body simply changes the nature of the punishment . . . Thus we find the widespread references in Christian thought to scenes of eternal punishment where the dead are not really dead; they are only unable to take flight from the misery that they have earned for themselves in their earthly existence.[13]

Origen, a third-century teacher, strongly objected to this notion of never-ending damnation in hell, suggesting some form of punishment that could be remedial and from which the damned could be released in due time, thus restoring the soul again to God's good graces. Origen's view was opposed by the Church and declared heretical in 553 A.D. at the Council of Constantinople. Thus St. Augustine and with him the Medieval Church looked into the mirror of time and saw there not only eternal heavenly bliss, but the face of a God who could damn man to the eternal fires of hell.

Though Augustine taught that hell is unending, he also insisted that

there is a temporary state of punishment for those souls not deserving of
hell but not yet ready for heaven. These souls needed a purgatory; in
fact Augustine hinted that all souls will need purgation. St. Bernard in
the twelfth century would be even more specific about purgatory. He
claimed there are three regions: Hell, where there is no redemption;
Purgatory, where there is hope; and Paradise, where there is the Beatific
Vision.[14]

Augustine also spoke of the power of demons in this world:

> We must flee out of the city of this world which is altogether a
> city of ungodly angels and men. Indeed, the greater we see the
> power of the demons to be in these depths, so much the more
> tenaciously must we cleave to the Mediator through whom we ascend
> from these lowest to the highest places.[15]

This idea of demons having power over human beings grew to huge
proportions in the popular imagination in the late Middle Ages. By the
eleventh century, artists would depict in gruesome detail the terrors of
those sentenced to purgatory and hell. Since popular art in the Middle
Ages (chiefly religious in content) served as a form of instruction for
large numbers of the people who could not read or write, these ideas
would spread to the populace across all of Europe. T.S.R. Boase
comments, "The human mind has a morbid thirst for horrors, and gradually
detailed torments became more and more specific."[16]

The third major theologian who was a major force in shaping late
Medieval Christian theology of time and death was Thomas Aquinas (1224-
1274) whose writings represented a rethinking of Aristotelianism with
significant influences from Neoplatonic, Boethian and Augustinian
thought. Aquinas' separate intention was to develop a comprehensive
philosophical base for Christian theology, a reconciliation between faith
and reason, without losing sight of his basic belief that all
intellectual effort has one goal: to know the scheme of salvation and how
to attain it.

Aquinas' teachings on suffering, aging and death involved two main
points that dealt with defending God as both just and merciful. The
first focused on God's role in permitting human suffering and the second
with God's role in permitting evil. Regarding the first, Aquinas tended
to treat God in the metaphor of an artist and the world as his work of
art. The perfection of the world, he believed, required many varied
beings among which are human creatures who are mortal and thus subject to
aging and death. Drawing a neat distinction between God's ordaining will
and God's permitting will, Aquinas pointed out that for the sake of the
good of the universe as a whole, God permitted, but did not ordain, that
suffering take place. An example of this was Aquinas' analysis of the way
death first came into the world. He believed the first human beings were
composed of warring elements that would lead to aging and death because
man is mortal like other animals.[17] However, through a gift of God
original integrity or a basic state of order, would have counteracted the
natural state of death. Human beings were given a gift of original
integrity by which soul so possessed body that it was deathless.[18] But
the first sin destroyed all this, unleashing those warring elements.
Thus Adam and Eve's actions brought disorder to the soul and death to the

body because sin took away original justice, which not only kept the
lower powers of the soul in subjection to reason but also kept the whole
body in subjection to the soul. This is reminiscent of Aristotle's belief
in the opposite humors that clash and destroy each other. Therefore,
aging and death are natural, because humans have material bodies. This
is Aristotle's belief as well, but for Aquinas, as for the Jews, death
is also a punishment for the sin of the first man and woman: "Death is a
punishment for sin."[19]

God, Aquinas taught, did not ordain death but only permitted it
because of the way things were structured prior to the first sin. Here
we come to Aquinas' second point, God's role in permitting evil. God
permits the possibility of sin, so that man can be free and thus choose
God freely. The moral order includes the element of freedom because
without it one could not give God love or merit the rewards of afterlife.
Like Jewish theologians, Aquinas taught that freedom makes man more God-
like; thus he maintained that the person must retain the power to sin.
Therefore, he argued, God permitted, but did not ordain, that sin be
possible because it is a greater good that humans retain their status as
free creatures.

Aquinas incorporated the Greek concept of immortality into his
model. The soul, he believed, continued to exist when the body died.[20]
We see Aquinas uniting the disparate ideas of immortality and
resurrection by claiming that the immortal soul, by its nature, demands
reunion with the body because they belong together naturally. But the
soul is a natural component of human nature; therefore, the soul and body
will reunite again in resurrection: "Nothing unnatural can be perpetual,
therefore the soul will not be without the body for ever. Since the soul
is immortal the body should be joined to it again. . . . The immortality
of the soul, then would seem to demand the future resurrection of the
body."[21] Aquinas claimed that not only the desire for God, but all desire
shall be stilled when the soul reaches heaven. Here he echoes Paul's
conviction that in heaven human joy will be complete: "What no eye has
seen, nor ear heard, nor the heart of man conceived, what God has
prepared for those who love him" (1 Cor. 2:9).

Death in Middle Ages

Strange partners, are the Christian and Greek traditions, one so
spiritual, the other so nature-bound; one so conscious of human choice
and responsibility, the other so driven by determinism. Given the
optimistic underpinnings of Christianity with its conviction about
resurrection, it is ironic that no other era has laid so much stress on
death as did the Christian late Middle Ages. One of its central themes
became *Memento Mori! Remember your death!* "In Northern Europe for two
hundred years . . . . death was the favorite topic of the preachers and
moralistic writers, it was one of the most common subjects for popular
art. . . . there was no object so frequently or so vividly before his
mind's eye as the skeleton he would one day become."[22]

In the early days of Christianity death was viewed simply as a
threshold to be crossed prior to the resurrected life. Christians
optimistically believed that ever since Christ triumphed over his death

by rising in a glorious form, they, too, could look forward to resurrection. However, a shift took place as Pauline tradition came under Neoplatonic influence. Enduring in this world was viewed as a kind of death in itself, with physical death affording the opportunity for eternal life. In other words, life was viewed paradoxically as death and death as life.

However, it must be remembered that most people in the Middle Ages did not fit into the picture of the devout Christian, who looked forward to death, believing the often-repeated phrase of the sermon "Death is better than life."[23] Ordinary people actually feared death, and this fear was destined to mount to extraordinary proportions. In the fourteenth century, dire physical conditions in Western Europe accompanied by the outbreak of the bubonic plague and other pestilences brought death with all its hideousness before the eyes of everyone, religious and irreligious, children as well as adults. Approximately 90 percent of those infected with the plague died from it. At least one-fourth of the population of the earth at the time perished as the outbreaks of black plague again and again spread throughout Europe, Asia and Africa between 1347 and 1383. Sanitary conditions were desperately inadequate. The population could not control other disasters such as fires and could not bury the dead fast enough. In addition, during these years death and torture were used as the official instruments of the Inquisition.[24] Food shortages and poor medical knowledge as well as widespread social disorder were accompanied by brutal carnage in warfare and subsequent torture and massacre of the conquered. Superstition and witch hunts attempted to assign guilt for the plague. Jewish communities were besieged for assorted reasons and were accused of being a cause of the plague as a result of their ancestors' alleged part in Jesus's crucifixion. Sometimes they were killed simply for monetary gain.[25]

In the late fourteenth century the arts reinforced in the populace an awful dread of death: "Toward 1400 the conception of death in art and literature took a spectral and fantastic shape. A new and vivid shudder was added to the great primitive horror of death. The macabre vision arose from deep psychological strata of fear; religious thought at once reduced it to a means of moral exortation."[26]

A popular folk tale, *The Story of the King Who Never Laughed*, illustrates the dark mood of the era:

> When asked the reasons for this sadness, he replied, "Because four spears are directed against my heart and would pierce it if I only show the slightest sign of joy; the first spear is the bitter suffering of Christ; the second, the thought of death; the third, the uncertainty of the hour of death and the possibility of sudden death without absolution, the last spear is the fear of last judgment."[27]

This dread of death can be associated with a growing awareness of the individuality of the human person. The Hebrew and earlier Christian emphasis on the community and collective destiny, what Aries calls *Et morie-mur*, "we shall die," gradually shifted, and when the question of death was raised, especially in the context of a growing fear and morbidity, there was the shock of discovery: the discovery of one's *own* death, *la mort de soi*. Aries, in discussing a mounting individualization of tombs from the eleventh century on, notes that a new awareness of the person as an individual came to be tied to the growing fear of death. The model shift he speaks of gave rise to consciousness of personal death. Putting this mutation into a metaphor, Aries says:

> Here we can grasp this change in the mirror of death or, in the words of the old authors, *speculum mortis*. In the mirror of his own death each man would discover the secret of his individuality. And this relationship which Greco-Roman Antiquity . . . had glimpsed briefly and had then lost, has from that time on never ceased to make an impression on our Western civilization.[28]

Following this discovery in the early Middle Ages, Western people gradually became resigned to the idea that we are all mortal. They looked at death from a new philosophical perspective.

Three prime themes connected with the fear of death emerged in the art of the fourteenth century. *The Dance of Death* theme originated in a poem of the late thirteenth century, "*The Encounter of the Three Living and the Three Dead*." This theme spread throughout Europe in sculpture, literature and painting. It tells of three knights who, while they are out hunting, come across three corpses and suddenly recognize them as themselves. A variation of the story is about a young and beautiful girl who looks into a mirror only to discover a skull as her reflection.[29] The *Dance of Death* theme depicted corpses dancing, arms entwined with living people, in a scene of unequaled emotional content. Death, the great equalizer, cuts down rich and poor, good and evil. Sometimes performed as a masque, the *Dance of Death* consisted of men dressed as skeletons dancing with figures meant to represent various levels in society. The fresco (1460) at La Chaise-Dieu in Haute Loire, France is one of the best preserved of these representations. A dangerous and forbidding realization of despair is expressed in these artistic discriptions: that the conduct of one's life, good or bad, has no bearing on one's fate. Serious doubts about resurrection and the promise of a happy afterlife appear on the popular level, accompanying the dismal prediction that, even if there is an afterlife, few will be saved and a multitude will be deserving of damnation.[30]

Fear of death ran rampant in the arts under the banner of the second theme, *Ars Moriendi*, the art of dying. "This new iconography is to be found in the woodcuts, spread by the new technique of printing in books which are treatises on the proper manner of dying; the *artes moriendi* of the fifteenth and sixteenth centuries."[31] A calm and peaceful deathbed scene is fairly typical in the art of the early Middle Ages, but in the late fourteenth century a strange phenomenon takes place. The scene becomes a dramatic contest between good and evil. An invasion of supernatural figures is shown in the bed chamber of the dying person; clustered on one side of the bed are the Trinity, the Virgin Mary and a whole court of angelic figures; and drawn around the prone figure on the other side are Satan and hordes of glowering demons. The purpose is to administer a final test to the victim. A final temptation besets the moribund by the army of monsters who try to bar his access to the kingdom of the blest by urging him to lose faith. God is present not as judge but to observe the resistance to despair of the dying person. Two important changes can be observed here. Judgment, instead of taking place on the last day of time, is interpreted as immediate, at the end of each life. In addition, it is depicted as taking place over one particular individual in response to his personal decisions.

By the fifteenth century it was thought that each person who died underwent a life review: his "entire life flashed before his eyes."[32] At the moment of his death he was offered the opportunity to give closure to his life by making a last decision, the decision to despair or believe, giving his life its final meaning. The shift in emphasis in the deathbed scene was toward more individual responsibility in the art of dying well.

The third theme of death in the arts was that of the *Triumph of Death* which appeared in fourteenth and fifteenth century frescoes in Italy. This theme emphasized death as taking the central place on a stage that is the death scene or burial procession. The death skeleton rides a horse that leads the procession and gestures to everyone to follow, underscoring the universality of the death experience. As the primary figure in the composition, Death was shown not as a messenger sent by God or even as his delegate, but as a power in itself with the spiritual dimension downplayed. If God or the saints appeared at all in the frescoes, they had minimal importance in the composition.[33] The art historian Carla Gottlieb comments, "The Italian *Triumph of Death* . . . shows death no longer as a delegate of God but as His substitute. Revolt at the injustice of fate, dread of the unknown, the abdication of God in favor of Death, these are the moving ideas of the fourteenth and fifteenth century themes."[34] In these three themes the only way one can overcome the dread of dying is to expose it, to see death's face in the mirror of time, to dance with death, or even to make death a god by allowing it to commandeer mammoth proportions of human psychic energy.

Preoccupation with the Inferno

The apogee of Christian literature of the Middle Ages is Dante's great masterpiece, *The Divine Comedy* (1300). Dante's marvelous knowledge of science, his complete grasp of the classical Greek poets such as Homer, the philosophy of Aristotle and the theology of Augustine and Thomas Aquinas, as well as his native genius converged to give deep allegorical meaning to his vision of the alternatives to life on earth. Dante wanted to show that, though man is beset by sin and ignorance, there is a source of relief in life after death. With divine inspiration during life and by means of severe spiritual discipline, one could achieve salvation and eternal bliss. The order of Augustine's universe is manifest in the architectonic and symmetrical form of the epic, which consists of the three canticles, "Inferno," "Purgatorio" and "Paradiso." Dante was guided through Hell, which was at the center of the earth, to Mount Purgatory, which protruded from the earth's surface, and up to the Garden of Eden from which Dante and his deceased wife, Beatrice, ascended to Heaven. Of the three realms, the "Inferno" left the deepest impression on the minds of poets and painters. Here Dante showed men's sins by a skillful system of retribution called by him *contrapasso*, a just correspondence between sin and punishment. For example, the gluttonous wallowed like pigs in their filth; the vain were marked by loathsome sores and scars, and liars were stricken by diseases of the mouth. All the damned souls were driven and tortured by beasts and monsters. From the fourteenth century popular ideas of hell, purgatory and paradise were largely shaped by Dante's vivid narrative, and *The Divine Comedy* was rapidly to become the authoritative pronouncement about belief in afterlife.

THE TIME OF LIFE IS BUT A MOMENT

As Christian theology developed through the late Middle Ages, certain factors, endemic to the Christian outlook about time, began to emerge. The Christian model of time was given a teleological interpretation. As in the Hebrew religion, Christians had always seen time as the field in which the gradual revelation and fulfillment of God's purpose grew. Therefore, life was considered precious and meaningful, a gift of God to be cherished as an opportunity to carry out his plan. In this sense, long years could be interpreted as part of that gift. Christians had a sense of optimism and expectation regarding life on earth, which contrasted sharply with ancient Greek pessimism regarding time, aging and dying. In addition, Christian tradition carried on the custom of respect for aging, although in general did not, as has been mentioned earlier, promise long life for faithfulness. The Christians came to have a strong tendency to think of life in this world as for the sake of the next. As Brandon puts it, "Although . . . implicated in the temporal process by God's will, the individual Christian has hoped ultimately to escape from time. The vision of God, the *Summum Bonum* of Christian endeavor, has been conceived as an eternal experience."[35] Therefore, the length of man's life on earth makes less difference than his preparation for the next life. In the Second Letter to the Corinthians (1:15) Paul urged the faithful to get away from the body and make their home in the Lord. Gerald Gruman notes that because of this focus on heaven things of this world seemed less important.[36] There was a sense of the transitoriness of things in this world. Paul had set the tone for this: "Though our outward man perish, yet the inward man is renewed day by day. . . . While we look not at the things which are seen, but at the things which are not seen: for the things which are seen are temporal, but the things which are not seen are eternal" (2 Cor. 4:16, 18).

Little or nothing is said about aging as such in the New Testament. The focus of the Christian Church was on the hope of life after death and the resurrection: "For we know that, if our earthly house this tabernacle dissolved, we have a building of God, a house not made with hands, eternal in the heavens" (2 Cor. 5:1).

Aging in the Middle Ages

The Christian Church's mandate, to baptize all nations, had opened the gates of myriad influences on its thinking. Significant was the Roman influence, which at least on the popular level helped mold attitudes toward time as well as aging and dying. As an example, in the latter part of the twelfth century, Lotario d'Conti di Segni, who became Pope Innocent III, wrote a treatise on the human condition, which included a description of old age that would reflect a very different

tone from the early Christian optimism of the New Testament. It rang
with the *memento mori* theme. A description of the overall mood of the
twelfth century, leading up to the reign of Pope Innocent III is given in
kaleidoscopic fashion by C.H. Haskins. The period was:

> . . . the epoch of the Crusades, of the rise of towns and of the
> earliest bureaucratic states of the West. It saw the culmination of
> Romanesque art, and the beginnings of the Gothic, the emergence of
> the vernacular literatures, the revival of Latin classics and of
> Latin poetry and Roman law; the recovery of Greek science, with its
> Arabic additions and much of Greek philosophy; and the origin of
> European universities. The twelfth century left its signature on
> higher education, on scholastic philosophy, on European systems of
> law, on architecture and sculpture, on the liturgical drama, on
> Latin and vernacular poetry.[37]

Pope Innocent III, who reigned from 1198 to 1216, was notable for
championing the supremacy of the pope in temporal affairs. He himself
cut a powerful figure in both the secular and religious scenes as the
world approached the thirteenth century. "He is one of the most clearly
defined, and dominant personalities; not only in the Middle Ages, but in
the history of Western civilization." [38] In a seven-year period of forced
retirement during the reign of his predecessor and foe, Celestine III,
Innocent III wrote a three book treatise titled *On the Contempt of the
World Following on the Misery of the Human Condition*. The tone of the
work was negative in that it portended dire future punishments for human
failings. The first book dealt with the baseness of man from the instant
of physical conception to maturity. The second book described man's sins
and the third his future torments. With repeated references to the
Bible, Innocent underscored the brevity of life and the miseries of
growing old. In chapters ten and eleven of Book I he rewrote a passage
from the Roman poet Horace (65-8 B.C.) but recast it in more physical
terms. In *Ars Poetica* Horace was interested in the behavior of old men
and described them as miserly, lacking energy but greedy for long life,
quarrelsome, critical of the younger generation, and endlessly praising
the good old days of their youth (ll. 169-74). Innocent III uses
Horace's passage, but focuses on unpleasant bodily accompaniments of
doting old age:

> However, when someone moves towards old age, at once his heart is
> weakened and his head is agitated, his spirit languishes . . . his
> face becomes red, he is stooped, his eyes become misty, his joints
> are unsteady, . . . his hair falls out, he is tremulous and
> disoriented, his teeth rot, his ears become deaf. An old person is
> easily provoked . . . is tenacious and greedy, sullen and
> quarrelsome, quick to speak but slow to listen--not slow to become
> angry; praises oldtimers, spurns contemporaries, vituperates the
> present, commends the past; sighs and is anxious, grows stiff. . . .
> Listen to the poet Horace: "Old age is surrounded by many
> disagreeable things. So, let not the elderly boast against this
> reality nor let young men be proud in the presence of a decaying old
> man; he was once what we [the young] are, and we shall be some day
> what he now is."[39]

The moral at the end epitomizes the *memento mori* of the medieval period, turning a Roman idea into a medieval one. These ideas spread quickly through France and England as well as Italy, becoming a well-cherished literary convention for old age in the medieval period and later.

Vincent of Beauvais, a Dominican friar who retired to a monastery at Beauvais in France, subsequently embodied Horace's negative outlook in his *Speculum Majus*, *The Great Mirror*, and the *Biblioteca Mundi*, *Library of the World*, which in many respects exemplified the dominant spirit of the thirteenth century and the high tide of scholasticism. These writings blended the authority of Roman and Greek learning with the Scriptures in an attempt to comprehend and reconcile them for the purpose of human salvation. Vincent's book blended scholastic method and the aims of Christian theology in a popular encyclopedia of vast scope for Latin readers of the thirteenth century. It contains several chapters devoted to old age. In them Horace's ideas are revamped again as old age is spoken of as the final conqueror and a matter for reproach. Using oxymora he presents longevity as a desired evil, a healthy sickness and a breathing death.

An English poém, "Pricke of Conscience," was a very well known work in the field of didactic and religious verse in the fourteenth century. The author is unknown, but the purpose was obviously the inspiration and religious education of the reader, whose conscience would be pricked so that the fear of hell would "stir till right dread . . . the conscience of lewed men." An encyclopedic review of the teachings of the Church Fathers, the poem includes Innocent III's ideas on aging with some additional unpleasant details. The physical aspects of waning old age are emphasized. Old age is said to begin at forty or fifty when one grows blind, weak and cold, his complexion and manners change, giving him a heavy heart, shaking hands and "his mouthe slavers, his tethe rotes." Absent mindedness, failed wits and an array of bad qualities, such as covetousness, follow.

In the latter part of the sixteenth century, William Shakespeare and his contemporary Elizabethans would echo this theme of the deterioration of physical prowess and mental acuity in old age. In the second act of *As You Like It*, which begins "all the world's a stage," old age is divided into several phases of progressive decline. The four early stages of man are followed by "green old age" which begins at fifty and ends with "decrepit old age" and second childhood, wherein the old person is left without everything:

> The sixth age shifts
> Into the lean and slipper'd pantaloon,
> With spectacles on nose and pouch on side,
> His youthful hose, well saved, a world too wide
> For his shrunk shank, and his big manly voice,
> Turning again toward childish treble, pipes
> And whistles in his sound. Last scene of all,
> That ends this strange eventful history,
> Is second childishness, and mere oblivion,
> Sans teeth, sans eyes, sans taste, sans every thing.
> *As You Like It*, 2.7.159-68

Restoration comedies of manners (1660-1700) further stylized old people in the same negative manner, often making them caricatures subject to ridicule. The destructiveness of time would become a preoccupying theme throughout portions of Shakespeare's powerful verse:

> O God! that one might read the book of fate,
> And see the revolution of the times
> Make mountains level. . . .
> The happiest youth, viewing his progress through,
> What perils past,what crosses to ensue,
> Would shut the book, and sit him down and die.
>   Henry IV, Part 2,3.1.45-7,54-6

> Ruin hath taught me thus to ruminate,
> That Time will come and take my love away.
> This thought is as a death, which cannot choose
> But weep to have that which it fears to lose.
>   Sonnets LXIV, 11-14

> Golden lads and girls all must,
> As chimney-sweepers, come to dust
>   Cymbeline, 4.2.262-63

Shakespeare depicts Time as "Wasteful time," "Devouring Time," "Time's fickle glass," and "Time . . . delves the parallels in beauty's brow." The poet's pen "has implored, challenged, berated and conquered time in more than a dozen sonnets. He condenses and surpasses the speculations and emotions of many centuries."[41]

Father Time

The hourglass has long been a symbol of time. In scenes from the *Dance of Death* Death, envisioned as a skeleton, raises its arm high and holds an hourglass, as he drags a young woman off to her fate. Here the emphasis is clearly on the medieval theme of death as the thief of youth. However, the hourglass would accompany another less morbid symbolic representation in Renaissance art of the fourteenth through the sixteenth centuries: the figure of Father Time. Here time is symbolized as a person, an old man with wings bearing a scythe and an hourglass, emblems of his function of cutting off life. These symbols recall Atropos, one of the three sisters in Greek mythology. After Atropos' sister had measured the thread of life, she snipped it off.

Antiquity had provided a basic image of time in the Greek *Kairos*, a crucial choice-point in human affairs represented by Opportunity, a figure with winged shoulders and heels, carrying scales representing balance and a wheel of fortune which stood for chance, decked with a forelock by which he could be grasped. Opportunity symbolized plentitude and power, but the hourglass focused on the fact that time is fleeting (and so is opportunity).[42] In the formation of the figure of Father Time holding the hourglass, Panofsky suggests that *Kronos*, the ancient and formidable god of agriculture, was confused with *Chronos*, the mythical father who devours his own children, and thus comes the significance of time as devouring its subjects.[43] This mistaken identity is perpetuated, according to one source, by the Neoplatonists, who saw *Kronos* as life, the symbol of cosmic mind and again fused *Kronos* with *Chronos*, the devouring father of all.[44] The scythe, or sickle, traditionally represents *Kronos'* association with agriculture or perhaps the act of castration of Uranus in Hesiod. Whatever the case, grimness was associated with the hourglass and the passage of time and later the clock became symbolic of the fatal significance of time's transitoriness. Shakespeare had mourned the passage of time as represented by the hands of the clock, which measures time:

> To be no better than a homely swain;
> To sit upon the hill, as I do now,
> To carve out dials quaintly, point to point,
> Thereby to see the minutes how they run
> How many make the hour full complete . . .
> How many years a mortal man may live.
> When this is known, then to divide the times.
> So many hours must I tend my flock.
> Henry VI, Part 3, 3.2.22

In iconography, Father Time is shown as a morose old man. Thus time, aging and death are explicitly associated, coalescing in the figure of Father Time, but without the heights of emotional content of the earlier days when the figure of death was the predominant symbol of time. Today Father Time is also depicted in popular art as an old man. He symbolizes the old year, which is dying away to make room for the child who will take his place as the new year.

Many of the symbols of time come together in Peter Brueghel's sixteenth century fantasy, *The Triumph of Time*. Father Time stands as the central figure and emphasizes both the creative and destructive aspects of time. In his left hand he lifts up a serpent that is, in its ancient symbolic form, biting its tail, representing the endless cycle of time. In the lore of alchemy, this symbol represented the idea of cosmic wholeness. An hourglass is positioned inside a rushing chariot, and poised above Father Time's head is a weight-driven clock, suggesting a growing awareness among the populace of time consciousness.

It should be kept in mind that few could expect a long life span in the Middle Ages. For example, in thirteenth-century England, male life expectancy at birth was estimated at 35.4 years, and in the second quarter of the fourteenth century this figure dropped to 33 years.[45] Of course, this does not make a case for the fact that some individuals did not live longer. Mainly, it is a comment on the high infant mortality rate. Robert Kastenbaum notes that "the struggle was to survive childhood and reach the early prime of life rather than to attain and enjoy a fruitful old age."[46] In addition, large percentages of males were killed in war or by other violence. According to one statistical study of the records of the day, about one-fifth of the members of a military cohort born after 1350 died by violence. Only slightly less than one-quarter of all those who actively participated in battle were to live to celebrate the age of fifty.[47]

Roger Bacon: Early Plans for Prolonging Life

As the dark vision focusing on the corruptibility of things physical began to fade, new thinkers and popular writers started to foreshadow, however dimly, some of the confidence and self-assurance that would later characterize the beginnings of modern science. Preventive therapies and methods of life prolongation were projected, offering a positive approach to disease cure and aging itself. Common sense, coupled with some daring, began to shift from fourteenth-century discouragement about early death and aging, to a more hopeful outlook. Thoughts of extending life and health well beyond all ordinary expectations began to enter the minds of a few farseeing individuals.

A Franciscan friar, Roger Bacon (1214-1294) author of *Major Works*, *Cure of Old Age and Preservation of Youth*, and *On How to Manage the Aging Process Together With Other Small Works on Medical Subjects*, took an unorthodox stand on old age, stretching beyond the Judeo-Christian conviction that longevity was a gift to be granted according to God's will. He was inspired by biblical reports of antediluvians. If, after the fall, individuals had the capacity for such long years, perhaps, he argued, the short lives of people of his century, barring wars, were due to human ignorance and neglect.[48]

Bacon was engaged in Latin alchemy, the doctrine and the practice of chemistry (popular between the thirteenth and seventeenth centuries) which was chiefly concerned with the transmutation of base metals into gold and the search for a universal remedy for disease. Alchemists believed that everything in the universe shared a degree of the same life force, a vital innate moisture. Bacon, like the Hebrews, believed that a diminishment of years was connected with sinful behavior; and, like Aquinas, he thought natural control of the body was lost by sinning: "Sins weaken the powers of the soul so that it is incompetent for the natural control of the body; and therefore the powers of the body are weakened and life is shortened."[49] He believed bad hygiene was a second element related to premature aging and short life and even suggested that this could be hereditary: "Thus a weakened condition passes from father to sons, until a final shortening of life has been reached."[50]

Bacon viewed old age dimly as an evil to be defeated, a progressive disease that could be counteracted by a process of rejuvenation of the body's moistures. Echoing Plato and Aristotle, he believed that a sound mind in a sound body was necessary for a good life. But, contrary to the ancients, he taught that an effort to retard old age was preferable to a philosophical acceptance of its physical limitations, thus hoping for compensation in the growth of wisdom. Bacon believed that one can attempt to slow down the onset of old age by means of proper diet, exercise, a modest life-style and good hygiene. He also believed that chemical therapy could cure disease and prolong life. Animals, he taught, had instinctive knowledge of the powers of healing in herbs and minerals, and humans could likewise have such knowledge through the use of pharmacology. As part of what he called "secret arts," Bacon listed all kinds of rejuvenating and curative substances: ground-up pearls, coral, rosemary, stag's heart, snake meat, and liquid gold, to list a few. Gruman comments on what was secret in Bacon's secret art: "what was novel and 'secret' about Bacon's attitude was the fact that he assessed [these substances] from an alchemical standpoint according to which everything in the world possesses a greater or less amount of vitalizing principle akin to the vital spirit [innate moisture] of living things."[51]

The vital principle in all things was ethereal, connected with "ether," the substance Aristotle and other ancients believed filled all space beyond the sphere of the moon and made up the stars and planets. Ether was always connected to life, the spirit and the divine. What is of particular interest is that Roger Bacon, though his methods were prescientific, was a thirteenth century scholar, who believed that life could and should be prolonged by active therapeutic intervention and not just passively accepted as given or taken according to a divine plan. Here we see the first traces of man seeing himself in an active controlling role *vis-à-vis* nature. This spirit grew through the fifteenth and sixteenth centuries and flowered in the seventeenth century. But Bacon did not think life could be rejuvenated indefinitely. However he did believe "life might be prolonged a century or more beyond the usual age of men now living."[52]

After Roger Bacon came another Franciscan friar, John Rupescissa (c 1362-?), who though an alchemist, became the first initiator of medical chemistry. Rupescissa's work stood at the transition point between medieval chemistry or alchemy, and medical chemistry, or iatrochemistry. His chief contribution was to show that there was not just a single substance, elixir, or philosopher's stone that would rejuvenate and cure disease, but many. Iatrochemists abandoned the dream of making gold from baser metals and turned to the study of human chemistry, identifying particular diseases and searching for particular cures. Paracelsus (1493-1541), in spite of his own dabblings in alchemy, became famous for his opposition to the humoral theory of medicine and lead the way to founding a system of chemistry that became the forerunner of modern biochemistry and chemotherapy.

A Humanistic Gerontologist

Humanism, a pervasive influence in the late Middle Ages, was the intellectual and cultural movement that emphasized the study of classical Greek and Latin literature and culture. This movement attempted to understand and to reconcile classical and Christian traditions and to apply the lessons history offered for the benefit of contemporary ethics and politics. The sixteenth-century humanists argued against a philosophy that would lead to arid disputation, preferring a philosophy that would focus on human interests, rather than the natural world or religion alone. It is not surprising, then, to find a famous Italian jurist, philosopher and theologian (who later became a cardinal of the Church and who played an important role at the Council of Trent) writing a major treatise on gerontology. The work of Gabriele Paleotti (1522-1597) entitled *Of Good Old Age (De Bono Senectutis)*, was written and published shortly before his death. It included the characteristic restatement of biblical and classical views on aging, with frequent quotes from Aristotle, Aquinas and Augustine, but it placed emphasis on a critique of classical treatments, remedies and attitudes toward old age. The book considered common complaints about the aged, but was for the most part an apology for the elderly: "the author obviously intended to prove that old age is not merely a negative phase of life, but has its specific value obtainable at no other period."[53] There were only a few references to the physical aspects of aging. What drew Paleotti's attention was the need for proper therapeutic measures for the treatment of aging persons, physically and mentally:

> [Certain writers] . . . deal with sadness which frequently oppresses the mind of old people greatly and they suggest remedies by which it is customarily alleviated. The following are considered a sort of healthy antidote, such forms of relaxation which delight the senses, as for instance, music, games, plays, conversations, dinner parties, pleasure drives, baths, parks, beautiful scenery and fountains.[54]

Quoting Aristotle and Thomas Aquinas, Paleotti notes that these psychotherapeutic methods are often helpful but have limited value because they cannot reach the hidden cause of the sadness which gnaws at the mind of elderly people.

Paleotti quoted from Augustine who, in deep grief over his mother's death, went to the baths for some relaxation but admitted later, that such therapeutic measures could not wash away the sorrow from the heart.[55] With uncommon practical sense, Paleotti discussed not only the state of depression found sometimes in older people, but also senile decline. Paleotti claimed that these states of mind were worsened because old people themselves realized their strength of mind was fading and that they had no hope of recovering youth and strength once they reached old age. Naturally, they became depressed. Paleotti, himself an old man, avidly denied the validity of popular proverbs that claimed, "Old age is a disease," or "To be an old man is not to be at all," or even "Throw people over sixty off the bridge." He pointed out the danger of these stereotypes. They assume attitudes that only worsen the old folks' last days, leading them into great mental agony. He argued that old age can be a fruitful stage of a person's life because wisdom, growth and the waning of fierce emotions of youth afford the person in his later years a unique opportunity for creativeness that was not accessible earlier.[56]

Hygienist-Gerontologist

Luigi Cornaro (1469-1565) stands as the prototype of a school of thought among writers about aging who were called hygienists because they believed that not secret arts, but a healthy life-style was the key to controlling disease and physical aging. They believed that human beings are born healthy, and in order to live long, free from disease, they must live a simple and moderate life. Cornaro was a Paduan nobleman of a very optimistic and lighthearted nature. The zest for life he displayed, typical of the spirit of the Renaissance, reaches the level of unbounded *joie de vivre* in his defense of the desirability of prolongevity. Cornaro in his own youth became gravely ill from leading an undisciplined life and was warned by his doctors that sobriety and better health habits were necessary to save him; therefore, he changed his life-style and lived to age ninety-eight. Like most scholars of his day, he took Greek and Roman ideas and combined them with his own theories, and in his case with his own experiences, in a completely novel way.

In his book *Discourses on the Sober Life* he gave reasons why it is wise to want to preserve life as long as possible.[57] Cornaro argued that not only can Christians attain everlasting life in heaven; they can and should, through moderate living, enjoy long and happy lives on earth. This optimism characterizes all his arguments. Old age is neither an enemy to Cornaro nor a disease to be cured, as Roger Bacon had intimated. Cornaro idealized old age and used this idealization as an argument for the prolongevist theory, which held that one not only can but should try to live a long life. He started his four *Discourses* at the age of eighty-three and wrote the last one at ninety-five. It was his wish that everyone should share such joy as he had in the experience of growing old. "For I have an ardent desire that every man should strive to attain my age, in order that he may enjoy . . . the most beautiful period of life."[58] Cornaro believed that one does one's best work in the later years of life because a qualitative maturing process takes place. It is "the time indeed at which men appear to the best advantage in learning and virtue--two things which can never reach their perfection except in time."[59] Finally Cornaro took over Aristotle's distinction between forced death, identified with disease or physical violence, and natural death, a gentle death associated with senescence, claiming that those who are temperate reach extreme old age and therefore will not suffer unnatural death.

Cornaro, like most Renaissance writers of his day, believed in the humoral theory of medicine wherein health consists of a proper balance of the four humors, and disease consists of their imbalance. Aging, again, was thought to be caused by using up one's vital principle or the innate moisture of the body. But this vital principle can be conserved, not by complicated drugs and exotic cure-alls, but by a healthy life regimen consisting of some commonsense rules about balanced diet and temperance: "it is impossible in the regular course of nature that he who leads the orderly and temperate life should ever fall sick."[60]

What Cornaro says that is different from his predecessors is that *everyone*, not just the exceptionally strong person, can live long, to between 100 and 120, and that one can conserve the vital force but not restore or increase it as Roger Bacon had thought. In other words his advice is to use the health regimen to retain health, because when consumed, it cannot be regained: "sobriety . . . is more conducive to the preservation of the radical [innate] moisture. . . . Hence we may reasonably conclude that the holy temperate life is the true mother of health and of longevity."[61] In addition, one must not rely on others for the maintenance of one's health: "A man can have no better doctor than himself and no better medicine than the temperate life."[62]

This section has moved from the optimistic Christian outlook of deep faith, which yearned for heaven, through the *memento mori* theme with its morbid preoccupation with the physical miseries of the human condition, particularly regarding aging, to the less pessimistic synthesis of death, aging and the passage of time in the symbolic figure of Father Time. Then it proceeded to the alchemical secret arts that Bacon offered to rejuvenate lost youth and to the first intimations of the discovery of medical science, and then to the humanistic apology for aging in Paleotti. Finally, it shows the burst of joy in Cornaro's unreserved idealization of the aging process. It is a long way from the Christian desire to escape from time, the oppressor, to the sixteenth century gerontologist who claimed, "I ceaselessly keep repeating: 'Live, live, that you may become better servants of God.'"[63]

In the fifteenth and sixteenth centuries an immense change took place. The man of the late Renaissance began to take a more active role in directing his life and his world, throwing off the pessimism and preoccupation with decay and death seen in the early Middle Ages and adopting an optimistic view about time, aging and death. This new consciousness is described by one author: "The man of the Renaissance experiences a boundless vitality, a sense of almost superhuman power and a feeling of being part and parcel of a wonderful wide world where there is no decay and destruction . . . only change and transformation."[64] In Renaissance man a spontaneous love of life and interest in the world, accompanied by a feeling for the beauty of nature and the preciousness of human years, had changed the Middle Ages' motto from *Memento Mori* (remember death) to *Memento vivere* (remember life).

THE SPLIT IMAGE

Man is only a reed, but a thinking reed.
                              Pascal

The theme of prolongation of life continued to develop in the seventeenth century, based chiefly on the work of René Descartes and Francis Bacon. Medieval people, ideally, had accepted their lot as God's will and placed their faith in salvation and eternal reward. Scientists of the late seventeenth century concentrated not so much on faith and acceptance of the lot of man as on an attempt to improve it. A new faith in mathematical physics, based on the power of human reason to grasp the first principles or fundamental laws of nature, arose. Once these principles were understood, it was believed that control could be extended over human life, aging and death. Yet Descartes was torn between the medieval Christian model of the world and the emerging scientific model of reality. His contribution to the scientific model led to the development of the mechanistic worldview and his definition of body and soul, as two distinct and separate entities, led to the problem of mind-body dualism that has plagued Western culture until the present. The Newtonian definition of absolute time which had its roots in Descartes' concepts of time and duration, entailed a revolutionary view, the advantages and disadvantages of which remain with modern science. Descartes' dream of a unified science, and Francis Bacon's scientific method gave birth to a renewed drive to prolong life and defeat death.

DESCARTES: A FOOT IN TWO WORLDS

René Descartes (1596-1650) was in the lead of the legion of scientists who, with Promethean confidence, shared the aim of "harnessing nature to the purposes of man." Of him, Leon Roth says, "The will o' wisp of his life was the conquest of death not only for the soul but also for the body."[1] In the seventeenth century, knowledge and scientific experimentation were pressed into the service of human control over nature, and Western philosophy and medicine would take a direction quite different from the past. To Descartes and other writers of the second quarter of the seventeenth century, the light of reason was the faculty given to man by God for the immediate apprehension of truth. In the following century the Enlightenment or Age of Reason would take firm hold on the mind and imagination of the West. Before that time men tended to look backward to the medieval view of the world, with Thomas Aquinas' Christianized version of Aristotelian theology, but now that model of the universe was challenged and men began to look forward to gaining a greater control through the use of reason. This century would be the age when science and scholarship would finally begin to cut loose from both superstition and ancient tradition and reason would be established as the foundation for all belief.

Descartes, who helped launch this new age, has been called the Father of the Enlightenment, but he was also a child of the Middle Ages, trapped between two models. While remaining a devout Roman Catholic, he espoused theories that made his work suspect in the eyes of the Church. He willingly suppressed one of his most innovative works on human physiology, in spite of four years of protracted anatomical study, because he learned that Galileo had been punished by the Church for advocacy of Copernican doctrine.

Deeply ingrained with the ideas of Aristotle and medieval philosophy, Descartes blended the logic of scholasticism with the Faustian dreams of medieval alchemists in a search for a means to extend life and prevent death. However he was torn between traditions of the past and new experimental science; between his belief in God's omnipotence and his faith in the power of man.[2]

Torn as he was, Descartes tried to hold these two sides together. He saw the Christian God as the creator of the laws of motion that governed the universe and believed this to be an intuition all men possess.[3] At the same time, he took a liberal view of religion, he even argued that the creation story should not be taken literally, but as a metaphor. Descartes believed the Bible ought not to be thought of as a source of scientific knowledge and that science and religion ought to be seen as having different ends. Therefore, with Descartes begins the division between religion and science.

The Machine Metaphor

In adolescence, Descartes became enamored of mathematics, a love that he never abandoned. In his early twenties he applied this knowledge of mathematics to simple experiments in mechanics, optics and hydrostatics (the science that investigates the pressure and equilibrium of water and other liquids). The story is told that it was his fascination with the hydrostatically controlled mechanical fountains at Sainte-Germain-en-Laye that was the source of his interest in mechanics.[4] He also followed the achievements of his scientific contemporaries, among them Galileo and Kepler, and was deeply involved and quite proficient in anatomy and dissection. It is said that he devoted the entire winter of 1629 to the study of anatomy. Daily he visited a local butcher's shop to witness the slaughter, often bringing home animals' organs for dissection. In the Middle Ages, reading authoritative works and engaging in disputation were believed to be the way to obtain knowledge. Science and medicine were enshrined in the library. Descartes was, without doubt, ridiculed and looked upon with suspicion for seeking knowledge in direct experience and for soiling his hands in this endeavor. Nevertheless, he believed in the direct approach.

Disappointed in the methods used in his own education, Descartes attacked all philosophical systems that were founded only on opinions of authorities. Therefore, he resolved that his life's achievement would be to seek to construct a comprehensive philosophical system based on the foundations of certitude: "Even should we have read all the arguments of Plato and Aristotle . . . so long as we are unable to arrive at a firm judgment of our own . . . what we are thereby learning is not science, but history."[5] This refusal to accept blindly the authority of the past and this insistence on finding a self-evident, indubitable point of departure for knowledge was the foundation of Descartes' philosophy. The problems he posed, the questions he asked, and his demand for absolute subjective certainty as a basis for knowledge served to undermine the whole tradition of Western philosophy.

Descartes used this certainty criterion as the test by which beliefs were evaluated. He thought one must begin by abandoning all preconceptions and unsupported assumptions, and systematically doubt everything that was not absolutely self-evident. He believed one could find, as in Euclidean geometry, a small set of first principles, or axioms of nature, that can be assumed without proof. He held everything in doubt until he could find a first premise that would be beyond doubt, and this would provide a starting point for his entire system of philosophy. The basis of subjective certitude, Descartes decided, was the indubitable, self-evident experience of himself thinking. Even if his thoughts were doubts he *knew* he was doubting. His conclusion, "*Cogito ergo sum*" ("I think; therefore, I am") is not really deducing anything. It simply is a pronouncement of an intuitive perception of self, a perception that no one can doubt. Yet, this revolutionary method of doubt, that lasts until subjective certitude is reached, led science and philosophy into the modern era. Descartes chose the machine as his metaphor. He viewed animal and human bodies as machines stating, "This will hardly seem strange to those who know how many motions can be produced in automata...[to] think of this body as a machine created by the hand of God."[6] Descartes' metaphor of the machine meshed well with his mathematical system of thought. He promised to uncover the "secret devices of things corporeal," so that one "would no longer be tempted to feel wonder regarding any product of human devising."[7]

The influence of Descartes' mechanistic metaphor has prevailed in medicine, as well as in other branches of science, to such a degree that anyone who attempts to question it is guilty of more than heresy and is subject to the accusation of opposing scientific truth.[8] Using Bertrand Russell's phrase, Colin Turbayne says that if one challenges the mechanistic model's ultimate categories, it is tantamount to, "beating his head against the brick wall of science, he is headed for disaster. . . ." since Descartes' metaphor became "a defining feature of science."[9] Mechanical laws "became literally identified with body processes. Bodies were literally seen as objects, mechanical entities that could be taken apart and put back together again," as if the whole of the person is the sum of its parts.[10] As René Dubos put it, "Many scientists that dedicate themselves to medical research tend to shy away from the problem peculiar to man's nature, and even those posed by other living organisms . . . and they deal by preference with questions pertaining to lifeless fragments of the body machine."[11] Along with other scientists who sought to master nature, Descartes zealously applied the mechanical model to all of biology and physiology and thus furthered medical knowledge in the interest of prolonging life.

Descartes' genius and creativity are found less in his new philosophical categories than in the questions he asked and the novel method they brought him to discover: Wherein can truth be verified? What is the beginning point that justifies knowledge?[12] By linking absolute verification of truth with the self, Descartes shifted the weight of the whole philosophical tradition from faith in the external order to confidence in the internal order, depending on the person's capacity for absolute subjective certainty for the purpose of validating knowledge.

Discovery of the Self and Mind Body Dualism

Descartes claimed that the souls of animals are different from the souls of humans, in which the seat of their self-consciousness resides. He insisted that in afterlife there would be more for man than for "the flies or ants."[13] Though "conjoined" to the body, the human soul is nevertheless entirely independent of the body. Descartes claimed that the soul of a person is immortal and is not bound to die with the body. He insisted:

> Death never comes through failure of the soul, but solely because some one of the principal parts of the body disintegrates. . . . The body of a living man differs from that of a dead man just as a machine . . . (a watch or other automaton when it is wound up. . .) differs from itself when it is broken and the principal of its movement ceases to act.[14]

In retaining his belief in immortality of the soul, Descartes retained a Christian solution to the fear of death. This can be seen in his comment that the belief in the soul's immortality was the source of his ability "to bear patiently the death of those I loved, but also to prevent me from fearing my own. . . . I know so clearly that they [souls] outlast the body and that they have been born for joys and bliss much greater than those we enjoy in this world."[15]

In the metaphor of the body as a machine, Descartes struck on a picture so familiar and current in the imagination of seventeenth century man that it made a lasting impression, providing a splendid concrete model for the exactitude and order of the universe of matter. However, he lacked a similarly engaging metaphor for the mind or soul, a metaphor that could equally take hold of the imagination as the body-machine image had. Burtt comments: "the common run of intelligent people who were falling into line with the scientific current, unmetaphysically minded at best, [were] totally unable to appreciate sympathetically the notion of a non-spatial entity quite independent of the extended world, partly because such an entity is unrepresentable to the imagination."[16]

The problem of understanding the mind, the seat of knowledge, was not solved, but was accentuated by Cartesian dualism. The realm of the soul, represented by an ambiguous and "vaporous" category, was doomed to fail: "God, the human soul and the whole realm of spiritual things . . . escaped imprisonment in the process of mechanization and were superadded presences, flitting vaporously amongst the cogs and wheels, the pulleys and steel castings of a relentless world machine."[17] Descartes would further provoke questions about the mode of body-soul interaction. He pointed out that just as a clock does not need a soul to tell time, so a body could operate automatically and without intervention of a soul as Aristotle proposed.[18]

Descartes created a gap between body and soul and interfered with the maintenance of a clear understanding of the category of "soul" by hardening his metaphor for the machine-body into a literal term. He did not merely picture human and animal bodies as machines; he literally treated them that way.[19] "In short, enthralled by his own metaphor, he mistook the mask for the face, and consequently bequeathed to posterity more than a world-view. He bequeathed a world."[20] By treating his own metaphor literally, Descartes thought not that man is like a machine, but that he is a machine. He no longer sought refuge in metaphor and fiction, Descartes finally stopped thinking of his metaphor as a hypothetical analogue of man and took his metaphor as a literal description of man.[21] A contemporary of Descartes, Thomas Hobbes, continued in the same spirit, describing the human person as material particles and life as:

> a motion of limbs . . . why may we not say that all automata (engines that move themselves by springs and wheels as doth a watch) have an artificial life? For what is the heart but a spring, the nerves, but so many strings; and the joints, but so many wheels, giving motion to the whole body.[22]

With such intellectual stirrings, the human person gradually is reduced to a machine that will run down, a body that will die.

A subtle shift was taking place in the intellectual environment in the last quarter of the seventeenth century. A preoccupation with astronomy and mechanics had intensified the spirit of scientific inquiry. What originated as a religious metaphor to represent the universe as a piece of perfect workmanship worthy of an all-wise and ingenious creator, would in the eighteenth century turn out to be something quite different. With the spread of the machine metaphor, the very relationship of the deity to creation was threatened. Descartes had assigned God not only the role of creator but also that of maintainer of the vast clockwork world and the famous scientist Robert Boyle (1627-1691) agreed with this. Newton (1642-1727) in the *Opticks* came to assign God specific tasks in providentially repairing the world when it broke down.

As time progressed, however, the successors of Descartes, Newton and Boyle, became increasingly aware that the machine-world could be explained as self-sufficient. Newton worried that eventually God would become superfluous. During this period a peculiar fascination, which almost amounted to an obsession about the body of a dead person, absorbed the popular mind. Knowledge of anatomy became fashionable. The anatomy lesson that was so often depicted in the engravings and paintings of the seventeenth century was, like the defense of a thesis, "a great social event that the whole town attended with masks and refreshment."[23] A new attitude appeared toward death; there was a lessening of awe regarding it and a willingness to manipulate the "zones" between life and death by scientific attempts at reviving persons apparently dead.[24] Death was no longer a threshold to be stepped over on the way to another world, rather, death was the enemy of the body, and the physician and scientist were to be death's master. The study of the body became not only fashionable, but necessary, if not to fight aging and death, at least to know God's world better.[25]

The secularization of death was seen in the physical separation of the church and the cemetery, the replacement of the importance of the clergy at the deathbed by the importance of the physician, and the first appearance of aging and death as problems to be solved, avoided, or even denied by medical professionals.[26] Monsters and devils in death rituals and art were replaced by the skeleton, which was not so frightening. The skeleton, like the one children play with today at Halloween, no longer reminded people of the demonic. The symbols of death that pervaded funerary art were less oppressive and less realistic; they were the skull and crossbones, the hourglass, the church clock and the scythe of Father Time. The human person gradually was reduced to a body that would die. The loss of soul as a category was the outcome of dualism, which led to the triumph of a "monsterous mathematical machine." Burtt comments, "Not only is his [the person's] place in a cosmic teleology lost, but . . . the things that made it alive and lovely and spiritual . . . are lumped together and crowded into their small fluctuating and temporary positions which we call human nervous and circulatory systems."[27] What was constructive and helpful in dualism's explanation of the world had been was lost and with incalculable effects.

Looking back on the notion of *psyche*, we see that the *psyche* (which Homer associated with the same principle of *life* that every living object shared) became for the Pythagorians and Orphic religions a spark of *the divine* in exile within man and for Plato the seat of personal intelligence and character. For Aristotle *psyche* took on the dignity of a source of balanced *rational action*. For the Greek philosophers, it was the antithesis of the body. The person, for the Hebrews, was made in the *image of God*. For Paul, it was through the gift of God that the life of man could be transformed and reborn as the recipient of divine life in resurrection. The Boethian definition would lay the groundwork for the medieval conception of the person as an *individual*, a spiritual being and an undivided whole, unique and valuable in himself and having an identity of his own. For St. Thomas, *immortal soul* and body belonged together; therefore, there was a demand for resurrection of the body and future glory. In the seventeenth century Descartes, by the radical distinction he drew between body and soul, paved the way for the popular philosophers of the eighteenth century to dispense with both soul and God and to think of man, the machine, as a material body alone. This is not to claim that the spiritual dimension of man in Western European life was entirely extinguished, but this age does give birth to the radical secularization of science.

ORIGINS OF NEWTONIAN TIME

Descartes dealt with material substances in spatial terms. Motion and change he conceived as physical, the change of a body from one position in space to another. Because of this emphasis on the spatial nature of bodies, Descartes emphasized the concept of space and not time in his writings. Basically, time, as it functioned in Descartes' system, "was conceived atomistically, . . . analogous to separate points which are only connected into a line by imagination."[28] In Descartes' last major philosophical work, he distinguished the concepts of time and duration. *Time*, Descartes believed, is a mode of thought, the number of motion existing only in our thinking. Time is the way humans quantify objects. But *duration* is the way things exist extended in space. As an inherent condition of existing things, objectively uniform and real, duration is what is measured by the human perspective according to some objective standard such as a day or year. *Time* is the work of the *mind*. *Duration* is the condition of *things in space*.

Charles Sherover insightfully points out that the metaphor that Descartes selected in speaking of the atomicity of time was the metaphor of a sequence of numbers, in that each number is separate, infinitely divisible, and independent of other numbers. Thus, spatial measurement is the key that acts as a mediator bringing together real duration in the world and human ways of describing it.[29] The important point here is that Isaac Newton, (1642-1727) with very little modification, based his first principle of the new physics on Descartes' spatial metaphor. Newton's famous definition distinguished between absolute, mathematical or *true time*, and relative, common, or *apparent time*:

> *Absolute*, true and mathematical time, . . . flows equably without relation to anything external, and by another name is called duration; *relative*, apparent and common time, is some sensible and external . . . measure of duration by means of motion, which is commonly used instead of true time.[30]

Absolute time (duration) was to become, along with absolute space, one of the two foundational categories of Newton's physics.[31]

In order to understand the decisive impact of spatialized time on the development of science and philosophy, it is necessary to review briefly the growth of linear time consciousness in Western Europe since its earliest discovery in Aristotle's thought. In defining time as the number of motion as to "before" and "after," Aristotle supplied the normative definition of time for the long history of philosophy. The metaphor of the movement of an object along a straight line was the metaphor of spatialized time. It is the time of objects because it is based on the examination of physical objects in time.

Mark C. Taylor pointed out that there are at least four results from using the Aristotelian concept of spatialized time: first, the moments of spatialized time are seen as homogeneous, that is, every segment is a point in space and each of these points in space is the same. Second, spatialized time emphasizes the quantitative aspect of time, that is, time measures quantity of motion. Some philosophers believe that this quantitative approach can underplay or even totally neglect qualitative considerations such as those of value. Third, spatialized time is universal insofar as it applies to all objects as homogeneous and quantitative, a grid upon which occurrences can be plotted, regardless of individual differences. Taylor goes further: "The fact that objective time derives from the perception of the motion of objects does not prevent this understanding of time from being used in connection with persons. When this is done, however, persons are treated in a manner similar to objects."[32] This results in spatialized time's tendency to have chronology as its main concern. Chronology, basically, is the science of arranging persons and events in serial order in a kind of time line, according to their occurrence, against a fixed standard of time. This way of dealing, for example with an aged person, would result in reducing age to simple chronological age and neglecting other important psychological and social aspects of the aging process. (The implications of this approach will be discussed later.) The fourth result of basing the concept of time on the view of space is that time is seen atomistically, as Descartes' theory had treated it. Time is described as discrete, temporal now-moments taken as objectively real. This conception of time raises serious questions about the nature of the continuity of objects and of persons. How can a person possess an enduring identity, which our experience seems to give overwhelming assurance of, if time consists of points that are viewed atomistically, that is, as separate and objective units?

Descartes tried to solve this dilemma by distinguishing time as the measurer's perception of duration, and duration as what is measured by that perception. But when Newton adapted Descartes' notion, he equated absolute truth and mathematical time with duration. Later, David Hume (1711-1776) would insist that the self did not exist except as a mere bundle of separate sensations and that it had no continuity at all. Hume's position was in keeping with a spatialized concept of time. Many years later, Kierkegaard (1813-1855) mounted an attack on the spatialized concept of time claiming, among other things, that it robs the individual of a sense of the three tenses and raises the issue of the continuity of the individual. Within this view, it would be possible to speak of the past, present and future, only if one could hold a position that is not within time. Kierkegaard calls this view outside of time the "Archimedean point," while Bronowski called it the ultimate gods'-eye view. It is the atomizing of time that leads to the necessity of reaching out for a kind of *deus ex machina*, which most modern philosophers believe is not within the grasp of any individual human being. Again we see that Descartes' categories, hardened by his followers, led to the dichotomy between subject and object that has given cause to much philosophical concern and debate.

Clockwork Consciousness

The history of the mechanical clock paralleled the gradual emergence of the clockwork model of the universe. Essentially religious motivation caused the technology of the clock to be improved. In medieval monasteries a kind of alarm clock aroused the sexton to call the monks to various hours of the Divine Office in an exacting schedule of prayer and work.[33] By the mid-thirteenth century, with the invention of the first verge escapement, the mechanical clock became the first ticking clock.[34]

The earliest public clocks were religious and astronomical in function rather than being merely timekeepers. Medieval Christianity with its other worldly perspective on life used the clock as it had used the hourglass as a symbol of the passage of linear time to remind the populace to prepare for timeless eternity. Religious activities were thus given a collective rhythm, organization and order. In addition, the religious person was reminded of his tasks by the clock which depicted "a perfection toward which other machines aspired."[35]

Within a short period tower clocks, with accompanying automata, spread throughout Europe:

> Suddenly toward the middle of the fourteenth century, the mechanical clock seized the imagination of our ancestors. Something of a civic pride, which earlier had expended itself in cathedral building, was now diverted to the construction of astronomical clocks of outstanding intricacy and elaboration. No European community felt able to hold up its head unless in its midst the planets wheeled in cycles and epicycles, while angels trumpeted, cocks crew, and apostles, kings and prophets marched and countermarched at the booming hours.[36]

Anticipating seventeenth century preoccupation with the universe as a machine, Nicole Oresme, a fourteenth-century scientist, compared the universe to a vast mechanical clock created and set in motion by the Creator.[37]

Odd as it may seem, linear time was developed into a generally accepted model not only by philosophers or scientists or even mathematicians, but also, in the thirteenth to fifteenth centuries by the mercantile class of Western Europe for whom time was money. This shift in the time-consciousness of the populace was accompanied by the growth of a sense of the person as an individual and by forces that secularized time.

Improvements in the technology of clocks followed with the invention of the coiled spring as a source of motion in 1450, the pocket watch between 1450 and 1460, and the pendulum by the Dutch physicist, Christian Huyghens, in 1657. Clocks became more reliable, and a new cult of precise measurement emerged in Renaissance science. Johannes Kepler (1571-1630) typified the clock consciousness of his age that focused on the continuity, regularity and predictability of both clocks and the mechanical laws of the universe: "I am much preoccupied with the investigation of the physical causes. My aim is to show that the celestial machine is to be likened not to a divine organism . . . . [But] as in the case of a clockwork, all motions [are caused] by a simple weight."[38]

The clock, first invented as a means of serving man's needs, became a metaphysical device, at first a metaphor or kind of fiction applied to the human body and then a model for the entire universe. Shortly it was taken more literally in mechanistic physiology and finally rose to a position of fostering a clockwork consciousness, an expression that represented science's preoccupation with absolute, spatial time.

In older time-measuring devices inaccuracy was commonly assumed. Timekeeping was essentially discontinuous or irregular, depending on the repetition of concrete phenomena such as the rise of the sun. Essentially, exactitude was neither needed nor desired. Early clocks, which struck the hour, had at first no dial and no hands, and then only an hour hand. With the pendulum, a minute hand was added but not until the eighteenth century was a second hand developed. "The clock provided a means by which time . . . could be measured concretely in the more tangible terms of *space* provided by the circumference of a clock dial."[39] The clock translated time into visual segments, atomized units marked off on a "face" and pointed to by hands.

Lewis Mumford has connected the clock with the change in mentality about time. He claims that the conception of time as a thing in itself (absolute time) has "dissociated time from human events and helped to create the belief in an independent world of mathematically measurable sequences: the special world of science."[40] Marshall McLuhan sees the same kind of dissociation between public time and private experience: "As a piece of technology, the clock is a machine that produces uniform seconds, minutes and hours on an assembly-line pattern. . . . Time measured not by the uniqueness of private experience, but by abstract uniform units gradually pervades all sense life."[41]

In this context one is tempted to look back at Aristotle's simple but searching question about the relation between time and the mind. One can recall also the answer that he later neglected to pursue: time does not exist apart from consciousness. It is ironical that Descartes, like Aristotle, stood at the threshold of a new perception that connected time and self-consciousness. Yet Descartes is seen as the discoverer of the problem of the modern self and the source of the Newtonian concept of absolute time, the time of things.

Descartes' Dream: To Defeat the Clock

On the night of November 10, 1619, Rene Descartes had a remarkable experience, one that would affect his career as a scientist and student of physiology. In a dream, he saw the Angel of Truth who opened to his gaze the treasure of all sciences, wherein "the human mind played no part." Through a kind of intuitive insight Descartes was confirmed in his conviction that there was only one single science that was the foundation of all others. This was the "Admirable Science" that would unlock the secrets of nature and the key to it would be mathematics. Jacques Maritian in his book *The Dream of Descartes* notes that Descartes' decision to put aside the traditional idea of the diversity of sciences and replace it with *the science* amounted to a "singular grave decision," the effects of which "are not yet fully realized."[42] The emotional experience of this dream was so deep and compelling that later, recalling the specific date of the event, Descartes would speak of the incident as a great revelation that marked a decisive point in his life and work.[43] But the dream would also give rise to a persistent conflict in his life because in the dream he was swept up by a powerful gale and thrown first toward and then away from a church. Descartes, deeply excited and disturbed, awoke with the question in his mind, "What path shall I follow in life?"[44]

We know what path Descartes followed after his nocturnal vision when we read his *Discourse on Method*, the original title of which reveals Descartes' optimism and enthusiasm regarding his scientific plans: *Project of a Universal Science Destined to Raise our Nature to Its Highest Perfection*. This was no ordinary endeavor that had been revealed to Descartes by the Angel of Truth. It would be *the science*, the universal science of mechanics that would underlie all physical reality: "To Descartes from that moment on, space or extension became the fundamental reality; motion, the point of all departure and, mathematics, the language of its revelation."[45] Once Descartes claimed that all bodies were governed by the laws of mechanics, he was in the position to make the grandiose claim, echoed in the rationalism of the Enlightenment, that "in principle we already know the answer to all the questions which can be asked" regarding the physical processes of nature.[46] This conviction spurred him on to believe that it would be in medicine that his most important discoveries would be made. He believed that if all bodily processes are governed by the laws of mechanics, then diseases of the body, once they are understood, must be capable of being remedied with the same certitude and precision as disorders of a clock. Out of this optimistic conviction would grow Descartes' dream of prolonging life. "I have resolved to employ as much of my life as remains, wholly in trying to acquire some knowledge of nature, of such a sort that we may derive rules of medicine more certain than those which we have had up to the present."[47]

But Descartes was dogged by "inner conflicts regarding his rationalism, utilitarianism and prolongevitism."[48] At one moment he seemed unwaveringly resolute in his prediction about the absolute success medicine could promise in controlling disease, in prolonging human life, and ultimately in conquering death. At the next moment he vowed to try not to desire the impossible and to accept submissively the world the way it is: "Making . . . a virtue of necessity, we no more desire to be well when we are sick, or to be free when we are in prison than we now desire bodies as incorruptible as diamonds or wings to fly like the birds."[49]

Descartes' doubts about his conviction that reason could solve any problem emerged again and again. In his confusion and alarm in the face of Galileo's condemnation, for example, Descartes suppressed his treatise on physiology. But his wavering did not dampen his ardor for solving practical problems, particularly in the medical area. Medicine, Descartes believed, was the means not only of healing and controlling human illness and suffering, thus promoting the "general good of mankind," but it would be the tool that would hold the promise of "rendering ourselves masters and possessors of nature."[50] Medicine would eventually conquer aging and death:

> Everything we know is almost nothing compared with what remains to be discovered, . . . we might rid ourselves of an infinity of maladies of body as well as mind, and perhaps also of the enfeeblement of old age, if we had sufficient understanding of the causes . . . and the remedies which nature has provided.[51]

Again, in *The Description of the Human Body*, Descartes speaks of his expectations about healing and retarding aging: "I believe it may be possible to find many very sound precepts for the cure of diseases and for their prevention and also even for the retardation of aging."[52] With this, Descartes declared his staunch intention "not to commit myself to any promise to the public which I am not sure of fulfilling."[53] He promised to discard traditional ideas and to develop a new image of man who would live a long and healthy life with the aid of a wholly new physiology that he would initiate. Concerned all his life about his own health, he spoke of the conservation of health as "the principal goal of his studies."[54] He claimed that everyone should be concerned to know the facts of physiology well enough that by age thirty, one could be his own doctor.

Even though he was little more than forty, Descartes expressed his concern about the swift passage of time. He often spoke about "the shortness of my life" and his awareness of how little time he had to accomplish the goals of his studies.[55] "I feel the greater obligation to make good use of the time remaining to me."[56] A letter written at the age of forty-two indicates Descartes' own hope for a long life. The letter is to Constantyn Huyghens, father of the scientist Christian Huyghens:

> I never took so much care to conserve myself as I do now and though I had thought formerly that death could not rob me of more than thirty or forty years, henceforth it cannot surprise me without depriving me of the hope of more than a century: since it seems to me evident, that, if we guard ourselves from certain errors . . . we will be able without other inventions to achieve an old age much longer and happier than now: but, because I need much time and experience to examine all that pertains to this subject, I am working now on an abridgment of medicine . . . which I hope will serve to obtain for me some delay of nature and so be able afterwards to better pursue my aim.[57]

Gruman, in commenting on this passage with its ambiguous wording, notes that either Descartes meant that he hoped to live to more than one hundred years or that he anticipated one hundred years in addition to the age he was when he wrote the letter. Gruman quotes a secondary source as saying that Descartes, though he did not himself promise to "render a man immortal," was "very sure it was possible to lengthen out his life to the period of the Patriarchs" (the antediluvians of the early biblical days.) The same source also noted that Descartes' hopes for lengthening human years were well known in Holland at that time.[58] So well known was his idea that upon his death from pneumonia at age fifty-four, Queen Christina of Sweden, whom he was visiting at the time, "could not help commenting on it sarcastically."[59] One of Descartes' most famous biographers notes that during his last days at Christina's court he spoke so hopefully of the long lives men might have that the Queen got the impression that Descartes deemed to live forever.[60]

Nevertheless, though his hopes soared, Descartes never detailed any method for prolonging life. In fact his work in biology is not, in itself, very innovative. What he did contribute to medicine's knowledge of aging was not so much original insight and certainly very few actual experimental findings, except for his small contributions in anatomy; it was his overall influence that was most beneficial, even crucial because his scientific optimism and his belief in the notion of progress inspired those who followed him to proceed toward the goal of controlling aging and conquering death. More concrete and lasting results would be the fruit of the hands of other more inductively and empirically oriented scientists and philosophers. Descartes' relentless experimentation with materialistic ideas and his application of the mechanistic method would be felt, at first, on the broad conceptual level but later, through the unceasing efforts of others, on the level of practical and concrete detail.[61] It has been noted that in the work of Descartes there is a highly concentrated deductive system of great economy and austerity: "By its mechanization it anticipated the structure that physical science was to assume in the future."[62]

The model of physiological mechanics was a splendid one for exactitude and order and would prove itself so successful that it would engage physiologists and would remain the dominant model in medicine even until the present. The first stirrings of the idea of progress can be seen in Descartes' conviction that nature can be mastered. The idea of prolonging life went hand in hand with the idea of progress.

FRANCIS BACON: LOOK, THERE IS TOMORROW!

One of the outstanding contributors to the prolongevitist movement was Sir Francis Bacon (1561-1626). If Descartes were to supply the dream of the future, Bacon would supply the experimental method to make the dream come true. Although Bacon died when Descartes was only thirty, he is considered here after Descartes because of the profound influence Bacon's method would have on modern science.

Whereas Descartes relied on the deductive and philosophical mode of reasoning, Bacon championed the inductive method and sought to reduce it to a set of steps and rules for use in scientific experimentation. Loren Eiseley described Bacon's work in his book, *The Man Who Saw Through Time* as a time-conscious "harbinger of the modern age."[63] The budding utilitarianism of his day advocated a practical application of knowledge to the problems of men. As Bacon put it himself, the call for the practical urged "the enlarging of the bounds of human empire, to the effecting of all things possible."[64] In his book, *The Masculine Birth of Time* (1603), Bacon said that science would be born from the light of nature, not the darkness of antiquity. Among the Hebrews, the Blessed Fathers were the authorities; these were the antediluvians. But for Bacon, authority came only in the new age of science when, after centuries of effort, scientists would finally progress exponentially in their knowledge: "'tis we [who] are the Fathers, and of more Authority than former Ages; because we have the advantage of more Time than they had, and Truth [we say] is the Daughter of Time."[65] The Scientific Revolution was the era in which man, theoretically and practically as well, began to turn away from the past with its cyclical interpretation of time. The prospects of the future that promised linear advancements would prove a lure that was irresistible. The result would be the Enlightenment of the eighteenth century and the idea of progress.

Oddly enough, as with Descartes' physiology of aging, Francis Bacon's theory and his regimen for the elderly proclaimed virtually nothing new. Rather, they were derived mainly from past literature and based on Aristotle's and Galen's humoral theories. Bacon claimed that aging leads to drying of body fluids and the cooling of the blood. Comparing youth and age in a way similar to Aristotle, only with physical degeneration in greater prominence, Bacon described an old person as he grew gray or bald and walked with a cane as "a monster with three legs."[66] Yet in all his writings on physical science, especially in his book *The History of Life and Death*, Bacon had as his central concern the prolonging of human life. As with Descartes and many other scientific prolongevitists of the seventeenth and eighteenth centuries, it was not so much concern for the pains of the aged that urged him on; it was more a concern for the transitoriness of time and a positive feeling for man's growing ability to control nature. But Bacon, like Descartes, was split between his religious convictions and his scientific appetite for progress. Nevertheless, he said,

> Life being a heap of sins and sorrows lightly esteemed by Christians aspiring to Heaven, should not be despised because it affords longer opportunity for doing good works. But the happiness of long life is, naturally to be desired although the means to attain it are hard to find.[67]

Bacon, too, had a foot in both the world of the past and the world of the future scientific age. Though he fondly listed the accomplishments of the ancients, he firmly believed they would be superseded by the medical experiments of his day. Bacon saw physicians as "coadjutors and instruments" whose efforts at prolonging human life would make manifest God's providence. Herein can be seen the fruits of what was a gradual shift, starting in the second half of the Middle Ages, from a passive acceptance of the will of God regarding aging and dying to an active intervention to prevent aging and prolong life and generally improve the lot of men by use of the physical sciences:

> For we have hope, and wish that it may be conducive to a common good; and that the nobler sort of physicians will advance their thoughts and not employ their time wholly in the sordidness of cures: neither be honored by necessity only; but that they will become coadjutors and instruments of the Divine omnipotence and clemency, in prolonging and renewing the life of man; especially seeing we prescribe it to be done by safe and convenient and civil ways, though hitherto untried.[68]

The methods he advocated for rejuvenation and life prolongation included the use of prophylactics, that is, medicine in the form of herbs, to strengthen the vital organs and drugs such as opium and nitrate. Along with many of his predecessors, Bacon suggested exercise, proper diet, massage and baths. His more innovative ideas included organ transplants and resuscitation of the dead.[69] Bacon also hinted at a genetic approach to medicine: advising investigation of "the length and shortness of life in men according to their races and families, as if it were a thing hereditary."[70]

In addition, it was Bacon's vision of science as a cooperative enterprise of shared scientific experimental efforts that led the Royal Society of Scientists, of which Newton was a member, to became the model of all scientific societies.[71] Bacon, like Descartes, had very little by way of practical innovative measures for prolonging life in the *History of Life and Death* or in his other writings. Mainly, Bacon's contribution was to lend to the prolongevitist movement his fame and prestige, which reached monumental heights. It has been said that: "The interest and significance of Francis Bacon . . . played a powerful role in getting English society to swallow, figuratively--the pill of science. . . . Society finally gulped down its medicine and turned to look in the mirror."[72]

What the seventeenth-century scientist saw in the mirror of time was the image of the future. Against the sufferings of mankind in the past, and even those still present among the common people and especially the poor, the aged and dying, the members of the scientific community would see relief and then release. Instead of relying entirely on the wisdom of the ages or on the providence of God, the leaders of this new scientific age would enthusiastically seize the reigns of progress and hitch up their chariot to the victorious methods of experimental science. Of all those who were split between the confinements of the past and the new frontiers of scientific exploration, "Francis Bacon alone walked to the doorway of the future, flung it wide and said to his trembling and laggard audience, 'Look, there is tomorrow. Take it with charity lest it destroy you.'"[73]

LIFE EXTENSION IN THE AGE OF ENLIGHTENMENT

Though nothing can bring back the hour
Of splendor in the grass, of glory in the flower.
William Wordsworth

The eighteenth century presented a dynamic and complex landscape in the history of Western culture. In order to clarify the status of the images of aging and dying that prevailed in that century and had a profound effect on centuries to follow, it is necessary to consider two main tendencies: one toward unbridled hope, the other toward dark despair. This is the period in which both the idea of progress and the dream of prolonging life reached their summit. It was the time when the science of geriatrics was born. It was also the age when religious fervor and belief in afterlife declined, a new death consciousness cast its shadow over the minds of many, a bold brand of philosophical skepticism was proclaimed and aging and dying were in turn idealized and dreaded.

THE ENLIGHTENMENT: MAN OVER MATTER

The Enlightenment is a cultural era closely linked with formal philosophical thought. A general movement known as an intellectual revolution spread through Western Europe. Its center was in France where it was associated with the Philosophes, a revolutionary group of thinkers and propagandist writers such as François-Marie Voltaire, the Marquis de Condorcet and Baron de Montesquieu. Whereas seventeenth-century rationalism was confined to an elite group of advanced thinkers, intellectual leaders of the eighteenth-century Enlightenment popularized their ideas among a relatively large, educated reading public. This was the century that optimistically championed a radical scientific prolongevitism. The scientist and American statesman Benjamin Franklin (1706-1790), summed up the positive spirit of this time in a letter written in 1780 to the renowned English chemist, Joseph Priestly. Franklin, who was later hailed by Condorcet as "the modern Prometheus" because of his creative inventions and forward-looking vision,[1] said:

The rapid progress of *true* science now . . . occasions my regretting sometimes that I was born too soon. It is impossible to imagine the height to which it may be carried in a thousand years, the power of man over matter. . . . all diseases may by sure means be prevented or cured, not excepting even that of *old age*, and our lives lengthened at pleasure even beyond antediluvian standards.[2]

Bernard Fontenelle (1657-1757), in his brilliantly successful popularization of the Copernican theory, *Conversations on the Plurality of Worlds* (1686), typified the fascination of the people of the Enlightenment with a mechanistic model of nature. He used the metaphor of nature performing on a gigantic stage. In the audience of spectators is one "mechanic" who yearns to jump up on the stage, dash behind the scenes and investigate the mechanisms that make up the stage scenery. Again, Fontenelle spoke with the wonder of a child about the clockwork universe: "I esteem the universe all the more since I have known that it is like a watch. It is surprising that nature, admirable as it is, is based on such simple things."[3]

For Descartes and most thinkers of the seventeenth century, God was still part of their model of the world. But in the Enlightenment the notion of an "absentee God" appeared as Christian Huyghens, Gottfried von Leibnitz, and the Deists pictured God metaphysically as the cause or creator of the world who instituted immutable laws involving a pre-established order that precluded alteration. He was the God who did all this and then stood back, leaving man to maintain it. This was the noninterfering God. Soon it would make sense to question the very need for a God at all: "While God was being deprived of his duties by the further advancement of mechanical science, and men were beginning to wonder whether the self-perpetuating machine . . . stood really in need of any supernatural beginning."[4] The metaphor of the world as an ongoing miracle, the work of an all-provident God, had shifted to the identification of the deity with the sheer fact of rational order and harmony in the world.

The bulk of thinking men, ever and inevitably anthropomorphic in their theology, could hardly sense religious validity in such theistic substitutes. For them, so far as they were considerably penetrated with science or philosophy, God had been quite eliminated from the scene and the only thing left to achieve was a single and final step to the mechanization of existence . . . an ultimate mechanomorphic hypothesis of the whole universe.[5]

Among eighteenth-century scientific thinkers, the power of man, as controller of nature, replaced the power of God.

This power of man over matter is particularly apparent in the progress made in the physical sciences. Physicians, such as Alfonso Borelli (1608-1679), had begun to apply mechanics to the anatomy of living organisms. Friederich Hoffmann (1660-1742), who considered Descartes an ideal, and Hermann Boerhaave (1668-1738), the most influential physician of the entire eighteenth century and the founder of modern clinical teaching of medical students developed and popularized the model of mechanics. They initiated a new physiological vocabulary, which was derived from mechanics and hydrodynamics and applied it to the teaching and practice of medicine. In 1747 Julien de LaMettrie (1709-

1751), a student of Boerhaave, shocked the intellectual world with his agnostic book, *L'Homme Machine, The Man Machine*. The book would achieve notoriety "second to none in Europe."[6]

In his book, LaMettrie claimed that man, like a beast, *is* a machine. Though he acknowleged a debt to Descartes for the metaphor of the body-machine, he deleted Cartesian metaphysics from his thought: "Let us conclude boldly then that man is a machine and that there is only one substance, differently modified in the whole world. What will all the weak reeds of divinity, metaphysic and the nonsense of the schools avail against this firm and solid oak?"[7] LaMettrie denied the existence of any soul whose essence was entirely distinct from extended matter. Soul for LaMettrie was conditioned by the organization of the body. He held that soul was only the functioning of the body:

> For in the final analysis, no matter what he says about the distinction of the two substances, it is obvious that [it] is nothing but a turn of phrase, a stylistic artifice, used to make theologians swallow a poison hidden behind an analogy that frightens the entire world, and which only they do not see. For it is just this, this clever analogy, that forces all scholars and true judges to admit that these proud and vain human beings, distinguishable more for their pride than for their name . . . are after all nothing more than Animals and Machines crawling perpendicularly.[8]

LaMettrie believed men differed from animals only in that their brain structure, bodily organization and needs are more complex. Thus he lent mechanism a new and extended form by denying the existence of an independent soul: "LaMettrie gave his formula a bolder statement than it had yet achieved, in his identification of man and beasts. Nothing before had been so pungently and paradoxically phrased as the *'Man-Machine'*."[9] Consciousness, sensibility and intelligence were explained exclusively in terms of the mechanics of the human body. Burtt marks the change in status of the human being in the mechanistic worldview:

> Man is but the puny local spectator, nay irrelevant product of an infinite self-moving machine, which existed eternally before him and will be eternally after him, . . . an engine which consists of raw masses wandering to no purpose in an undiscoverable time and space and in general wholly devoid of any qualities that might spell satisfaction for all the major interests of human nature, save solely the central aim of the mathematical physicist.[10]

The rapid elimination of God and the change in the category of "soul" would have a profound impact on eighteenth century attitudes toward aging and particularly toward death. No longer intact was the old defense system for meeting death calmly with the attitude of faith and the knowledge that heaven was at hand. Subsequently, there appeared a new realization of the fragility of life, and this brought with it, Aries believes, "an anxious sense of nothingness, which finds no solace in hope of the beyond although this hope continues to be expressed. Eventually it culminates in a kind of indifference to death."[11] LaMettrie expressed such an attitude toward death when he noted, "These are my plans for life and death; throughout life and until the last breath [I will] be a sensual Epicurean; but a firm Stoic, at the approach of death."[12]

Another philosopher, Baron Paul-Henri d'Holbach (1723-1789), defended
atheistic materialism in his *System of Nature* which denied the existence
of God and soul.[13] This book became a classic text for the philosophical
expression of modern science.

In the war over rationalism and empiricism, Cartesian dualism, which
"had been dragged along like a tribal deity in the course of the
campaign," had at last been torn asunder.[14] D'Holbach explained matter
and motion as totally determined. He claimed that the "soul" is simply
an illusion and that the only acceptable method of scientific endeavor is
the investigation of matter from an empirical and rational point of view.
Regarding the fear of death, d'Holbach echoed Aristotle's rational
approach. He insisted that one ought to face life and the inevitability
of death bravely, becoming familiar with the idea of death as unavoidable
and thus conquering the only true enemy, fear. He also noted wryly that
the recognition of the fact that there is no afterlife was ultimately
liberating because it broke the power that priests had over people.[15]
Aries comments, "Once deprived of the soul, the body was nothing but a
handful of dust, which was returned to nature."[16]

Seeing Death in the Mirror

As the eighteenth century came to focus on the discrepancy between
the order of reason and the as yet uncontrolled acts of nature which
bring suffering and death, the need to master nature became more
prominent. On one hand, death was recognized as present at the heart of
everything physical: machines wear out! On the other hand, death mainly
remained hidden, lurking under the surface of things. Aries illustrates
this point poignantly by pointing out a painting by the artist Furtenagel
in the Kunsthistorisches Museum in Vienna, that shows a husband and wife
as they view themselves in a looking glass. "But in the back of the
mirror, as if at the bottom of a pool, one can see a death's head."[17]

Paradoxically, faith in progress stood hand in hand with a new
realization of the temporal limits of human existence. Traditional
Christian preference for other worldly aspirations was countered by a new
dream which envisioned "a veritable heaven on earth."[18] Heroic efforts
in behalf of longevity initiated daring counter attacks on death itself.
Methods of resuscitation were earnestly sought. Benjamin Franklin, John
Hunter (1728-1793) and others experimented with methods of suspended
animation by freezing. Death must be defeated and the dead resurrected by
scientific means.[19] Franklin wrote a letter in 1773 to Barben Dubourg
discussing the "observations on the causes of death and the experiments
[he] proposed for recalling to life those who appear to be killed by
lightning."[20] Apparently in a playful mood, he noted that he heard it
remarked that flies drowned in wine could be revived by the rays of the
sun. Again, half seriously, he conjectured in the same spirit of
impatience for progress:

> I wish it were possible . . . to invent a method of embalming
> drowned persons, in such a manner as they may be recalled to life at
> any period however distant, for having a very ardent desire to see
> and observe the state of America a hundred years hence, I would
> prefer to any ordinary death being immersed in a cask of Madeira

wine, with a few friends, till that time, to be then recalled to
life by the solar warmth of my dear country! But since in all
probability we live in an age too early, and too near the infancy of
science, to hope to see such an art brought in our time to
perfection, I must for the present content myself with the treat,
which you are so kind as to promise me, of the resurrection of a
fowl or a turkey cock.[21]

The Philosophes, in their efforts to apply the knowledge of science
to push forward the frontier of life consistently attempted to defuse
the vision of death as a mysterious and awe-inspiring human experience.
But, given all their convictions about the potential of scientific
control over nature, at the same time there appeared "the first
manifestation of the great modern fear of death."[22] Until then anxiety
over death was speakable in words and rituals, but as the last half of
the eighteenth century approached, "People started fearing death in
earnest, they stopped talking about it."[23] This silence started
ironically with clergymen and doctors. The great French *Encyclopédie*
said:

> Men are afraid of death the way children are afraid of the dark,
> only because their imaginations have been filled with phantoms as
> empty as they are terrible. The elaborate ritual of last
> farewells, the weeping, the mourning, the funeral ceremony, the
> last convulsions of the machine that is breaking down: these are
> the things that tend to frighten us.[24]

There was a dark and cynical side to the eighteenth century that
qualified the optimism in the idea of limitless progress. The Marquis
de Sade (1740-1814), from whom the term "sadism" derived, was a child of
the Enlightenment in whose character two attitudes merged: the contempt
for the body and the radical rejection of immortality.[25] He gave
detailed instructions in his will that his body was to be buried
"without any ceremony" or "any sort of display" and that acorns should
be planted on the fresh ground, so that in time to come the site would
be once again as thickly wooded as before; thus he said "the traces of
my grave will disappear from the surface of the earth, just as I am
pleased to think that my memory will be erased from the minds of men."[26]

Self: The Straw Man

The French Philosophes forthrightly denounced Christian philosophy
and declared war against the Old Regime of French Royalty in the
political arena. Promising to hang the last king with the entrails of
the last priest, they publicly renounced the authority of the Church and
the Bible, placing their faith, instead in human progress.[27]
Nevertheless, most of the Philosophes, who went as far as atheism,
believed that this materialist philosophy was too sudden and strong a
pill for many. They agreed that the need for good order dictated that
Christian "superstitions" be allowed to remain, for the present time at
least, among the masses of common people who, in fact, were hardly
touched by the Enlightenment. D'Holbach, for example, ordered that
atheistic doctrines never be discussed in his salon when the servants
were present.[28]

But thinkers of the day proceeded with the application of the mechanical and materialist model to the social sciences as well as physiology:

> In the hands of the "physiologists" of the French *Encyclopedie* like LaMettrie, d'Holbach, Condorcet and Cabanis, man became nothing but a machine; consciousness became a secretion of the brain just as bile was a secretion of the liver; and the physical and physiological laws as they conceived them were taken as the norm of the laws not only of mind, but also of history and the historical process of society.[29]

Psychologists, too, joined the relentless quest for measurable certainty. David Hartley (1705-1757), founder of the associationist school of psychology, was the author of *Observation of Man* (1749), the first treatise that incorporated into psychology the main assumptions of the philosophy of mechanism using Newton's method and vocabulary. He was also the first Englishman to employ the title "psychology" to the subject matter that inaugurated a science of behavior, which before was seen primarily as an extension of physics.[30] The philosopher David Hume (1711-1776), in his *Treatise on Human Nature*, "hoped to duplicate, in the realm of mind, what Newton had accomplished in the realm of nature."[31] Hume's skepticism, turning its back on Descartes' central concept of intuition as a basis of certitude, claimed that all ideas are merely copies of sense perception or "impressions." Therefore, nothing other than what man experiences can be conceived. Against Descartes, he argued for the premise that a fact can never be proven by reason alone; it must be discovered in experience or inferred from an experience. Hence metaphysical systems telling of the existence of God or the origin of the world or other matters transcending human experience were meaningless and to be abandoned. On this basis, Hume presented tightly drawn philosophical arguments against the possibility of proving the immortality of soul except by religious faith. Hume was not in the mood for faith:

> The metaphysical arguments for the immortality of the soul are equally inconclusive . . . the moral arguments and those derived from the analogy of nature are equally strong and convincing. If my philosophy, therefore, makes no addition to the arguments for religion, I have at least the satisfaction to think it takes nothing from them, but that everything remains precisely as before.[32]

Regarding the self in philosophy, Hume held that when we are self-conscious we are aware of *fleeting* thoughts, feelings and perceptions. But our experience tells us that there is never a continuous impression of the self; therefore, the idea of the self is in fact a fiction, a figment of our imagination. He believed that by habit we jump to conclusions confusing the conglomerate of our sense perceptions, which happen to be juxtaposed in time and space, with the idea of a permanent substantial and enduring self:

> It must be some one impression that gives rise to every real idea. But the self or person is not any one impression, but that to which our several impressions and ideas are supposed to have a reference. . . . There is no impression constant and invariable . . . passions

and sensations succeed each other and never all exist at the same time. It cannot, therefore, be from any of these impressions . . . that the idea of self is derived, and consequently there is no such idea.[33]

Hume claimed we are fooled by the customary assumption that we are surrounded by stable objects. But he thought we ought not to be deceived by this habit of mind. The fact is that everything is always subtly changing. What we observe is really a sequence of impressions. We do the same thing when we think of ourselves. Nevertheless, there is, in reality, no stable self underlying the sequence of impressions we perceive. Hume claimed, "I never can catch *myself* at any time without a perception and never can observe anything but the perception."[34] The "self," if the term has any validity at all, is merely the impressions themselves. Hume's concept of the self was "nothing but a bundle or collection of different perceptions, which succeed each other with inconceivable rapidity and are in a perpetual flux and movement."[35] He used an analogy: "The mind is like a theater, where several perceptions successively make their appearance, pass, repass, glide away and mingle in an infinite variety of postures and situations."[36] Hume reduced the idea of an enduring self, as the basis of human experience, to a figment of the imagination.

The interesting part of the story, for the purpose of investigating theories of aging and dying, is that Hume had invented the notion of the enduring self in order to banish it just as one sets up a straw man just to destroy it. Lyons says in his book, *The Invention of the Self: The Hinge of Consciousness in the Eighteenth Century*, that Hume in creating the category of the enduring self, that underlies all experience, appealed to the modern imagination and left to posterity a philosophical concept that has remained since: "it is the invention rather than the disposal [of the self] which has impressed everyone who has thought about the matter since, even though they, too, have often cast off the self."[37]

It is also interesting to note that like many of his contemporaries, Hume suffered from an acute fear of what was to come after death. When only thirty-seven, Hume became very sick, and often talked with great perturbation of the devil, hell and damnation; however, at the time of his death from stomach cancer at age sixty-four, he had controlled his fear and accepted death's inevitable seal and demonstrated this by a cheerfulness and equanimity that astounded his friends.[38] Hume's progressive thinking and Scottish practicality can also be seen in his advocacy of active euthanasia as a mode of "courageous escape" from debilitating and painful disease or old age.[39]

Origin of Geriatrics

While mechanism and skepticism and the idea of progress occupied philosophers, in England and on the continent physicians were achieving a growing knowledge of both physiology and pathology. They were tracing the signs of disease through life and seeking explanation of aging and death through postmortem dissection or autopsy. The eighteenth-century *Encyclopédie* advocated that everyone ought to have a knowledge of anatomy:

Knowledge of the self presupposes knowledge of the body, and knowledge of the body presupposes knowledge of a network of causes and effects so prodigious that there is not one that does not lead directly to the notion of an all knowing and all powerful intelligence. . . . The knowledge of anatomy is important for man.[40]

In 1628 William Harvey (1578-1657), distinguished founder of modern physiology whose discovery of the model of the circulatory system of the body formed the cornerstone of modern physiology, performed an autopsy on Thomas Parr, who was reputed to be 152 years and 9 months old at the time of his death. Harvey, the father of anatomical studies, ascribed the death to a sudden change of climate and the rich diet eaten by Parr when he was brought up to London by the earl of Shropshire to be exhibited to the king as a prodigy of longevity. The influence of this classic autopsy was widespread, and other physicians studied the body through postmortem observations, comparing their results with Harvey's.

The English physician Sir John Floyer (1649-1734), by use of autopsies, studied many diseases connected with the elderly. He is considered the father of modern geriatrics for his work in compiling and evaluating established medical knowledge about aging in *Gerontological Medicine or Galenic Art of Preserving Old Men's Healths.*[41] Writing on standard hygiene and moderation themes, Floyer borrowed many of his ideas from Francis Bacon but was also responsible for extending and clarifying Bacon's thought. He was one of the first to devise a "Physician's Pulse Watch," which brought together for the first time the technology of the clock with the science of geriatrics.[42] Floyer drew up extended therapeutic methods and regimens that were tailored to individual needs and constitutional types of elderly individuals.

Another philosopher-physician who stressed the tradition of hygiene and moderation through health maintenance, coupled with the prolongevitist theme, was Christoph Hufeland (1762-1836), the German author of *Makrobiotik*, which he translated as *The Art of Prolonging Life.* Hufeland claimed that the art of medicine had as its goal the preservation of health and the extension of life. People who lived the simple life would live longer, according to Hufeland: "Only among the classes of mankind who amidst bodily labor, and in the open air, lead a simple life agreeable to nature, such as farmers and gardeners, hunters, soldiers and sailors . . . attain to the age of one hundred forty and even one hundred fifty."[43] This gerontologist's method aimed at instilling strength and vigor into the bodies of the aged. With many others he believed that at birth the body possessed a certain amount of vital power that was used up according to one's life-style. Therefore, he prescribed a code of hygiene even more extensive than Cornaro's. In his writings, Hufeland cleared away much of the misunderstanding and quackery, current at that time regarding treatment of the aging. There was a wave of enthusiasm for his advice which was called the "Hufelandist Movement."

In Hufeland's writings there is a hint at the psychology of aging and dying typical of the eighteenth century. He talked about fighting fear of death by rationalization and psychological methods. His advice carried with it vestiges of hope for a better life beyond the grave.

Hufeland was convinced that the fear of death, the most unhappy of all fears, shortened one's life. In fact he said: "No one who feared death ever attained a great age."[44] Offering several points of advice to dismiss this fear, Hufeland, like d'Holbach, suggested that one must "look this unavoidable enemy in the face until it [death] has at length become to him a matter of indifference." Thus one can learn to dispose of this fear.[45] He argued, that since death is painful only to spectators, as those who have been resuscitated all agree, and since life is only a transition or preparation, a medium not an object in itself, one ought not to have exaggerated fear of dying.[46] Stressing psychological factors, Hufeland listed, among others, the proper treatment of the aging, the fostering of a "pleasant frame of mind" by regular association with children and young people, the involvement of the elderly in new and exciting projects, such as building houses or laying out gardens, but cautioned that tasks that threaten the aging person should not be undertaken.[47]

At the same time that prolongevitism flourished, a contrary idea arose. What Hufeland hinted at was a harkening back to the Renaissance model of "natural" death. It is the kind of death where, with everything provided for and in a comforting atmosphere, one merely slips away, dying peacefully and uneventfully in the company of family. Gruman associates this with the financially independent man of the upper middle class and calls the model an "idealization of bourgeois comforts and values that illustrates a mood of complacency among the Philosophes . . . [who describe the bourgeois man] supposedly freed by 'philosophy' from any worries about religious matters, and dying placidly and uneventfully in his home."[48]

Major medical breakthroughs that laid the foundation of the scientific approach to the medicine of old age took place as the result of the work of several prominent physicians in the middle and toward the end of the eighteenth century. Among these is Johann von Fisher (1685–1771), who was responsible for the first medical work on old age that made a major break from medieval tradition and approached the subject in a truly modern spirit.[49] Another is Giovanni Morgagni (1681-1771), who was the proponent of a method of diagnosing and explaining diseases of old age in terms of pathologic anatomy, a method still used. Benjamin Rush of Philadelphia (1743-1813), Benjamin Franklin's private physician, made the first American contribution to the medicine of old age with his *Account of the State of the Body and Mind in Old Age With Observation on Its Diseases and Their Remedies*, which was based on the author's own observations. Rush considered what he saw as both the physical and mental characteristics of old age. The work became the foundation for the further pursuit of knowledge about the aging process in the New World.[50]

Mind Over Matter: William Godwin

With few exceptions, the thinkers who founded the field of geriatrics were primarily scientists and physicians. But in 1793 William Godwin (1756-1836), an English political and moral philosopher, entered the arena as an outspoken advocate of victory over the death of the body by prolongation of life. The difference between Godwin and his predecessors lies in his method, which urged control by means of mind over matter. One of Godwin's major works, *Enquiry Concerning Political Justice and Its Influence on Morals and Happiness*, laid out his direction of thought.[51] In it he staunchly defends a form of Newtonian mechanism reminiscent of d'Holbach's *System of Nature* with its deterministic universe embodying an eternal succession of causes and effects. However, he rejected out of hand d'Holbach's materialism with its emphasis on physical causes and its reduction of mind to the physical organ of sensation. Mind, Godwin argued, is determined psychologically, not physically. Therefore, he also rejected Hartley's theory which he saw as "a system of material automatism."[52] Godwin rejected relativity, hedonism, and the French philosophers' concept of subjective truth.[53] Deeply influenced by Platonic thought, Godwin embraced a doctrine of external and immutable truths that was not dependent on the supreme will of a Creator-God.

Most interesting was Godwin's concept of the self. On one hand, it is not basically different from the sensationalist school of psychology, in which the person is seen as a passive receiver of impressions, a vehicle that is operated by causes.[54] But, on the other hand, Godwin claimed that the person has an immediate intuitive knowledge of the existence of his thoughts, ideas, perceptions, or sensations. This consciousness constituted the self. Even though Godwin considered Hume's rule of association to be part of the mind's way of operating, he claimed it must be supplemented by reflection.[55] Godwin recognized, but did not dwell on, the existence of unconscious impressions or associations claiming that consciousness consisted of "supplementary reflection," or second thought. One of the reasons why he minimized the unconscious was that he believed in mind over matter. Though Godwin admitted that we do not understand how mind and body interact, he cited many everyday experiences to prove that they do, for example:

> The different cases in which thought modifies the structure and members of the human body are obvious to all. First, they are modified by our voluntary thoughts or design. We desire to stretch out our hand and it is stretched out. We perform a thousand operations of the same species every day and our familiarity annihilates the wonder. . . . Secondly, mind modifies body involuntarily. . . . Hasn't a sudden piece of good news been frequently found to dissipate a corporal indisposition? Is it not still more usual for mental impressions to produce indisposition, and even what is called a broken heart?[56]

Godwin expressed faith in the perfectability of mankind, that human nature is capable of "perpetual improvement."[57] Not only can man perfect himself, but he *will* do so. This momentum toward the future would continue not only indefinitely but exponentially because once the taste for truth is developed in an individual, he will tend to follow it throughout life. Those who are not aware of their priorities and who do not plan rationally for the future sow the seeds of their own destruction. "Error contains in it the principle of its own mortality. Thus advocates of falsehood and mistake must continually diminish and the well informed adherents of truth incessantly multiply."[58]

Godwin's Socratic faith in the *omnipotence of truth* carried with it a belief that the fruits of good judgment result in good behavior. In short, he assumed that humans were capable of ongoing improvement toward objectivity of mind. This kind of faith in the improvement of man through ethical insight followed by ethical behavior would have been scorned by a philosopher like d'Holbach who had little or no faith in the perfectability of man if it depended on the growth of virtue based on increased knowledge. Education for proper behavior, in d'Holbach's mind (as it would be later for Watson, Skinner and the Behaviorist school), would not appeal first to reason, but would be more like "animal training."[59]

Godwin counted more on the individual's mental discipline, the person's power to control his own mind. For example, he claimed that a person's mental life can affect premature aging:

Why is it that a mature man loses . . . elasticity of limb, which characterizes the heedless gaity of youth? The origin of this appears to be, that he desists from youthful habits. He assumes an air of dignity, incompatible with the lightness of childish follies. He is visited and vexed with cares that rise out of our mistaken institutions and his heart is no longer satisfied and gay. His limbs become stiff, unwieldy and awkward. This is the forerunner of old age and death.[60]

Disease and even death, he believed, are the concomitants of dullmindedness, stagnation and a loss of good cheer, but there is little reason to believe that aging necessarily must bring on these problems. Godwin thought, "Through the voluntary power of some men over their animal frame, they prevent this. . . . There is also little plausibility in thinking that these powers are beyond the limits of the human mind. . . . [Remedies proposed for controlling the infirmities of the body] may contribute to prolong our vigor, if not to immortalize it and, which is of more consequence, to make us live while we live."[61] However, he does not claim that immortality of man is a plausible goal, "It would be idle to talk of the absolute immortality of man."[62] He clearly disassociated his ideas from those of Franklin, Bacon and Condorcet. These scientists, he claimed, operated within a model that gave priority exclusively to the experimental method, careful quantitative calculations, pathology and scientific technology, and emphasized professional objectivity. Godwin insisted there was another model of medical practice, infinitely neglected, which was of equal importance in that it related the conscious mind to the health of the person, using a personalized and preventive approach and making the individual responsible for his health and life-style. Godwin insisted that it is of extreme importance for all people to be aware of their own ability and responsibility to control their health.[63] This is an anticipation of what today is called "psychosomatic medicine," with the one difference: Godwin's notion of control of the body by the mind was exclusively conscious. Today both conscious and unconscious factors are considered.

But Godwin's insight was not destined to dominate health care. Gruman notes that this "mind over matter" approach has "not found many followers in the history of medicine for it has been undermined by the same factor which swept away Cornaro's model of personal responsibility for prolongevity." What Gruman refers to here is the "development of

impersonal, standardized therapy with drugs, sera and radiation . . .
combined with complex . . . methods of public health."[64] Finally
emerging were the effects of the "Faustian dream" of those who succeeded
Descartes: the dream of manipulating the clock and conquering both death
and the effects of aging through engineering the body mechanism. The
pill of Francis Bacon's "new science" finally was ingested by his
Promethean followers who stole the spark of life from the hands of the
gods and gleefully claimed the rights of ownership for themselves.

The Perfectibility of Man

Marquis Marie-Jean de Condorcet (1743-1794), Enlightenment
philosopher, mathematician and founder of the social sciences, stands
out as the culmination of faith in progress. He looked to the advances
of science as the most direct means of achieving the perfectibility of
man. Through him and Godwin the prolongevitist movement reached its
summit: "If man can, with almost complete assurance, predict phenomena,
when he knows their laws . . . and forcast the future on the basis of
his experience of the past, why, then, should it be regarded as a
fantastic undertaking to sketch . . . the future destiny of man on the
basis of his history?"[65] His *Sketch for a Historical Picture of the
Progress of the Human Mind* (1795) was a kind of last testament, the tone
of which bears witness to the fact that it was written under threat of
death.[66]

Condorcet expressed his belief in ongoing future progress that
would exponentially increase life expectency, built on environmental
improvements and advances of the medical sciences. Believing that life-
styles of both the very rich and the very poor were disadvantageous,
Condorcet advised moderation and improved health through amassing and
studying scientific data. Thus, mankind would be allowed a life span
that would increase indefinitely as scientific accomplishments extended
themselves into the future, with death approaching only when it was
welcome:

> Would it be absurd . . . to suppose that this perfection of the
> human species might be capable of indefinite progress; that the day
> will come when death will be due only to extraordinary accidents or
> to the decay of the vital forces, and that ultimately, the average
> span between birth and decay will have no assignable value?
> Certainly man will not become immortal, but will not the interval
> between the first breath that he draws and the time when in the
> natural course of events, without disease or accident, he expires,
> increase indefinitely?[67]

Condorcet was a visionary and idealist who condemned inequality of
all kinds: in wealth, in education, as well as between the sexes. He
was an outstanding forerunner of the movement for women's rights.[68] He
also focused on public health as part of the eighteenth-century social
and political reform movement, part of which advocated social
legislation in France for the amelioration of the lot of the poor
through old age pensions and allowances for widows and orphans.
Combining an ardent disposition and an avid optimism with coolheaded
objectivity and with a passionate hate of injustice, Condorcet was

referred to by D'Alembert, the French mathematician and encyclopedist, as "a volcano covered with white snow."[69]

Condorcet's aim was not only the quantitative prolongation of life, but a qualitative state of permanent health. This was proudly announced in his work, *Atlantis*. "Just as a watchmaker by his skill can keep a timepiece in perfect running order, so a physician can do the same for the human machine."[70] Gruman notes that Condorcet's concern for indefinite prolongevity distracted attention from questions about terminal care.[71] In the nineteenth and twentieth centuries a kind of scientific optimism emerged that proved both blessing and curse for the aged and for the terminal patient. This was ironical, given Condorcet's dedication to the belief that merely surviving is not enough. He held the ideal of an improved humanity, of furthering the welfare of all men, and through scientific, political and economic means, of solving problems that cause pain and misery to all human beings. Condorcet, bolstered by his idealism, himself had "Socratic fortitude" in the face of his own death. He remained buoyed up by his hope for the realization of his dreams through human strivings that are part of the "eternal chain of human destiny." The very last words Condorcet wrote in the *Sketch* bear marks of profound optimism for the future that apparently never left him. In describing the tenth and highest stage of progress that man could attain, he deemed those who strive for this progress virtuous and its enemies criminals:

> These are the questions with which we shall conclude this final
> stage. How consoling for the philosopher is this view of the human
> race, emancipated from its shackles, released from the empire of
> fate and from that of the enemies of its progress, advancing with a
> firm and sure step along the path of truth, virtue and happiness. .
> . . He dares to regard these strivings as part of the eternal chain
> of human destiny. . . . Such contemplation is for him an asylum . .
> . there he lives with his peers in an Elysium created by reason and
> graced by the purest pleasures known to the love of mankind.[72]

THE ROMANTICS: ROUSSEAU AND THE JUGGERNAUT OF PROGRESS

Jean Jacques Rousseau (1712-1778) belongs to the period of the Enlightenment, and yet his ideas go beyond those of the time. Although he had his roots in the general movement of thought in eighteenth-century France, it is the very optimism and faith in progress that accompanied the typical mechanistic interpretation of the world that was criticized by Rousseau in his *Discourse on the Origin of Inequality*, published in 1753. He was the son of an expert watchmaker, whose erratic behavior toward his son, as recounted in Rousseau's *Confessions*, marked Rousseau's disposition for the rest of his life. A gifted writer, musician and philosopher, Rousseau led a tortured life of introspection, self-doubt, and later, isolation from society and eventual insanity.

A highly spiritual man, Rousseau argued for three general principles: God is good, nature is good and man is good. These basic categories are shown in his writings which argued against inequality. But Rousseau distinguished between what he terms "natural inequality" and "social inequality." Natural inequalities such as unequal talents or natural endowments and the like, he believed, were good and should be accepted; while inequalities of social position, rank and inherited wealth, he believed, as Condorcet did, were evil and should be abolished. Unlike Condorcet, however, Rousseau located the source of these inequalities in man's desire for progress. He condemned especially the institution of private property: "The first person who, having fenced off a plot of ground, took it into his head to say *this is mine* and found people simple enough to believe him, was the true founder of civil society."[73] Before he wrote *Discourse on Inequality*, Rousseau had lived a comfortable life and was received into the homes of the wealthy, associating with influential friends such as the Encyclopedists and the d'Holbach circle. Later, disgusted with the pomp, deception and artificiality he felt was inherent in that life, he chose to "reform" and to engage in a simpler style of living. Renouncing any plans he may have had for gaining good fortune through self-promotion, Rousseau resolved to pass his remaining days in "poverty and independence," breaking the bonds of concern for "what the world might think." He deliriously proclaimed himself free from the shackles of conventional time with its clockwork consciousness: "I gave up my gold lace and white stockings. . . . I took off my sword and sold my watch, saying to myself with incredible delight 'Thank Heaven, I shall not want to know the time again!'"[74] After escaping from the constant rounds of social life, Rousseau meditated on the source of his own and his society's misery:

> I buried myself in the forest where I sought and found the picture of those primitive times, of which I boldly sketch the history. I demolished the pitiful lies of mankind; I dared to expose their nature in all its nakedness, to follow the progress of time and of the things which have disfigured this nature, and comparing the man, as man has made him with the natural man, I showed him, in his pretended perfection, the true source of his misery.[75]

Rousseau described the difference between "natural," or savage man and "civilized," or socialized man, attacking the idea of "enlightenment," progress of the sciences and arts, as inherently dangerous. Admitting that such men as Newton, Descartes and Bacon were "great scientists," Rousseau, nevertheless, insisted that they failed in that they did not give people sufficient direction on how to live well. Still more stinging was his criticism of the Philosophes, a "crowd" of lesser writers who "try" to disseminate philosophy but only serve to destroy faith and virtue.[76] Glorifying natural man as he came from the hands of nature, Rousseau claimed him to be the "pure self," wholly detached and totally at one with himself. He was the self for whom all else is wholly other. Rousseau claimed that primitive man lived entirely within himself, in total isolation, without language, thought, memory, or foresight. The pure self, Rousseau believed, existed naturally in the immediate present as pure consciousness and was undivided in that it was the object of its own love and unaware of any other. But Rousseau probed further: If man were born free, why does he find himself everywhere in chains? Is it because the faculty of self-perfectibility, though it distinguished man from beast, destroys the blissful and innocent state of natural man? Rousseau searched for a self not fettered by its own strivings, a self that was free to explore the horizons of its own subjectivity, individuality and feelings. In order to embody his vision he turned to the only categories he knew, Cartesian-Newtonian concepts. Thus he shut the gate that imprisoned the self in a lonely cell in the bastion of objectivity. Herein Rousseau set up the question that initiated a new philosophy of the self. It was the same question that Kant, who read Rousseau avidly, was addressing at that very time in Koenigsburg in eastern Prussia. The man-beast, with childlike unselfconsciousness, knew nothing of the gift of self-perfectibility with its relentless striving, and, therefore, thought that he could lose nothing when time caught up with him. When natural man was forced to face the inevitabilities of aging and death, he was not as disappointed as was the man who sought a kind of immortality in the perfection of himself and his society. Rousseau argued that civilized man, a corruption of natural man, was forced to split from his pure self and enter into competitive and vain activities. Civilized man was like a child who, playing unselfconsciously, suddenly saw that he was being observed. Thus surrendering his innocence, civilized man became subject to all kinds of self-created problems and pain especially in old age:

> Why is man alone subject to become imbecile? . . . while the beast, which has acquired nothing and which has, moreover, nothing to lose, always retains its instinct--man, losing again by old age or other accidents all that his *perfectibility* has made him acquire, falls back lower than the beast itself?[77]

In Rousseau's mind modern society caused the shift from *love of self*, which makes man what he truly is, to *anxious reflection* that induces man to compare himself with others. Rousseau thought that this limiting of man's vision created illusions which caused him to take pleasure in seeing the misfortune or inferiority of others. For Rousseau, social progress becomes an irreversible juggernaut that gains ground and feeds on its own momentum, crushing the pure self.[78] The very consciousness that sought to overcome man's alleged imperfections, he believed, is itself the cause of man's misery. The attribution of imperfection to the natural state is itself the origin of the present inequalities and human sufferings. But Rousseau himself was aware that there could be no sudden shift in models and ultimately no total return to nature. Thus he attempted to mount several solutions in the areas of government in his *Social Contract*, education in *Émile* and social life in *The New Héloise*. In all three he championed not discipline and moderation as ways of improving life, but self-expression and freedom, natural impulse and individual feeling. This was his proposal for blending the natural strands of life with civilized human experience.

During the last sixteen years of his life, Rousseau abandoned these speculative solutions to the problems of man and society and took up instead a solitary search for the lived experience of pure selfhood. His experience turned out to be a difficult one. At the opening of the twelfth chapter of *Confessions* he said of this period: "Here commences the work of darkness . . . in which I have been entombed, without ever having been able, in spite of my efforts, to penetrate its frightful obscurity."[79] He grew morose, fearing real or imagined persecution from the outside world. From 1772 to 1774 the author set about penning his dialogues, one of the "strangest, supposedly maddest and still little understood works" and it bears the "schizophrenic title *Rousseau, Judge*

of Jean-Jacques."[80]   Here we find a description of the experience of a
tortured consciousness that, looking into the mirror of time, attempted
to see only the pure self, the object of its own love. This search,
accompanied by a bitter longing for individuality, insofar as it had
entirely given up its bearings in the world, brought with it a souring
taste and futile sense of loneliness. The seeds of this agony of
aloneness can be found in the very first lines of *Confessions*:

> I desire to set before my fellows the likeness of a man in all
> truth of nature, and that man myself. Myself alone! I am not made
> like any of those I have seen; I venture to believe I am not made
> like any of those who are in existence. If I am not better I am
> different.   Whether   Nature   has acted rightly or wrongly in
> destroying the mould in which she cast me, can only be decided
> after I have been read.[81]

With Rousseau, the new romantic age was born.

Rousseau could have been dismissed in his day, and by later
generations, as simply a tortured soul or a madman. Nevertheless, his
influence has been widespread. His dynamic spirit had immense impact in
Germany through Kant, Herder and Schiller. In England his influence is
seen in the works of Godwin, Wordsworth and Keats. In France Rousseau's
work supported the revolutionary spirit of the day. The value of the
legacy of this man of letters to later generations was partly due to his
powerful vision of regenerated human nature; for, although he often
nostalgically pictured the innocence and simplicity of early times, he
also saw nature as a dynamic force. The version of man's perfectibility
that Rousseau condemned was the desire for progress that was not
progress in his sense at all, but a dead end of artificial pretense that
foments a split between man and his natural self. The vision of man as
he *might be*, Rousseau believed, could transform human existence as it
is.   Nature possessed the potential for legitimate progress, if
civilization could keep the flame of natural man alive within itself.

Another reason for Rousseau's singular influence is seen in the
unrestrained self-revelation exemplified in the *Confessions*, considered
one of the most masterful autobiographies in literature. It was his
subjectivity, his individualism and his indulgence in lyric expression
in relating his own personal experiences and his glorification of nature
that made this tragic visionary the Father of Romanticism. Intelligent
young people of the late Enlightenment period were enchanted by Rousseau
as well as with the lure of sentiment accompanied by honest yearnings
for a nobler humanity. Wordsworth's lines embody the overall spirit of
Rousseau's vision:

> One impulse from a vernal wood
> May teach you more of man,
> Of moral evil and of good,
> Than all the sages can.[82]

The Romantics: Beautiful Death

In the last part of the eighteenth and the first part of the nineteenth century the Romantic Movement arose in opposition to traditional intellectual conceptions and prevailing artistic and literary standards. Artists experimented with changes in images. Friedrich Schlegel (1772-1829) first employed the term "romantic" versus "classic" to characterize this opposition. These terms have been overdrawn and unduly simplified, nevertheless, the broad distinctions hold, at least for a general understanding of the cultural elements involved. Classicism was generally marked by simplicity, directness, nobility and perfection in achievement. The Romantic threw himself into his work, which showed his own personality, feelings, longings and the ideals of his spirit. His tendency toward the infinite, he believed, could never be fully represented by the finite. Romanticism endeavored to give expression to the strange and mysterious side of life and in the bold spirit that undertook boundless aspirations.

The generation of the Romantics that came of age at the end of the eighteenth century developed a profound sense of contempt for the ideals of the Enlightenment. Wordsworth's lines in "The Tables Turned" typified this:

Enough of science and of art;
Close up these barren leaves;
Come forth and bring with you a heart
That watches and receives.[83]

Romantics gave the concepts of reason, nature and progress unique interpretations. What the Philosophes saw as reason was conceived by the German Romantic tradition as understanding. Reason for the German Romantics gave priority to intuition. Nature, which was orderly and measurable and lawful for the Mechanists, was for the Romanticist primitive and wild. Progress, instead of being physical and predictable, in Romanticism took the form of a process of organic growth.

Under the pseudonym of "Novalis," Friedrich von Hardenberg (1772-1801) became a lyric poet, philosopher and scientist who wrote a series of brilliant, if mystifying works. Novalis, considered by many the greatest and most profound of the Romantics and their most characteristic spokesman, influenced both English and French Romanticism. In his opposition to the ideas of both the Enlightenment and early Classicism he presented his vision of the Romantic life by furnishing the age with a description of the poet, who by his art leads man who is "homeless" to the safe harbor found in the depths of his own soul. Novalis thought that man's aimlessness originated in the narrow concept of his own nature as time-bound. As a finite being he seeks infinity and the poet can help him attain this vision by the discovery of his true self, which unveils the meaning of life that has been entombed in mechanistic explanations. Thus man's imagination is released and the opposition between man and nature overcome. Bringing to birth a form of magic idealism, Novalis described man's power to control reality, to invest objects with new and hitherto unknown value. In his romanticizing principle he described the human power to improve things from a lower to a higher quality by thought and imagination alone. In order to accomplish this there was a need, Novalis pointed out, to employ the as yet untapped potential of the mind. All knowledge, he believed, is mystical in its nature and the ability to make the world over comes from man's power to turn inward, as Rousseau, and release this coiled spring of inner strength. As Novalis put it:

> Life is a twilight softly stealing;
> The world speaks all of love and glee;
> Grows for each wound a herb of healing,
> And every heart beats full and free. [84]

In typical fashion of the Romantic, Novalis, who died at the age of twenty-nine, glorified death. He believed that the full spirit of the romanticizing principle of life was death. Through death, life is not destroyed but strengthened[85] because through death man puts behind him the finite and opens himself to the infinite. Death, therefore, is not a culmination or end of living, it is the secret goal or perfection of life. Since life begins the dying process, death is both the end or goal and the beginning of life.[86] Merging will and emotion in his poetry, he proclaimed that poetic genius may be able to attain the strength to bring about death by the direct action of will alone. This notion was very attractive and deeply affected later writers such as Dostoevsky (1821-1881) and Albert Camus (1913-1960). Novalis' meditations on death began a long history of such reflections which became the hallmark of Heideggers' thought as well as existentialist thought.

Aging Idealized: Wordsworth and Keats

Romantic probing into the death of the individual personality was accompanied by meditation on old age, especially in poetry. It is interesting to note that many of the famous Romantic poets lived close to death themselves and died young. Lord Byron (1788-1824) lived to thirty-five, John Keats (1795-1821) to twenty-six and Percy Bysshe Shelley (1792-1822) to thirty. Changes in nature and the wonders of the changing universe were the central preoccupations of the Romantic poets. Unlike the Mechanistic scientist who was confident that he held the secret of life and death in his hand, the Romantic poet spoke of nature as a mysterious "Living Whole" of incalculable splendor, an incomprehensible gift and an immeasurable wonder.

Romantics were anxious to scrutinize all stages of life from youth to old age. Prior to this period, old people were often drawn in literature either in the image of comic figures or as representatives of doting old age who should not be taken seriously. However, with the Romantics, the old man was taken as a central and symbolic character as in Samuel Taylor Coleridge's (1771-1834) "The Ancient Mariner," Shelley's "Rousseau" and Wordsworth's (1770-1850) "Old Cumberland Beggar." Wordsworth raised some probing questions about social issues as he described the "aged beggar" he met on a walk in the mountains of northern England.: Should the elderly, poor and infirm be institutionalized, or should local communities, allowing them to move about freely, take responsibility for their sustenance? Wordsworth believed the "aged beggar" served a purpose within the community which would benefit spiritually from his presence.

> Though narrow be that old Man's cares, and near,
> The poor old Man is greater than he seems:
> For he hath waking empire, wide as dreams;
> An ample sovereignty of eye and ear.
> Rich are his walks with supernatural cheer;
> The region of his inner spirit teems
> With vital sounds and monitory gleams
> Of high astonishment and pleasing fear.[87]

Wordsworth regularly idealized old age:

> What though the radiance which was once so bright
> Be now forever taken from my sight,
> Though nothing can bring back the hour
> Of splendor in the grass, of glory in the flower;
> We will grieve not, rather find
> Strength in what remains behind;
> In the primal sympathy
> Which having been must ever be;
> In the soothing thoughts that spring
> Out of human suffering:
> In the faith that looks through death,
> In years that bring the philosophic mind.[88]

Reminiscent of Plato, these lines spoke of an aged person as becoming a philosopher through the experience of maturation. Wordsworth painted a picture of old men who were quiet and remote, representing senescence as honored passivity.

The idealization of the decrepitude and poverty of old age as shown in Wordsworth's need to see the elder man as always tranquil was criticized by Simone de Beauvoir as spiritual posturing. "This mystical twaddle is indecent," she wrote, "when we look at the real condition of the immense majority of old people; hunger, cold and disease certainly bring with them no kind of moral gain."[89]

Rather than signaling peaceful acceptance of old age, Thomas McFarland believes Wordsworth's old man who "wanders about alone and silently" indicated Wordsworth's own fear of solitude. He notes:

> Only as a figure representing what for Wordsworth was the possibility of existence *in extremis* is the old Leech-Gatherer so important. It is his role as an embodiment of Wordsworth's own anxieties that makes him a central rather than a peripheral figure. For Wordsworth, not death but solitude was the ultimate dread.[90]

McFarland believes that rather than finding old people tranquil, Wordsworth, to stem his own fear, needed to "tranquilize" old people, lest they force him to feel failed. Nature may have been glad in most of Wordsworth's writing, but he, as the observer of nature was dogged more and more by a dim sadness at the thought of the isolation incumbent on advancing years. Wordsworth lamented:

> We Poets in our youth begin in gladness;
> But thereof come in the end despondency and madness.[91]

Romantic poets regularly glorified nature and death that brought the person back to nature. Shelley often remarked, "How wonderful is death."[92] Melancholy became a sign, for the Romantic, of a person's great sensitivity. Early death became almost a norm, death either by illness or by suicide. Lives were radically fragmented, some by drugs, others by madness.[93] But the Romantic combination of emotion and will, as well as the lucid depiction of personal agonies of soul, typified the creative Romantic poet-philosopher, who was usually shown as a misunderstood and agonized genius.

Keats, who suffered the premature deaths of many loved ones and died of tuberculosis at twenty-six, answered death and old age in a different voice. Keats shouted back at death with a booming energy of spirit. He emphasized the need for exerting immediate energy in the face of death. He did not believe in the theories of man's perfectibility. Things change too quickly. "Verse, Fame and Beauty are intense, indeed, But Death intenser-Death is Life's high meed."[94] In "Ode on a Grecian Urn" Keats suggested that life itself is better than art if life is lived with energy. The central theme in all his work was that change is inevitable, but that life can still be happy. Keats has no time to dabble with the illusion of eternal youth; the urn itself bore witness to this. Keats, who was aware that he would die young, wrote his immortal lines in the "Ode to a Nightingale":

> Now more than ever seems it rich to die,
> To cease upon the midnight with no pain
> While thou art pouring forth thy soul abroad
> In such an ecstacy![95]

Unlike Wordsworth, he does not see meeting death and aging either with tranquillity or as its tranquilizer. For him old age is no wasteland but a time for discovering fresh insights. In his description of a climb up Ben Nevis, Scotland's tallest mountain, Keats called the mountain "Old Ben" and used it in part to symbolize the changes that occur in old age. He described the mountain veiled from a wide view by large clouds. We cannot see all at once and in all directions because, "Even so vague is man's sight of himself!" Nevertheless there are breaks in the mist revealing glimpses of reality: "Mankind can tell of heaven." [96] About this passage David Luke comments:

> We can see clearly here how for Keats metamorphosis is as much a matter of emergence and discovery as of dissolution. . . . Insofar as his account of the geological and atmospheric processes of "Old Ben" is partly a symbolic comment on the circumstances of old age, it suggests that, if old age dramatizes the disappearance of things, it can still reveal an intermittently developing energy as well . . . a fresh prospect. In short Keats' "Old Ben" is as much a symbol of life as of death.[97]

Keats' energy and boldness in the face of the vicissitudes of living can be traced not only in his contention that old age is a time to live vigorously, but also in his conviction that death is not to be dreaded. He insisted that we are mistaken if we think that the greatest pain is to die, because death is merely an awakening from the dream of life which entails only transient pleasures. In his poem "On Death," Keats said:

> Can death be sleep, when life is but a dream
>   And scenes of bliss pass as a phantom by?
> The transient pleasures as a vision seem,
>   And yet we think the greatest pain's to die.
> How strange it is that man on earth should roam,
>   And lead a life of woe, but not forsake
> His rugged path; nor dare he view alone
>   His future doom which is but to awake.[98]

There was a paradoxical strain on eighteenth-century faith in man over matter. Some were full of self-confidence, in spite of their absentee God, but their faith encountered the bold objections of Romantics and anti-Enlightenment zealots. High expectations were dogged by brooding anxiety. Skepticism, first about Divine power and then about human power to control threats to human life, was coupled with a bright touch of hope as geriatrics and knowledge of physiology and pathology gained momentum. As the paradox mounted, belief in the perfectibility of man, countered by a genuine distrust of its actual outcome, sought its outlet in an exclamation of yearning for some strange beneficent source of relief in idealized old age and death.

BEHIND THE LOOKING GLASS⁷

Man himself is the mirror in which and by which
reality is reflected.

Konrad Lorenz

The Greeks looked into the mirror of time and saw the order of nature;
the Judeo-Christians observed the magnificent creation of God. The
leaders of the Enlightenment saw in the mirror of time an earthly
paradise of endless predictable progress. But Rousseau envisioned the
breakdown of the dream of the Enlightenment because of its failure to
address the serious problems related to human values. In his unhappiness
with the conventions of the day, Rousseau's tortured consciousness is
clearly reflected in Johann Wolfgang von Goethe's (1749-1832) character,
Werther, in *The Sorrows of Young Werther*.

Goethe, who will be treated first in this chapter, is usually counted
as part of the Romantic movement, but his thought verged intellectually
toward that of the revolutionary founder of contemporary philosophy,
Immanuel Kant. Werther, born out of disillusionment with the
Enlightenment, dramatized many of the notions Kant was simultaneously
analyzing in his famous critiques; and Goethe's character, Faust,
directed his audience to one of the main insights of Kant's critical
philosophy. The last part of this chapter will deal exclusively with the
monumental thought of Kant and his philosophy of time.

FROM WASTELAND TO HEAVENLY HEIGHTS

The Sorrows of Young Werther was an autobiographical novel first
published in 1774 and reissued in revised edition in 1778, the year of
Rousseau's death. Its hero was a gifted and articulate young man, a
typical late Enlightenment enthusiast, who was optimistic but self-
indulgent and willful. As with the Romanticist, Goethe's Werther,
experiencing mounting frustration and disappointment with his own and
society's accomplishments, gradually became disenchanted with the
artificial conventions of his fellow men. He arrived at an ideal

conception of a "truly natural society." In a highly sentimental but impossible love affair he discovered that traditional moorings of faith and reason did not secure him from potential destruction. Losing his way in a wasteland that lacked values, Werther experimented with skepticism and fell into a deep depression and a profound sense of abandonment. In experiencing several seemingly meaningless catastrophies and deaths, Werther suddenly discovered that the world was full of senseless destruction and that he had no reason to think his life had any meaning other than blind suffering. Finally, as a victim of deep pessimism, he took his life in an attempt to cure his hapless existence. Goethe described himself in all the events of Werther's life except his suicide. The pointless waste of a young man's life was symbolic, in Goethe's mind, of the failure of the traditional vision of an orderly world and a subsequent sense of disorientation that was shared by the leaders of the late eighteenth and early nineteenth centuries:

> Goethe himself fled from a situation which was driving him, perhaps to suicide, but which certainly had revealed to him the failure of the terminal Enlightenment solution. . . . Order, meaning, value and identity were lost and for the first time the problem of nineteenth century man is revealed. He cannot begin building a world from a lost paradise, from attainable heaven or even attainable hell, or from a perfectly structured world in which he lives. He must begin in the wasteland.[1]

A totally new orientation must be set up, Goethe believed, wherein the self is seen as the source of value. He possessed a basic fear and repulsion for the medieval attraction to the gore and horror of death.[2] As his career developed, he moved more toward a Neoclassical version of happiness and long life through moderation and self-discipline, reminiscent of the Cornaro tradition. In *Poetry and Truth* Goethe described a series of stages of inner growth and development toward meaning and quality in long life, which Gruman notes is an anticipation of Erik Erikson's developmental categories.[3]

Goethe reached new heights of brilliance in *Faust* where he presented tragedy in a new light, the light of modern man's dilemma: an inability to face his own inadequacies and failures, and to accept his finitude. Typical of a romantic hero, Faust, in his dying moments, had a vision of his soul ascending a high mountain with the saints, including his beloved Gretchen, bearing him to the heights of heaven. In a crescendo, the chorus proclaimed that the transcendent things of time are merely a symbol of what cannot be known or expressed in human terms. The ultimate tension of the human condition was laid bare. This vision was the result of Faust's genuine love for Gretchen, who reappeared in the figure of Helen of Troy. Goethe's final announcement was not that a plunge into the true or totally detached self affords salvation and vision of the infinite; but that it is in the soul's discovery of the "other," the non-self, that rescues the self from oblivion. The discovery of the highest self comes not in detachment, not in reaching some new depth of inner isolation, but in all the ambiguity and striving entailed in the process, the journey, that is the tale of Faust.

The traditional Faustian theme of the man who sold his soul to the devil for the sake of infinite knowledge, gratification and riches, a form of eternal youth and pleasure, symbolized a Promethean defiance of basic mortality. But Goethe's *Faust* makes a different point: the true hero must face the failure of his own power to defy. As Peckham put it, "man's adequacy lies in his power to face his inadequacy." Tragedy followed when he was unable to do this.[4] This need to face human limitations and to master, not nature (as Descartes had wanted) but man's fear of admitting his inadequacies and his limitations in time, was a theme that anticipated the *angst* of the twentieth-century existentialists.

HERALD OF CONTEMPORARY PHILOSOPHY: KANT

Rousseau said in *The New Heloise* that each of us has a divine model of order and perfection inscribed in our hearts, and fortunately, we do not have to be philosophers to distinguish right from wrong. Like Rousseau and many of the Romantics, Immanuel Kant (1724-1804) believed that the morality of a person's acts resides in his good will. Kant was deeply influenced by Rousseau, seeing in him "the Newton of the moral world."[5] However, Rousseau had trouble deciding whether man's conscience was a feeling or a judgment. Kant took it as his task to address this issue. In order to accomplish this he constructed some firm categories about the self and its relation to time, and he related these two categories to the moral life. He also explored man's capacity to know about the existence of God, freedom and immortality. As ambiguous and whimsical as Rousseau and the Romantics were, so Kant was logical and structured in his thought. His difficult and often abstruse writings bore witness to the intricacy of his mind. His conservative life-style attested to his serious mindedness and lack of whimsicality.

Kant's fundamental intention in his philosophy was to establish a firm basis for a deterministic Newtonian universe governed by rational law and order, while retaining a basis for belief in the autonomy of moral choice. This twofold aim was directed toward what was the "foremost philosophic problem" resulting from the movement initiated by Descartes' mind-body dualism.[6] Kant's momentous contribution to modern philosophy can be appreciated more when one reflects on the fact that the issues he raised and the categories he used stood at the beginning of almost every modern movement in philosophy in America and in Europe. He served for those movements as founder, as inspirer, or as target for refutation. It was, fundamentally, his commitment to human freedom, as well as to science, that had much to do with the impact he made on the history of philosophy. As part of his ingenious thought, which tirelessly hammered out a unique philosophy of knowledge, Kant took a new look at time, placing it as the centerpiece of his epistemology. "Kant finally brought time out of the shadows," and thus laid the groundwork for new ways of viewing aging and dying.[7]

Existentialism, phenomenology, pragmatism and many varieties of linguistic philosophy were largely shaped by an evaluation of Kant's notion of experiential time. Because of the complexity of Kant's philosophy it is necessary to concentrate on those elements that directly affect the subject: his concepts of time, the self and immortality.

Time and the Limits of the Mind

Kant reacted against David Hume's thought, which dissolved the self
and advocated skepticism. Kant disallowed skepticism as a permanent
position. Blaise Pascal (1623-1662), William James (1842-1910), and Kant
made roughly the same point: one must go on living and making decisions,
but a state of permanent doubt forbids the decision-making process to go
forward. "Skepticism is . . . a resting place for human reason, where it
can reflect upon its dogmatic wanderings and make survey of the region in
which it finds itself, so that for the future it may be able to choose
its path with more certainty. But it is no dwelling-place for permanent
settlement."[8]

In spite of his disagreement with Hume's skeptical stance, Kant
claimed to have been awakened from his dogmatic slumbers by Hume because
in Hume's work he perceived a grave question about the human capacity for
certitude in its knowledge about the world. Kant criticized Hume for his
shortsightedness, claiming him "one of those geographers of human reason"
who think they have solved the problem of the self by disposing of it,
claiming it is outside the horizon of human reason. But Kant argued,
Hume had done this without first determining the nature of that
horizon.[9] This realization jolted Kant into asking the question that
cast the mold for his whole system of thought. The question with which
he initiated his first major work, *The Critique of Pure Reason*, is: What
are the limits of the mind? It was a question that asked what is beyond
and what is within human cognitive competence. Kant's answer to this
inquiry about the limits of human comprehension not only gave his thought
its basic direction, but it also challenged the age-old gods'-eye view
and the Christian teaching that proof of God's existence and of
immortality can be established on a rational basis. In order to
understand Kant's answer, it is necessary first to see the overall aim of
his critical philosophy.

Kant, as a scientist as well as a philosopher, defended Newtonian
views and sought to ground the validity of the new physics by refuting
Hume. At the same time, he was a moral philosopher who sought to provide
a safe foundation for moral freedom. In his work Kant attempted to draw
together the seemingly opposite threads of rationalism and empiricism and
to weave them into a single unified tapestry of philosophical thought.

The Copernican Turn: Dismissing Certitudes

The problem that Kant saw Hume raise, that so jarred his
philosophical sensibility, led him to question the ancient distinction
between beliefs and experiences of the world and reality itself. Kant
pointed out that ideas, concepts and language do not merely correspond to
reality; they constitute reality. In this sense, Kant suggested that
systematic knowledge of the world comes from an active interrogation of
nature and not from a passive observation of it. Unlike the Platonic
epistemological stance (wherein the forms are derived by the mind from
nature) Kant suggested that the forms by which we order experience are
derived from the human mind. Speaking of metaphysics as a battleground
where unanimity has failed so far, Kant reflected: "Hitherto it has been
assumed that all our knowledge must conform to objects . . . [now] we

must make trial whether we may not have more success in the tasks of metaphysics, if we suppose that objects must conform to our knowledge."[10] He was shifting the metaphor for the mind from one of passive reflector to one of active participator. The mind, Kant insisted, "constitutes" our knowledge just as a constitution gives the grounds for a nation by providing rules and structures within which it is able to operate.

For Plato, sense perception, thought and memory relied on copies or images as in a mirror.[11] For Aristotle the senses passively receive impressions as a piece of wax receives the impress of a signet ring.[12] For John Locke (1632-1704) the metaphor for mind is a blank piece of paper, or *tabula rasa*, which simply receives the ready-formed images of sense experience.[13] All these metaphors emphasized the passive role of the mind in knowing. But for Kant, we actively constitute our own experience by the "categories" of our mind. The categories, Kant pointed out, are the rules or structures according to which we experience the world. For example, we experience objects in space and time. Kant believed that this is not just a habit, but the *only* way we can experience the world. Space and time are the two forms in which human perceptions occur; they are *forms* of the mind that are empirically real because we experience them. For Kant the mind is neither a spark of the Divine in exile, nor a fragment obediently following ironclad principles of the cosmic order of Nature, as it was for the Greeks. The thirst for order is, in Kant's view, a human thirst. We cannot receive data except in a temporally ordered form and without this ordered form, coherent experience is impossible. Temporal categories that exist in the mind prior or before they are put to use are what the mind contributes to make data understandable. The traditional focus of philosophical analysis was on the natural world, the world as it *is*, the gods'-eye view. Abandoning this viewpoint, Kant shifted to a focus on an analysis of the knower and the ways the knower can come to understand his world. This shift represented a fundamental philosophical turn so radical that it has been called the Copernican Revolution of Philosophy.

Kant himself used the metaphor of the Copernican shift, from the earth-centered, Ptolemaic universe to the sun-centered, Copernican universe to represent his revolutionary turn from the study of external reality to the study of the categories whereby the human mind constitutes reality. Copernicus, Kant claimed, "failing of satisfactory progress in explaining the movements of the heavenly bodies on the supposition that they are revolving round the spectator . . . [he questioned] whether he might not have better success if he made the spectator to revolve and the stars to remain at rest."[14] In Kant's view the *objects*, or rather, what was for him the same *experience* in which alone the objects can be known, conforms to the concepts or categories of time and space, which are the ways the mind works. The only possible mode in which legitimate cognitive claims can be made about the world as we perceive it is by making use of concepts that are temporally structured, and these can ground the validity of empirical ideas about the world. Time is not only the principle of order in our understanding; it is also the principle of all intelligibility. Therefore, absolute knowledge of unchanging laws of nature is out of human reach. All theories are hypotheses for Kant. Yet Kant does not doubt that the temporal categories that structure experience turn out valid scientific knowledge. In other words, science is still possible, though it does not afford absolute certitude. The experiencer does not concoct his world. To put it in Kant's words "experience is not invention . . . sense not imagination."[15] In fact, Kant had a dread of idealism wherein the mind creates the object it knows. His was a critical idealism wherein the mind of the knower structured only the sense object but not the matter of which it was made. Again, "form is not to be looked for in the object-in-itself, but in the subject to which the object appears, nevertheless, it belongs really and necessarily to the appearance of this object."[16]

This was Kant's answer to his question "What are the limits of the mind?" "How far can human cognitive competence reach?" Time is the essential form of any possible sense experience and, therefore, of all knowledge or awareness, and this is the inherent outer boundary to cognitive competence. The mind can reach only within the limits of its temporal categories, leaving the area beyond to be investigated from a different standpoint and with different tools. Just as the true hero in Goethe's *Faust* must face the final failure of his Promethean defiance and find his adequacy in the power to face his inadequacy, so in Kant's vision, the true philosopher must forfeit his Promethean-Cartesian certitude and in so doing, discover his adequacy, his powers of objective scientific knowledge in accepting the limitations of the temporal and spatial forms of the human mind. He must finally acknowledge that the temporal categories of the mind afford only symbols of reality, which one cannot know for sure to be reflections of the way things are in themselves. This was the sense in which Kant finally abandoned the gods-eye view.

Therefore, Kant left behind traditional metaphysics with its categories that afford objective and absolute knowledge. In addition, Cartesian rationalism was challenged as Kant insisted that temporal creatures are only able to know the world in which they find themselves and only by means of concepts that are temporally structured and able therein to enter the field of time in which all our experiences take place. A person's capacity to frame or organize his experience as data that is present, past, or future, is, then, the capacity to have any intelligible experiences at all. Here the mind acts as a "synthesizer" or "unifier." As pearls are strung to make a necklace, so individual temporal events are strung together or given unity, by the work of the mind. Thus Kant internalized time as a structure of the mind.

Nevertheless, Kant retained the linear analogy in his notion of time in that he depicted time as atomized points on a line, a succession of discernible moments. In this regard Kant, like Rousseau, did not get beyond the dual notion of time that he received from Descartes and Newton. This is not at all so surprising in that Kant's aim in the first place had been to ground the new physics which embodied a strict causal determinism. In physics, which uses the time of objects, present phenomena are seen in their temporal succession, in terms of the past causal events that yielded them. In like manner, the same causal chain enables prediction of future events. Physics is, therefore, necessarily deterministic. Kant understood the limits of this quantifiable concept of linear time. Therefore, in the second half of his philosophical project, in which his aim was to establish a safe foundation for human morality, he eliminated quantifiable time concepts from the realm of the moral life. His attempt, it must be remembered, was to save morality and human freedom without weakening the grounds of the new science, so he segregated moral reason and the realm of values from causal determinism. In the end, Kant knew that the self, if not in the realm of scientific knowledge, at least in the area of morality, cannot be reduced to a Cartesian-Newtonian series of atomistic moments along a line. Thus the self steps *behind* the looking glass.

Stepping Behind the Looking Glass

Kant claimed that Hume, when he looked for a self among fleeting human experiences, was not able to find it because he was searching in the wrong place. He searched *in* the mirror itself, that is, within the fleeting and temporal thoughts, feelings and perceptions of the person. Kant thought that the place to find the self was *behind* those fleeting experiences. However, he believed Hume was correct in one way--the *self*, Hume said, is not empirical; it is not an *object* of experience. Kant maintained that the self is the *subject* of experience, a subject that stands behind the experiences and threads them together. The temporal self is the necessary condition for the possibility of any kind of experience at all. Kant used the metaphor of self as a synthesizer that actively combines varying impressions into the unity of an object. The self is presupposed and logically necessary if any sense perception, concept, or system of thought is to be built. This temporal self is essential for any self-consciousness, wherein we can watch ourselves doing what we do. In this sense, Kant argued, *the self is both observer and mirror because the self sees itself and is the provider of the categories of time by which it is seen*. Time, then, is the key category in Kant's definition of the self. It is the drawing together of these two categories, the self and time, that is the hallmark of Kant's philosophy of knowledge, and this merger brought with it revolutionary effects on the philosophy of aging and dying in the following century and a half.

The "transcendental ego," as Kant called it, stands behind self-consciousness and is responsible for it. Actively constituting the self the way it is, the transcendental ego enables the person to apply his own rules and to structure empirical data as his own experience. The self, as the mirror of time, can structure human experience and thus make both the experience of self-consciousness and objective knowledge possible.[17]

In the Kantian formulation there were two conceptions of self. The first is the "transcendental ego", the conception of self as self-consciousness. This is what makes us human and is necessary if we are to be a self at all. Kant thought, we experience this self in as real a way as we experience anything else. Kant's second conception of self was the "empirical self," which makes us not just human beings but also individual persons. It includes all those specific qualities we have that make us different from other persons, our strength, our body, our posture, as well as our different past experiences and memories. Here Kant projects a totally revolutionary model for conceptualizing human understanding. His new critical philosophy maintained that the attainment of human knowledge is a time-bound activity which can have cognitive competence only in relation to material that can be presented within temporal categories. As knowers, we must supply the rules and structures, the categories for our own experience. There are, however, serious dangers incumbent upon a misunderstanding of Kant's point here. A natural question must arise, and "relativists" answer it affirmatively: Can different people supply different rules, structures and categories? Can truth or reality be different for different people? Kant's work is often cited as bolstering, and even inspiring the German Romantic tradition associated with the Schlegel brothers, August and Karl (1767-1845 and 1772-1829), Novalis, Friedrich Schliermacher (1768-1834) and Friedrich von Schelling (1775-1854), who was the most typical figure in the tradition (and the figure with whom it culminated). For these German Romantics, Kant's notion of the active self which *constitutes* its own experience, categories and reality is shifted to the self that *creates* its own reality.

Kant authored a classic pamphlet in 1784 titled "What is the Enlightenment?" He thought his own work was firmly enlightened and in the mainstream of eighteenth-century thought. But his use of faith and intuition to ward off a radical dualism in his system proved to be a temptation for many of a different brand of thought. Kant would have been horrified had he known how some nineteenth-century philosophers, from Johann Fichte (1762-1814) to Georg Hegel (1770-1831) to the Romantics, would interpret his ideas. For example, the Romantics and others took Kant's word "transcendent" and used it very differently from what Kant had intended. It is essential here to make quite clear that Kant held the word "transcendent" to mean that all persons would share a *common* set of rules or structures that are part of a *common* human experience about which there is not a choice but a rule. In short, for Kant, there is only one reality.

Determinism, Freedom and Immortality

In Kant's system man is not only a rational but a moral being. "Pure reason" is Kant's term for reason's first function as speculative or theoretical. Reason's second function is concerned with "practical reason," which is involved with moral action. In the *Critique of Pure Reason*, Kant argued that when we try to prove that God exists or that man is free or that the soul is immortal, we necessarily find that our arguments are inconclusive.[18] But Kant did not thereby give up his search for proof about the existence of God, immortality and human moral freedom. Science and determinism offer theoretical knowledge, but humans exist in a moral mode as well. Kant claimed there are moral arguments that can offer a kind of certitude, and thus he took up the defense for the existence of God, immortality and moral freedom, from the standpoint of practical reason. When we need to *know about* something we turn to science where every event, including certain predictions about human actions, comes under deterministic laws: "Reason . . . must approach nature in order to be taught by it."[19] He believed this on the theoretical level, but on the practical level, when we need to live, to decide to *do* something, our wills are the sufficient cause of our actions. In his *Critique of Practical Reason* he said we act *as if* we are totally free. We have to think of ourselves as free and thus assure our freedom:

A need for practical reason . . . is based on a duty to make something (the highest good) the object of my will so as to promote it with all my strength. In doing so, I must presuppose its possibility and also its conditions, which are God, freedom and immortality; for these conditions I am not in a position to prove by my speculative reason, though I cannot disprove them either. This duty is based on . . . the moral law.[20]

Morality must presuppose freedom as a property of the will. Determinism requires a closed future, but moral freedom needs an open future.

It is well known that personally Kant was committed to belief in God, freedom and immortality:

I must not say "It is morally certain that there is a God, etc." but "*I am* morally certain." In other words, belief in a God and in another world is so interwoven with our moral sentiment that there is little danger of my losing the latter, there is equally little cause for fear that the former can ever be taken from me.[21]

Moreover, Kant believed that to deny certainty to knowledge "of God, freedom and immortality is to make room for *faith.*"[22] He believed man is better off without conclusive theoretical arguments about such matters because then he is left to his own free actions and decisions of faith. Why, Kant asked, must the average person with common sense have to wait for philosophers to tell him whether there is a God or a future life? In regard to the most important matters of life, Kant insisted, "The highest philosophy cannot advance further than is possible under the guidance which nature has bestowed on even the most ordinary understanding."[23] But it was not blind faith or religious experience that Kant relied on for his argument's security. It was the moral law in each person.

Using the language of "indefinite progress," but not in the way Godwin or Condorcet used it, Kant issued a thesis that claimed it is the moral destiny of our nature to maintain "infinite progress" toward complete fitness to the moral law.[24] Ever sensitive to the time-bound nature of finite man, Kant gave not a logical, but a moral argument for the conviction that there is a future life, an argument for immortality of soul on the grounds that this life is too short for full moral development to take place within it. The highest good, he insisted, is the union of happiness and virtue. But while happiness can be attained in this life, which is so limited in time, perfect virtue (holiness) cannot be. Therefore, an infinitely prolonged existence is required in a future life to make possible infinite spiritual progress: "endless progress from lower to higher stages of moral perfection is possible to a rational but finite being."[25]

Again the question about relativism can be raised, this time in the moral realm. Is Kant saying that different individuals supply different moral rules for specific situations because they have internal convictions about the moral law? Kant would answer, "Certainly not!" The sense of *duty* he spoke of is a "categorical imperative," a command or imperative, an "ought" that is "categorical," according to a universal law of reason or an objective and universal principle, about which there can be no doubt. Moreover, this sense of duty is the product of both autonomous reason and rational will, independent of all personal feeling or self-interest. For Kant morality is never a case of individual

feelings about particular situations but a "common reason of mankind."[26]
He declared that the behavior of an individual ought to serve as an
example for all mankind. This argument saw man as bondsman and God as
master over life and death:

> Human beings are sentinels on earth and may not leave their posts
> until relieved by another beneficent hand. God is our owner; we are
> His property; His providence works for our good. A bondsman in the
> care of a beneficent master deserves punishment if he opposes his
> master's wishes. . . . No matter what torments I may have to suffer,
> I can live morally. I must suffer them all, including the torments
> of death.[27]

The Priceless Person

One last point is essential: Kant's entire ethic was built on the
notion that the moral agent must be regarded as a person rather than a
thing as in Descartes' *res cogitans*, a thinking thing.[28] Kant clearly
stated, "Act so that you treat humanity, whether in your own person or in
that of another, always as an end and never as a means only."[29] A person
for Kant must always be an object of respect because he possesses dignity
as a human being, that is, an agent of the moral law. In Kant's way of
thinking persons, unlike things, are priceless: "In the realm of ends,
everything has either a price or a dignity. Whatever has a price can be
replaced by something else as its equivalent, on the other hand, whatever
is above all price, and therefore admits of no equivalent, has a
dignity."[30] Kant believed that a person does not have a mere relative
worth or a "market price," but "intrinsic worth" or dignity[31] by virtue
of the fact that, as a moral agent, he is free from external
deterministic rulings: "as an end in himself, he is destined to be
legislative in the realm of ends, free from all laws of nature and
obedient only to those which he himself gives."[32] This is a concept that
Goethe cried out for, the recognition of the person as the source of
value. Kant internalized within the person universal moral law, just as
he internalized time, but claimed in both cases that he did not fall into
relativism because humans share a common sense of time and a common sense
of duty. In addition to the dignity afforded to persons who, unlike
things, are subjects and moral agents, Kant attributed a similar dignity
to the human body as opposed to other kinds of bodies, which are simple
objects. He said, "when the concept of body is brought under the
category of substance, it is thereby determined that its empirical
intuition in experience must always be considered as a subject and never
as a mere predicate."[33] Unlike Descartes and the mechanists, who saw all
bodies the same and thus subject to the external laws of time and space,
Kant believed that the human body is not a mere object; rather in his own
words, "the very same being which, as outer appearance, is extended, is
(in itself) internally a subject, and is not composite, but is simple and
thinks."[34] Here Kant attempted to undercut mind-body dualism in which
the soul thinks and the body is radically different, merely an object
existing in time and space. Kant said we must abandon the thesis that
"only souls think" because "it is men who think."[35]

But it was not Kant's moral arguments for the existence of God, for
freedom and for immortality that were taken up as this ingenious

philosopher's legacy to the nineteenth and twentieth centuries. Kant's philosophy of knowledge, which embodied the thesis that time is the foundation from which man's cognitive limits arise, acted as a leaven for contemporary philosophies. The more this thesis is worked over, raised to prominence and pounded down again, the more it seems to appear in new and different forms in contemporary thinking. Kant's novel approach represents the profound thinking through of the meaning behind the primacy of Descartes' *cogito* that initiated modern philosophy. Without Kant's insight about the horizon of human comprehension and without his heraldic proclamation of the need for a deeper penetration into the area of the temporal form of the human mind, the philosophies of aging and dying of the nineteenth and twentieth centuries undoubtedly would have been quite different.

Kant may have seen himself as a man of the Enlightenment, but he was a long way from either the mechanistic materialists, who with scientific certitude envisioned the "Man-Machine," or the faith-renouncing Philosophes. In fact, Kant renounced the skeptics who boldly dismissed the possibility of any knowledge of God, soul or immortality. Kant was in tune with the few moderate and more psychologically oriented geriatricians who placed their faith in the power of the mind and the decisions of the will in improving the conditions of human life. Yet he would be less sanguine in anticipating the almost unconditional perfectibility of man as it existed in Condorcet's thought. Certainly, for Kant a radical belief in indefinite scientific progress would be too extreme. Though Kant sensed the value of Rousseau's pure self along with the role of the will in the life of moral agents, he would totally reverse Rousseau's idea of the "*detached timeless pure self*," which has access only to the immediate present and, as pure consciousness, stands without access to any other as an object of its own love. Though both Rousseau and Kant shared the Newtonian model of time, Kant ultimately recognized the need to abandon this view as applicable to the moral dimension of human experience. But he did not go to the opposite extreme, as some of the Romantics did in their belief that the mind creates reality.

With Goethe, Kant searched for a concept of self that did not entirely fall under the totally objective and deterministic rules that science used for bodies that are "in" time and space. Nor would Kant's self become a necessary victim of the subjective loneliness of a magic idealism that lost touch with and remained silent about the meaning of reality.

In the moral realm, Kant envisioned judgments of the will as based on a universal natural law that is internalized within every person, thereby giving him a dignity as an irreplaceable human subject, as distinguished from an object, which can be duplicated. But most important of all, Kant contributed his paradoxical vision of a new kind of Prometheus, who finds his power not in defiance but in acceptance of the intrinsic limits of man's temporal nature. Kant's entire theory of knowledge was founded on his conviction in the primacy of the time-structured subject, which serves as the ground of certainty, meaningfulness and anticipation in human experience of the self and the world. This is what made Kant the herald of contemporary Western philosophy which placed time as the keystone of its many edifices.

THE SHATTERED MIRROR

Each age is a dream that is dying
Or one that is coming to birth
Arthur O'Shaughnessy[1]

The Victorian age (1838-1901) was a period of rapid change, that some interpreted as an era of progress and others as a rush toward destruction.[2] The assessment of whether mankind was advancing or declining with the passage of time and incumbent social change, it seems, was affected by the experience, disposition and sometimes the temperament of the person addressing the question of whether a dream was dying or being born.

An awareness of the transitoriness of time, the precariousness of life and the inevitability of death loomed large in the Victorian imagination, accompanied by a sense of the puniness of man in the face of the vast universe. Victorians became progressively concerned about the measurement of public time in a scientific and objective way. There was also a growing fascination with what was seen as the potential for the creation of life from nonliving matter. Some artists and thinkers were enamored of the idea; some horrified, not by the potential of scientific progress in itself, but by the question of the capacity of man to handle the challenge without destroying himself in the process, as Francis Bacon had warned.

The change in the way the elderly were seen represents a turnabout from the American colonial view which ideally revered old people as the custodians of virtue, as veterans of a productive lifetime and as models for the young. American Romanticism brought with it a sentimentalized version of this veneration, but exaggerated esteem may have merely masked a growing dread of aging and death. By the end of the Civil War in 1865, this sentimental pretense collapsed with the recognition of changes in metaphysical, religious and social traditions. Suffering, and the liabilities of the aging process were expressed more realistically and aging, viewed scientifically, was treated more objectively. The shift involved a change in perception, a transition in the value placed on the elderly as such. An unprecedented denigration of older Americans took place, and this happened independently of immediate or dramatic changes in demographic or socioeconomic situations. It took the first several decades of the twentieth century for modernization to have a profound effect on the actual living conditions and self image of the older generation.

Shifting perspectives are evident. The American colonial death system can be compared to Romantic views and practices which focused more on the family than on the larger community. Mourning customs and ceremonies reveal popular views of the meaning and value of life and death. Elaborate death customs and displays of mourning, characteristic of the Victorian era, started to diminish and people began to cope with death more by denial and silence.

VICTORIAN TIME CONSCIOUSNESS: PROGRESS OR DECADENCE

The idea of progress, and the perfectibility of man that had so preoccupied the previous century would continue as a popular view of unprecedented optimism and faith in the future. Nevertheless, what was seen by many as advancement would by others be redefined as a prediction of inevitable decadence. Debates about the validity and meaning of scientific discoveries and theories were reflected in newspapers and magazines, as new ideas about the age of the earth and the origin of life challenged fundamental theological premises. The task of the Victorians was basically to adapt the fundamental values of their tradition in an age of bewildering change. As Jerome Buckley put it in 1966:

Whatever the late Victorian journalistic exploitation of the ephemeral, their major spokesman, at least, retained until the end a respect for the historical past and a concern with the large concepts of progress and decadence. Their best commitment to the present, essential as it was to the direction of their own energies, was made with neither complacency nor despair, yet in the full consciousness of time.[3]

Conditioned from earliest years to general instability, the nineteenth-century citizen had to make peace with twin aspects of hope and fear. A new and affluent class of farmers and landlords was brought into being by the growth of industry which brought with it great wealth. In urban and rural life, a new middle-class arose and began to imitate the gentry, initiating social competition and an urge toward visible display both in life patterns and in the customs surrounding death. A typical middle-class Victorian aimed "to secure a double crown of respectability in life and salvation after it."[4] Wealth and gracious living were intimately connected with respectability and salvation, and the Victorian was keenly conscious of the part the age in which he lived played in the development of a new and more "modern" world. A new consciousness arose in Western man that his relationship with the world was changing. No age before had been possessed with such a unique concern for time, progress, aging and death.

In the fourteenth and fifteenth centuries, the theme of the "Triumph of Death" represented death at center stage. Death, which took the place

of God, was accompanied by an attitude of revolt at the injustice of
fate. Peter Brueghel's sixteenth-century fantasy, *The Triumph of Time*,
emphasized both the creative and the destructive aspects of Father Time.
In the nineteenth century, Shelley used a similar metaphor to depict his
(typically Victorian) attitude toward time. His poem "The Triumph of
Life" was a dream allegory, written while sailing off the coast of
Italy.[5] It was his last poem, unfinished because of his own sudden death
by drowning. The poem depicted time as a four-faced charioteer,
blindfolded in all directions including the past, the present, the future
and the eternal now. The horror of the vision lay not only in the ill-
guided rush of the chariot toward inevitable destruction, but also in
showing the entire human race dancing madly behind the chariot:

> Maidens and youths fling their wild arms in air . . .
> Like moths by light attracted and repelled,
> Oft to their bright destruction come and go . . .
> One falls and then another in the path
> Senseless. [6]

Like the juggernaut that crushed its blind followers, Shelley's chariot
attracted even the elderly, who did not have enough wisdom to predict
inevitable disaster:

> Old men and women foully disarrayed
> Shake their gray hairs in the insulting wind,
> And follow in the dance, with limbs decayed.[7]

The human race is led to its own destruction, as a stream of slavelike
creatures, down a wide highway behind the victorious chariot of time. In
Shelley's version, mankind as a whole had been deluded by false dreams
about earthly existence. The cruel irony is that *life* leads man to *death*.
The fact that humankind goes forward, without consciousness of its fate
is the point on which Shelley muses.

Other writers feared that mankind could subject itself to a slavish
existence, harnessed to time's drudgeries because of lack of vision
regarding the future. Poets, like Shelley, sought refuge, beyond the flux
of incessant change, in the artistic life which they saw as the greatest
source of stability and meaning. In his poem Arthur O'Shaughnessy
depicted the poet as one who can foretell things that are to come. Poets
are "dreamers of dreams." They are also "the movers and shakers of the
world for ever."[8] The Victorian poet believed that poets were the image
makers who warned ordinary persons, often blinded, that there is a need
to examine the direction and timing of the rushing chariot that bears
life forward.

As the nineteenth century wore on, pessimism grew. In England as
well as in America writers gave warnings of their misgivings about the
future. Jerome Buckley notes, "To all modern men, life and time seem
inseparably linked, and most are content to be led aimlessly through the
drift of experience. But the more sensitive ones demand some perspective,
a sense of time's course or meaning."[9]

The Cartesian interpretation of the self in the Enlightenment
dictated a radical change in the traditional Western interpretation of

the person. It brought about a breakdown in the medieval worldview of
man, and of his place in the larger community. By the nineteenth century,
the modern *self* was destined to stand in isolation against all else in
the world. As one peered into the mirror of time, the question about a
person's individual identity could no longer be answered by defining
man's human position and destiny in terms of a community of being, a
stable teleological order, or a religious or metaphysical system. Like
Rousseau, the average late Victorian found himself unable to explain his
life in terms of an eternal system that gave it meaning. Nineteenth-
century man meditated with Pascal: "When I consider the short duration
of my life, swallowed up in the eternity before and after, the little
space which I fill . . . engulfed in the infinite immensity of spaces of
which I am ignorant . . . I am frightened, and am astonished at being
here rather than there."[10] Yet the Victorian poets longed for a larger
metaphysical context. They "are forever looking before and after,
impatient with the mere flux of things, and eager to find a way once
again of measuring their brief lives under some eternal aspect."[11]

Thus, in this century--especially in Victorian England and America--
there emerged for the first time a truly modern attitude toward time.
The Victorians became progressively obsessed with time and with the means
used for measuring it. In the scientific view material objects took on
less fixity and became a mass of "charged energies" in a space-time
continuum. Rapid change was seen as the basis of life. "If the discovery
of space has proceeded rapidly ever since the late Renaissance, the
discovery of modern scientific time belongs largely to the past one
hundred and fifty years."[12] The reliable measuring of time was a
critical component in the complex set of factors that brought on the
Industrial Revolution in England and America. Time-keeping (an
interesting term in itself) and the discipline associated with it became
a necessity. Prior to the Industrial Revolution, clocks were primarily
used on public buildings and churches. The routines of country people
were governed by the length of the hours of daylight and by the rising
and setting of the sun. By the eighteenth century, and more so in the
nineteenth century, the Protestant work ethic (with its belief in virtue
connected with hard work), coupled with the growth of industrialization,
resulted in a people most concerned with the clock and the importance of
time well spent. A connection between time and money further entrenched
itself along with the growth of commerce and new methods of cost
accounting that accompanied the manufacture of standard products.

Industry and science dealt mainly with objective, linear time, which
measured all things quantitatively, according to a standard. This is a
kind of shared, neutral, "public" time. In this sense in the industrial
and scientific order time was necessarily treated as a commodity to be
measured, accounted for, and saved. By the end of the nineteenth century
there existed a general public image of the magnitude of history, and an
overall public realization of its length, compared with the brevity of a
single individual life. These realizations, in turn, reinforced the sense
of time as fleeting and life as uncertain.[13] But the scientific
imagination also produced some spectacular experiments that fueled
excitement in poets like Byron and Shelley and his young wife, Mary. The
artist, it was believed, whether poet or novelist, would represent human
time. "Private time," in contrast to "public time," was seen, especially
by the Romantic, as relative to personal emotions, possessing its own

pattern of variations in tempo.

Search for the Secret of Life

The artist is most often the one who asks questions about the nature of human life and its value. Shelley's last line in the "Triumph of Life" was: "Then, what is life, I cried."[14] He and Byron are well known for the long conversations in which they discussed the question of the principle of human life and whether or not science had discovered "the spark of life" in recent experiments with electricity. One such experiment was performed by Erasmus Darwin (1731-1802), who it was reported had personally observed a piece of vermicelli come to life in a glass container.[15] Earlier, in Bologna Luigi Galvani (1737-1798) had combined his knowledge of electricity and anatomy in his theory of "animal electricity." Galvani became known as the father of galvanic electricity with his discoveries that legs severed from a newly killed frog contract when touched at different points by electrical discharges.[16] In 1802 Giovanni Aldini used electric shock to induce muscle spasms in the corpse of a criminal hanged at Newgate. As with Galvani, the momentary twitching of the muscles was thought to give conclusive evidence that electricity was related to the origin of life.[17] It was in this milieu that Mary Shelley conceived of her image-making novel entitled *Frankenstein or The Modern Prometheus*, published in London in three volumes in 1818. John Godwin's daughter, Mary Shelley, was the quietest member of the illustrious circle of thinkers and writers that included her husband, Percy, the famous and erratic Byron and a mad young doctor, John Polidori. She conceived of her tale during the summer of 1816 after a discussion with them about the potential for creating life from inanimate matter. The story fused moldy Gothic terrors to a scientific context, raising an issue that had long dogged Mary Shelley's sensibilities: the relationship between the newfound powers of science and the awful potential for destructiveness hidden in the modern self. The existence of the monster in the story raised all kinds of ethical questions that the scientist, Frankenstein, had to face.[18] Once he had created the monster out of dead matter, by an electric charge, he was filled with horror and disgust at what he had done. The monster story, though fiction, was Mary Shelley's way to question progress.[19] Important questions are posed, not only by the original story, but also by hundreds of versions of it, which for the most part retain the central themes. In perpetuation of the myth of the new Prometheus, especially in America through films, the public has taken for its own Mary Shelley's questions as well as her fascination with alchemy and the occult. In general, it was nineteenth- and twentieth-century fear of time, life and death that was being reflected.

In the scientist's belated awareness of his moral responsibility, Kantian-like issues were raised: man's awareness of the difference between persons and things and the responsibility of the scientist to consider the ethics of life and death. As alchemy had promised men cosmic power over life and death by the use of a single simple philosopher's stone or an elixir, science now projected a popular faith in its own seemingly limitless and God-like powers to discover the ultimate secret of human life. The sixteenth-century scientist's desire to prolong life by defeating aging, to push death back, or even overcome death entirely had extended itself to the desire to create life. In *Frankenstein*, the very distinction between the living and the dead was blurred by the monster's existence as half-human and half-machine, perhaps the logical extension in the public imagination of LaMettrie's machine-man.[20]   The question at the end of the book remained: "Will the monster be able to die?" or "What is death for a man who is, at least in part, a machine?"   Martin Tropp says, "On one level, the monster was symbolic of the mechanistic attitude behind man's new technology; its construction out of the parts of dead corpses was a logical extension of the reductive equation in which living things are not distinguished from inorganic matter."[21]

Tropp thinks that the fact that most people confuse the name of the scientist, Frankenstein, and the nameless monster, which they call Frankenstein, indicates that they are intuitively acknowledging their suspicion that the creator realized in some way his creature was none other than himself.[22]   Whether or not Tropp is right, a growing awareness was coalescing that the failures of the mechanistic model were the failures of its image makers.

IDEAS OF OLD AGE IN VICTORIAN AMERICA

Popular perceptions of aging specifically by Americans can be said to have shifted from the period between the Revolutionary War and 1830, again between 1830 and the Civil War, and finally, in the post-Civil War period. W. Andrew Achenbaum in his analysis, *Old Age in the New Land: The American Experience Since 1790*, aptly points out that it is not at all unusual that, given the worldview of Americans before 1830, the symbol for devotion to country so deeply cherished at that time was personified in Uncle Sam, "a sinewy old man with long white hair and chin whiskers...dressed in red and white striped pantaloons and a blue coat bespangled with stars and sporting an unabashedly old-fashioned plug hat."[23]   The aptness of this symbol sprang from the fact that early Americans believed that the new republic depended for its success on the commitment of citizens of all ages; Americans before 1830 counted on the aged as well as the youthful to share their work and wisdom in making the infant republic a viable new nation. Little distinction was made between age groups; nature was seen as bestowing both gifts and liabilities on persons at every stage of development. Although there were occasional evidences of fear or hatred of the aged, the blessings of old age were generally seen to afford experience, wisdom and accumulated insight into the meaning of life and death. Ideally, old people were revered because they were perceived as custodians of virtue and seasoned veterans of productivity.[24]   Elderly persons were expected to participate in community activity, which for them often meant (as it had for Plato) holding public office unless affected by serious disability, and they themselves were expected to evaluate when they could no longer be active in public affairs. In short, in the early nineteenth century the general perception was that the elderly were to be esteemed for simply having achieved old age. Young people were in turn instructed by ministers and writers alike to heed their advice and example about how to succeed in life and achieve a happy longevity and to accede to their insights on how to bear the inevitable sufferings and pains they had to endure. Their resignation, patience and tranquillity were seen as signs of a philosophy that helped put the ultimate meaning of life into perspective. Writers such as Godwin and Condorcet were read and re-read and their advice, not only about the possibility but the desirability, of prolonging life through temperance and moderation was extolled. Generally, Americans believed that one's mental and personal habits were extremely important and that older men and women ought to be ascribed an important function in that they had demonstrated life-styles that had effectively promoted longevity. Thomas Bailey notes in the *Records of Longevity* in 1859:

> I mean—notwithstanding the instances which will be found in these records to the contrary—to establish the truth...that temperance, industry and exercise are the great elements of longevity. A few slothful men have attained to extreme old age, and so have a few gluttons and drunkards, or at least, hard drinkers, but for the most part, and in incomparably greater proportion, long livers have been distinguished for their sober and industrious habit.[25]

Early Victorians believed in the value of suffering. One example of this view can be seen in James Hinton's book, *The Mystery of Pain: A Book for the Sorrowful*. Hinton believed that life itself could be measured by man's ability to endure pain.[26] In this period in America, suffering was often interpreted as having a higher purpose or as a cleansing or trial by fire. Later, Emily Dickinson (1830-1886) wrote in the same vein:

> My first well Day -- since many ill --
> I asked to go abroad,
> And take the Sunshine in my hands,
> And see the things in Pod -- . . .
>
> My loss, by sickness -- Was it Loss?
> Or that Ethereal Gain
> One earns by measuring the Grave --
> Then -- measuring the Sun --[27]

Americans between 1790 and 1830 did not exult in pain or in the liabilities of old age, but its poets, philosophers and clergymen represented it as a part of living that everyone must accept with a stoic or orthodox Christian attitude.

As the century moved on, American Romantics idealized old age, emphasizing the subjective challenge to each individual. This emphasis was less on the liabilities presented by passing years than on aging as a part of everyone's experience. The problems and sufferings of growing older were represented as each person's chance to grapple with the meaning of his own individual destiny. One author of that period, Albert Barnes, urged young people to observe the actions of old people who may serve as role models in accepting both aging and oncoming death and make appropriate preparations for the life to come. "There is a manner of meeting death which is appropriate to man's manner of life," he said, "which will be a proper completion or rounding out of the character as a man leaves the world."[28] A peaceful, natural death was a sign, therefore, of a righteous life. In keeping with tradition, the American Romantic writer saw old age as a special period of life. Rather than just one of the equally important stages of life, old age was *the transitional* stage of development on the "path to immortality," the *ultimate* stage of life.

By the advent of the Civil War, old age was generally considered the
perfect vantage point of virtue that enabled the person to be closest to
immortality and thus have the best view from which to instruct others on
how to reach it. What has been said of the European Romantics can be
reiterated of American Romantics. Sentimentalization of old age and death
functioned to conceal dread of isolation and pain in the consciousness of
the population. Thomas Cole put it this way: "The sentimentalization of
old age and death reflects the cultural hegemony of the middle class and
degrades the very objects it claims to exalt. . . . The sentimental view
masks the hatred of old age and denial of death that emerge more clearly
at the end of the century."[29] However, after the Civil War, this
idealization process diminished and was replaced by a more dispassionate
image. Between 1865 and the First World War (1914) many elements
contributed to a shift to a lower esteem for the aged. The new model of
time and the new science, as well as the incumbent shift from an agrarian
to an industrial economic basis, caused a reassessment of both the early
republican view and the Romantic view of the value of the aged. The
former general acceptance of the positive value of suffering, and the
liabilities of the aging process, began to break down. This shift in
attitude can be detected in the words of Emily Dickinson, who in a poem
written in 1875 says:

As Summer into Autumn slips
And yet we sooner say
"The Summer" than "the Autumn", lest
We turn the sun away,. . .

So we evade the charge of Years
On one attempting shy
The Circumvention of the Shaft
Of Life's Declivity.[30]

The metaphysical answer that pain was to be accepted because there are
higher purposes in the ultimate scheme of things, could no longer bear
the weight it once did when the great moral design held sway of men's
imaginations. Pain and blind necessity, the grindstone of life, became
things to be controlled. In the midst of Victorian conventions it was
becoming increasingly problematic, for a culture that was bent on more
comfort and material progress, simply to excuse or ignore suffering.[31]
By 1870 the new American middle class, which aimed at stabilizing and
reforming industrialism along with capitalism and establishing its own
image, began to rationalize old age and death.

In a harmonious society based on scientific laws and guided by
social engineers, old age and death became matters for the
management of experts. . . . Redefining old age as human
obsolescence, academic, social and biomedical students
conceptualized aging as a series of problems whose solution lay in
the intervention of trained professionals.[32]

Physicians, biologists and sanitary engineers were initiating steady
improvements in public health, habits of hygiene and infant care, and
slow but steady growth in efficient hospital care. Previously, hospitals

were viewed as stations on the way to the grave, as almshouses for the elderly and poor. They afforded protection to the community from communicable diseases by isolating sick persons, rather than acting as a step towards health. Gradually, by the late nineteenth and early twentieth century, Americans increasingly began to realize the value of hospitals as indispensable agencies for relieving social needs and as educational institutions or as training grounds for physicians, medical students and nurses. American doctors were slower than Europeans to improve medical analyses of the diseases of old age. However, later in the century, the American public came to respect the scientist and medical professional, more than the older person himself, as sources of knowledge regarding prolongevity. Old age was viewed less as a state of wisdom and more as an incurable diseases: "Experts on health matters convinced the general public that old people suffered incurable pathological disorders."[33] In his 1906 article, "The Quest for Prolonged Youth," Carl Snyder gave the following pessimistic evaluation of the process of aging: "If there is any disease in the world it is this [aging]. No one looks forward to it with eager anticipation. Nobody welcomes it, nobody enjoys it. It is a disease, that is to say, it is a pathological condition. But for it there exists no therapy, no cure."[34] Mere survival was no longer seen as a virtue and there was less connection made between moral virtue and the aging process. For example, the philosopher William James (1842-1910) commented in his *Principles of Psychology* that everyone will, as an older person, become more rigid and less ready for new ideas. He conceived the term "old fogyism." James believed, "Most of us grow more and more enslaved to the stock conceptions with which we have once become familiar, and less and less capable of assimilating impressions in any but the old ways. Old-fogyism, in short, is the inevitable terminus to which life sweeps us on."[35]

Thomas Cole notes that a dichotomization between the young and the old that had begun as early as the end of the eighteenth century, culminated in actual contempt for the aged. He blames this on an increase in individualism and the intrusion of the market into the lives of the American family:

> The emergence of a class of wage earners, stripped of private productive property, initiated a splitting process that ramified throughout nineteenth century America: home was separated from work; the male from the female "sphere;" public from private life; the healthy from the sick, work from leisure; the criminal from the virtuous; the poor from the rich; youth from age and life from death.[36]

The labor force was required to be efficient and nimble in body. A tough, realistic approach to work, time and money replaced the Romantic idealization of aging. In 1861 the first federal retirement regulations appeared, and private industry, too, began moving in the same direction. Early nineteenth-century practices excluded from work only the elderly who were ill and relied on the individual aged person to decide when he ought to retire. Twentieth century regulations, for the most part, applied uniformly to all persons of retirement age. All the virtues formerly ascribed to the elderly: insight into the meaning of life, wisdom and the role of the examplar, were gradually shifted to the

young. Although the rhetoric about respect and value for old people
continued long after the Civil War and into the early twentieth century,
aging would soon come to be connected directly with dying, and the aged
would be avoided by young people who feared being near the dying.
Achenbaum notes that the new "realistic" attitudes toward life perhaps
surprisingly gave rise to a denial of death:

> Perhaps even more ironically, this new, tough, realism was
> premised in part on the denial of death. Death had not lost its
> sting, of course, but new ideas and conditions prevailing in society
> did enable contemporaries to reach the conclusion that the reduced
> probability of dying young was a clear indication of the march of
> progress in the United States. Hence, more and more Americans in
> the last decades of the nineteenth century overcame death by
> ignoring it in youth and associating it with age.[37]

Modernization, in the form of demographic, economic and political
shifts that began at the end of the eighteenth century, brought with it a
sweeping cultural reorientation of popular perceptions of aging and a
"new emphasis on youth, progress, equality, technology and material
satisfactions which led to a redefinition of the ultimate meaning of
life."[38] The earliest practical effects of modernization and
industrialization did not include the older generation as much as other
age groups and thus had less impact on the elderly themselves than on the
rest of the population. In addition, there is little evidence that
before the twentieth century there was any marked change in the self-
image of older Americans.[39] The real consequences of modernization on the
elderly were seen between World War I and World War II when society's
expectations of the aged changed. But more importantly the way the older
generation saw itself shifted, especially in the segment of the
population over 65 not gainfully employed and living on fixed income.

The most dramatic shift in the image and self-image of the aged in
America was accompanied by a move to study and assist them as a social
group. David Fisher says that there were entirely new attitudes,
assumptions and expectations: "Old age had always been a social problem.
. . . But there was something new in the modern world--an instrumental
attitude which lay at the center of modernity itself. . . . It is a style
of thought which made an artifact of society, itself and government a
tool for its improvement."[40]

DEATH IN VICTORIAN AMERICA

Along with the changed perceptions of aging in America in the
nineteenth century, great shifts took place in popular attitudes toward
death during the Victorian age, which Howe says, "marked a crucial--
probably *the* crucial--transformation in the United States."[41] John Morley
notes that the Victorian age revealed its soul in its mourning customs
and ceremonies and that no one could possibly understand the makeup of
this remarkable era without knowing something of its attitudes and
customs related to death.[42] Furthermore, Lawrence Taylor claims, death
rituals thus can serve "as a key to the inner structure of a period."[43]
In order to understand Victorian attitudes toward death, it is necessary
to look back to the colonial age and its approach to death. In early

colonial America members of tightly knit communities held common ground in their confrontation with sickness and death. It was, as David Stannard puts it:

> ...a world in which all manner of social stress was absorbed and responded to by a fluid, informal, complementary network of family, church and local government, a world in which there was little distinction between public and private or among one's activities or associates in workplace, marketplace, house of worship or home.[44]

In early America, Wordsworth's question about the "Old Cumberland Beggar" was answered: the elderly, the physically or mentally ill and even criminals were considered to be part of the local community's responsibility. It was the community that functioned as the defining unit of colonial America's worldview. When a death occurred, the community order or integrity was disturbed; therefore, it was necessary by means of its death system to reaffirm that unity and to reestablish that integrity.[45] The "death system" helped deal with the uncontrollable by providing acceptable behavior patterns, customs and language that constituted a response to death. Through the activities of public funeral rituals and shared symbolic gestures such as simple common meals, a public shared grief was expressed. Everyone, whether rich or poor, young or old, whether a member of a large family or a single survivor, was recognized in death by the members of the group. David Stannard notes that this was especially true in communities with closely shared cultural and religious values:

> for the century and a half from the earliest days of settlement until the era of the Revolution . . . death in most of the New World's towns and villages brought with it a general outpouring and sharing of grief and sorrow, and a general participation in the funerary ritual. In death as in life, the experiences of any individual touched the lives of everyone else.[46]

The burial place was amidst nature, and the burial customs were simple. The box that was used as a container for the body was homemade, the body was washed and prepared and dressed at home in everyday clean clothes, and the procession to the grave included all the residents of the town. Later in the Victorian era this changed, and so did the attitude of early settlers toward suffering. The view that this life is a wilderness to be passed through on the way to a better life began to decline in America. Pious rhetoric would be retained, but, as with suffering of all kinds, death would gradually become less acceptable and the attitude toward the future of the dead more ambiguous. Therefore, death was seen as more disturbing and needed to be made more tolerable; "the living demanded that . . . its harsh reality [be] muted and beautified."[47] A new way of treating death emerged. Other influences made an impression on nineteenth century mentality, but the influence of the images of Romanticism largely determined the nature of Victorian emotion.[48] Romantic sensibility brought a new feeling for the loss of a loved one. The affection that formerly was diffused was now concentrated on a few close persons. The sense of traditional community and the sense of the individual as part of that community that had developed in the Middle Ages gave way to a sense of privacy and family affection. What was mourned was the physical

separation from the loved one which, it seemed could never be accepted.
Reunion with the loved one was longed for in a future life. The death
scene was viewed within a new metaphor, not as tragic but as beautiful.
This is illustrated in Romantic deathbed scenes, in the development of
the rural cemetery, and the revision of funeral rituals.

Romantic Deathbed Scenes

There was a spate of deathbed scenes in nineteenth century
literature; Victorians were in practice more involved with deathbed
surroundings than almost any other aspect of dying. Family mourning, one
of the most deeply entrenched customs of the period, became almost a
fetish, partly because of an intense preoccupation with separation from
the loved one and preparation for reunion in heaven. John Reed says,
"Mourning the dead is an instinct as old as man, but in no era had it
become such an iron-bound convention as in the Victorian age."[49] The
Romantic deathbed scene, it was believed, allowed the opportunity to
afford emotional comfort and reassurance both to the dying and to
relatives and friends gathered around the dying person, especially if
they witnessed a "calm clear-eyed death," a death with composure and
resignation. The powerful lesson of death, it was thought, ought to
inspire everyone with Christian fortitude by being a "final outward sign
of inward grace evidenced by the departing."[50] In addition, the deathbed
gathering offered a last opportunity to all to encourage, forgive,
repent, or offer last wishes perhaps admonishments. Reminiscent of death
scenes in the Middle Ages, a kind of gothic element entered this period,
but with less force than in former times. Victorian etiquette called for
behavior to be proper, even if the gap between pretension and performance
was wide. Victorian authors sentimentalized and romanticized death
chamber scenes. The custom bore a great importance for the Victorian
writer. It served as a means of pointing out the basic importance of the
moral scheme underlying much of the literature of the period. Reed says,
"Offensive as many modern readers now find the deathbed convention, it
was, for its time, a truly immediate reality that bound fictional
convention and social fact together."[51]

However, as the nineteenth century passed, Victorian consciousness
alternated between hope and fear, public faith and questioning of
spiritual realities. "Distant echoes of their positive faith and stronger
reverberations of their misgivings reached down the years."[52] Conviction
about afterlife waned, and gradually mortuary practices changed, and the
deathbed convention, once so prominent, was no longer practiced. One
notable element leading to the abandonment of this convention was the
increased faith of Americans in the advancement of medical theory and the
gradual acceptance of the hospital for the cure of the sick and even as
an acceptable place for the ordinary person to die. The effect of this
widespread appreciation of better health care and antiseptic methods in
the twentieth century finally removed the death scene from the home. The
circle of participants in the hospital setting became more limited.
Instead of neighbors and friends, including children, only the closest
relatives, sometimes just the spouse, were allowed to visit the dying
patient, and then only at certain hours. As Aries notes, the hospital
would increasingly become "the place of solitary death."[53]

The Rural Cemetery Movement: The Garden Model

An attitude of indifference toward the location and maintenance of gravesites was common in colonial America because the body was regarded as unimportant, simply a shell to be left aside after death. Therefore, there was very little concern about burying the remains. A typical town graveyard was often an unkempt section of land where graves and markers might well be trampled upon by people and cattle.[54] William Cullen Bryant's poem of 1818, "The Burial Place," illustrates this casual attitude toward graveyards:

Naked rows of graves
And melancholy ranks of monuments
Are seen instead, where the coarse grass, between
Shoots up its dull spikes, and in the wind
Hisses and the neglected bramble nigh,
Offers its berries to the school boy's hand[55]

By the 1830s however, the rural cemetery movement appeared. The Romantics saw the city as a place that had been made unnatural by society. They therefore established the rural cemetery—a kind of garden area, in beautiful, private and rustic environments in the countryside, far from the noise and ugliness of the city. Much of the impetus for the development of this garden model for burial places could have come from prominent American figures, such as Thomas Jefferson, who planned such a gravesite in Monticello as early as 1771.[56] George Washington's grave was also a typical garden gravesite of the plantation country.[57] These rural cemeteries, which contained personalized plots carefully cared for by gardening techniques, were also used for parks and places of recreation. Their peace and the setting of the natural landscape reinforced the Romantic attitude of death as beautiful and peaceful. Even the term "cemetery" was new. It meant "sleeping place" and was applied to the place of interment, which was considered a reminder of heaven. H. F. Gould writes:

And sweetly secure from all pain they shall lie
Where dews gently fall, and the streams ripple by;
While the birds sing their hymns, amid airharps that sound
Thro' the boughs of the forest-tree whispering around.
And flowers bright as Eden's, at morning shall spread,
And at eve drop their leaves o'er the slumberer's bed.[58]

The Romantic metaphor for death was that of natural order and therefore death was to be accepted and even embraced as symbolic of the cycle of growth and decay and a source of succor and moral instruction related to family life. It was believed that shared mourning made for a unified family, which stood against profane society or the society of accumulation. Unable to mourn publicly with the extended community, the family enclosed itself in the sanctuary of the home and sought personalized and private location for the gravesite of their dead loved ones. Wilson Flagg cites an address delivered at the consecration of a rural cemetery which designates the burial site as "a school of both religion and philosophy" that has as its function to help "form the character, and govern the conduct of the living."[59]

The Late Nineteenth-Century Funeral

In the later decades of the nineteenth century, funerary customs became very elaborate. Whereas simple dress both for the deceased and the mourners was acceptable earlier, now the mourning costume became more pronounced and the rules of etiquette an unbreakable code. The simple shroud as the dress of the deceased was changed to the custom of clothing the body in the deceased person's best suit or dress. The simple coffin, made by the family or local carpenter, became a casket, named after a *casse,* a small chest or box used for jewels or other precious items. The casket, rather than being hexagonal and vaguely body-shaped, became rectangular, and some were mass produced in factories. Later caskets were enclosed in outer burial boxes and metal caskets appeared, some elaborately adorned with name plates and plumes. The simple wagon was replaced by the hearse, which became so ornate that it resembled a parade float.[60] The American spirit of the nineteenth century was to ignore, avoid, or disguise the forces of death and decay with whatever custumes, rituals and technologies were available. Expensive monuments, strict rules of etiquette and mourning costumes and jewelry, memorial cards and other paraphernalia became common.

By the close of the century the custom of the family, church and community caring for the deceased person's body was replaced, and the mortuary business was instituted. Prior to this time the body had been washed, dressed and laid out by family members and friends, who also dug the grave and buried the body. The nineteenth century ushered in the church sexton, and later the commercial funeral director took over his tasks. Respectability was connected with wealth, both in life and death, and it was essential that a family maintain the standards of its class in conducting a funeral for one of its members. The funeral, it was thought, might even add to one's social status. John Morley notes that even the poorest classes felt this way and illustrates his point stating that in 1843 it was reported that paupers at times were known to leave their youngsters' dead bodies in the street rather than accept the charity of a parish funeral.[61]

From Display to Denial

During the last years of the nineteenth century, however, the strict codes for mourning began to relax somewhat. Books of etiquette allowed more leeway in codes, dress and participation in rituals. The methods Americans used to cope with death began to change. Though still preoccupied with death and dying, Americans began denying it rather than embracing it. Even the use of the word "death" was avoided in literature and popular conversation and replaced by euphemisms. Not only did the nineteenth-century way of displaying death wane, but it was openly criticized. Popular literature advised that elaborate displays of grief were self-aggrandizing. Supported by official professional undertakers' associations, people began to bypass earlier customs, which were based on family-centered or community-related death rituals. "By . . . the twentieth century Americans were seeking different ways of reconciling the fact of death with what appeared to be the realities of time. . . . As they embarked on a new social journey, their principal method of accommodation assumed various forms but was basically simple denial."[62]

Direct exposure to death was minimized by the intervention of hospital and funeral parlor.   Therefore, the visibility of death, and hence its shock value, decreased.

Perpetual care of gravesites was also introduced further distancing mourner and deceased.   By the Second World War, only vestiges of the Victorian funeral remained.   Time and resources were diverted into channels other than saving for one's funeral.   Death could be more easily denied by the young because, death among the young became rarer. Most frequently, it was old people who died.   People openly criticized any display at funeral services.   Charles O. Jackson notes that, although the aspects of the funeral that are often attacked in the twentieth-century have always been around, "only the anger directed at them is new."[63] People of the twentieth century sometimes prefer no funeral service at all.   Jackson points out some of the difficulties that arise as a result of twentieth century death denial, for example, that the dying are treated as an embarrassment and alienated from the living. A system of death denial does not function very well as a death system because it does not help the community or the individual mourner to heal by shared expressions of grief; and when the connection between the communities of the living and the communities of the deceased is ignored, historical roots are lost.   In addition, Jackson says, if our roots in the past community of the dead are lost, death appears to become an absurdity, calling for further denial. Life, too, becomes absurd, and there is philosophical bankruptcy in the face of death. Jackson states that denial becomes entrenched; the longer the situation of denial is allowed to exist as a society's chief coping mechanism, the harder it is for the young to develop another.[64]

BROKEN IMAGES

. . .the final terror of self-consciousness
is the knowledge of one's own death.
                              Ernest Becker

As the Victorian age began to wane, some thought progress, at least in the sciences, had reached its peak and that there were few if any discoveries left to be made. Some professors of physics were advising their graduate students to switch to other fields that might offer more promise. At the end of the nineteenth century the head of the United States Patent Office recommended that the office be abolished because everything that could be invented had already been invented.

But the twentieth century brought new surprises. One of the most significant was Einstein's theory of relativity, published in 1905. New metaphors for time were in the making; amidst all the ferment of the age those who would formulate new models of aging and dying were at work. Quantum physics, which was launched at the beginning of this century, brought startling discoveries that would seriously challenge the mechanistic view of reality. However, the general public did not understand relativity and was, through the first half of this century, largely unaware of discoveries in quantum physics. Not until the detonation of the atomic bomb near Alamogordo, New Mexico, on July 16, 1945 would the implications of the atomic age begin to intrude on Western world-consciousness.

Almost from its beginning the twentieth century witnessed periods of disruption and division. The First World War was brutal with its use of poison gas and the slaughter of innocent civilians. Between the World Wars there was a short period of euphoria, a boom in economic growth. It was a frenetic era known as the Roaring Twenties. But this quickly came to an end with the Wall Street panic of 1929, which led to the Great Depression of the 1930s. In Germany, it was the pledge to quell this economic crisis that helped launch Adolf Hitler on his march to absolute power. Soon the depression was offset by an escalation in the production of weapons as nations prepared for a new conflagration. In the Second

World War old rules were abandoned as nations depended on cost-efficient delivery systems of destruction such as rockets and bombers. Whole cities, with millions of inhabitants, were destroyed. Not even the elderly and sick were spared. With the images of Auschwitz and Hiroshima, the specter of mass death and the human capacity for limitless destruction lodged itself in the public consciousness.

Out of the chaos and horror of the two world wars a different philosophical focus emerged. "Existentialism" became a catch-all term that focused on general discontent and the tragic and disordered state of the world. The new image-makers rejected absolutist ideologies and distrusted the facile answers provided by nineteenth-century deterministic materialism. Existentialism represented a search for meaningful actions in an absurd and meaningless universe. It was not a philosophy, but a label for many divergent forms of revolt against traditional thinking. Though it cannot be reduced to set philosophical tenets, the very refusal of the existentialists to accept any body of beliefs, especially systematic metaphysics and normative ethics, appealed to a world that was beginning to question traditional values. A new song of the self was heard echoing Dostoevesky's *Notes from the Underground* (1914). This time it was not the classical, biblical, or romantic version of the self, but a wretched and anguished self. In his influential work, *The Wall* (1939), Jean-Paul Sartre fused existential motifs of loneliness, the absence of meaning and mindless brutality to depict an indifferent universe. Sartre's agonized reflections on commitment, dread and confrontation with death are brought to life by his personal experience as a soldier and fighter in the French Resistance movement. Anxiety over human mortality and the constant threat of self-deception in the face of adverse power are familiar themes for existentialist writers, but if any primary concept pervaded their thought, it was the sovereignty of individual choice as a central fact of human nature. Conveying their ideas in essays, novels, plays and poetry, these thinkers were heard throughout the Western world. Their themes reverberated in psychiatry, psychology and religion. Albert Camus, who won the Nobel Prize in literature in 1957 for his book, *The Plague*, wrote repeatedly about violence, absurdity and death. He called on the world to strengthen the dignity of life and death and dispense with worn-out ideologies.[1] Old images were being broken, old mirrors shattered. New model makers were already working to integrate the fragmented reflections of those who had looked death in the face and taken temporality and the human condition seriously. A new covenant was being established between the self and time.

At Harvard University, Alfred North Whitehead (1861-1947) was formulating his new philosophy of organism. The same center of intellectual activity had spawned pragmatism, later known as contextualism, a school of thought that took the human temporal situation as its touchstone. It originated from the ideas of Charles Pierce, revised by William James and later by Stephen C. Pepper, Nelson Goodman and others. Contextualists saw philosophical systems as hypotheses that allowed people to make sense of their world and help solve human problems. They saw philosophy as a way of world-making.

This chapter will review the contributions of several philosophers who, reacting to the dilemmas of modern life, explored the weaknesses of what they saw as old philosophical models with reified metaphors. This necessitates a brief return to Augustine the philosopher-theologian whose ideas regarding time have led some to cite him as a forerunner of existentialist thought. Next the discussion will turn to Martin Heidegger, whose philosophical work powerfully influenced the existentialists. Heidegger rethought the ideas of time in the history of philosophy and led the way to the reevaluation of the concept of time in the second half of the twentieth century. Along with Albert North Whitehead and Stephen Pepper, Heidegger recognized the bankruptcy of mechanism and the need for a way of thinking in which time would be given a human dimension. Lastly it is important to mention the development of quantum physics in the first half of this century and the part it played in preparing the groundwork for what may become a significant shift in Western attitudes toward aging and dying.

IN YOU, O MY MIND, I MEASURE TIME[2]

Augustine's ideas about time belong more to modern philosophical thought than to the fourth and fifth centuries in which he lived. For this reason these ideas are best discussed as an introduction to the models of time that were proposed by Heidegger, Whitehead and Pepper.

Stepping outside his Neoplatonic model, which dictated that time was a perpetually revolving image of eternity, Augustine took a revolutionary step by searching for the meaning of time in human experience. In his passionate self-examination, in the *Confessions* we can almost hear him thinking aloud about the riddle of time. Crying out with an almost existential anxiety, wondering whether his own inability to express his experience of time was not the problem: "By 'not knowing' do I perhaps mean simply that I do not know how to express something which is in fact known to me?"[3] Augustine's search led him to the conclusion that time was so inextricably tied to the mind that the two could not be separated without the loss of the distinctive character of human experience itself.

Observing the need for a new approach to the subject of time, Augustine proceeded to express his concept in a metaphor that had a modern ring. The mind, he claimed, "distends" itself so that past and future can exist in the present; thus time can be perceived and measured. By careful inspection, Augustine struck on the internal character of the temporal process. Playing out his analogy, he saw time as nothing else than an extension, perhaps "an extension of the mind itself."[4] Next, Augustine searched in his own experience for the answer to what this meant and came to the conclusion that time is the consciousness of a certain duration, which cannot be exhaustively defined in passive spatial terms. Time is an active stretching out of the mind as it performs three functions: expecting future events, attending to present events and remembering past events.[5] It seemed to Augustine that time is the endurance and identity of the mind's experience of these three acts of expectation, attention and memory. Augustine further argued that it is only for creatures who can perform these acts that time possesses direction. Events by themselves have no direction. Nature, in itself, possesses no history. Only the soul is capable of observing history. Therefore, only in human lifetimes could either tragedy or fulfillment occur. The human perspective, Augustine argued, is not analogous to the passive wax that received the imprint of the signet ring. The mind is dynamic. The subject experiences itself as tying together past-present-future.

Augustine observed that although in our own minds we seem to know what we mean by time, there still remains an element of mystery in it. We talk paradoxically as if past and future exist in the present, but we also recognize that we stand at a point on a time line with past as finished and future as not yet. Augustine claimed that while the present is all that is really available to us, it still appears that there are three times: "A present of things past, a present of things present and a present of things future."[6] With an anguished cry over this seemingly impossible inconsistency, Augustine asked: "What, then, is time? I know what it is if no one asks me what it is; but if I want to explain it to someone who has asked me, I find that I do not know."[7] The origin of this apparent paradox may be found in Augustine's entering the perilous straits that Descartes tried to pilot, into the choppy waters of mixed metaphors, or the shifting images of time. While he retained his old commitment to the Judeo-Christian model of historical time, interpreted quantitatively in Aristotelian fashion, Augustine simultaneously insisted on a new approach to time, with its locus in the continuity of the individual self as it stretched into the future. Hans Georg Gadamer refers to this as the "ontological paradox of time . . . which can never be in the present and yet is nothing but a succession of all-consuming presents, the light of the inner experience which the soul has of itself as it presses on to meet the future."[8]

Augustine's unexpected connection between time and active consciousness is reminiscent of Aristotle's question about measuring without a measurer and time's relationship to the soul. Augustine disagreed with Aristotle's answer that time is external and objective by claiming, "It is in you, my mind, that I measure time."[9] In the last analysis, however, Augustine made a truce with objective time. Like Aristotle, he could not escape his prior commitments. For Augustine, the psychological element was ultimately swallowed up in a metaphysical and religious model.

From then until the rise of modern philosophy, time either was not a subject for discussion or was simply interpreted under the Aristotelian and later the Newtonian objective and spatial model. It would take the Copernican Revolution of Kant to throw a spotlight on internalized time once again in order to challenge what has been called "The quasi-divine power of the human mind to know necessary and changeless truths that exist beyond time."[10] It would take twentieth-century philosophers to spell out a theory whereby human transcendence of time amounted to more than a Platonic escape from it or a Newtonian quantification of it.

HEIDEGGER: TIME AND DEATH

Martin Heidegger (1889-1976) in his foundational work *Being and Time* spoke with a previously unheard of force, sharpness and depth about the inextricable connection between the self, the limits of time, and dying.[11] The questions Heidegger posed about death and the human experience of the passage of time gave focus to many of the concerns that plagued the Western mind in the early twentieth century. Heidegger stated that his aim in *Being and Time* was to investigate "Time as a possible horizon for any understanding whatsoever of Being."[12] Thus he used as the centerpiece of his system of thought Kant's first principle: the primacy of the temporal dimension of human experience. Guided by this central insight, Heidegger determined his field of focus and then went further than Kant, pointing out that the very existence that the self carves out is essentially achieved through time-bound experience.

In illustrating the link between the self and time, Heidegger drew a careful distinction between persons and things. Unlike persons, things endure through time, that is, their relation to time is an external one. They exist in time as a block of wood exists in space. Humans, on the other hand, are conscious of time having an internal relation with the passing of events.[13] Kant had retained the Newtonian model of time and suggested that the work of the transcendental self was to string together separate moments into a unity, like pearls into a necklace. Heidegger rejected decisively this model of time. When examined in its actual context, he reasoned, the self does not experience momentary segments; time is not lived in bits and pieces. Actual life experience, he insisted, recalling Augustine's metaphor, is found stretched out in durational spreads.

Heidegger focused on the self as the subjective ground of human awareness. It is the self that gives unity to the past, present and future by the way it defines these experiences for itself. The past is conceived of in personal terms as part of the present because, like a treasure chest, it can be retrieved, seized and broken open. Unlike the old Newtonian model, the past is never simply over and gone, but is vital in the present. For example, Heidegger argues that what human beings have grown up with, as their traditional way of interpreting themselves and their world, becomes the way they understand the present and the way they interpret the possibilities of the future.[14] The past is not important to the present only insofar as it has aftereffects on the present situation; rather the person *is* his past, his *own past*. All the events that have taken place in his life he carries along into the present, and these events steer him toward the future.

Heidegger believed the future is part of the present. He called this ability of the human being to project himself into the future "anticipatory resoluteness." We can draw our future toward us, helping to bring it about. Out of all the possibilities that could have been selected, the commitment of our time, our plans and energies, helps bring a specific future into being. Together, Heidegger concluded, the past, present and future function in terms of enabling possibility.[15] In characterizing time as "durational spreads," Heidegger unfolded his thesis about the human dimension of time: persons as selectors of possibilities give these possibilities their meaning and their life. What is crucial is not only the awareness that such choices are possible, but also a recognition that they are not value-free, but involve personal preferences. Similarly, societies must act as "shepherds of being," choosing alternatives about what the future will be. Individuals, nations and united nations make peace or war, harmony or holocausts. Heidegger's picture of human involvement in time:

is that of a moving field of focus directed by what is of interest or concern, which at any point lights up what is yet ahead of us-- like the light on a miner's cap which *now* illuminates the path on which he *will* walk bringing his habits from the *past* into the walking.[16]

As the person selects his way, certain paths "stand out" before him.

This selection process was the key to Heidegger's concept of human freedom, a freedom that was intimately tied to his concept of time. But Heidegger in no way insisted that human beings are possessed of unlimited freedom. On the contrary, the fact that humans are creatures of time presents a limit situation from which there is no escape. Heidegger believed that the human person, in making certain choices, is limited by his own temporal situation. Each judgment, once made, becomes an unalterable, irrevocable historical fact; his past cannot be undone, repeated, or changed. When presented with numerous possibilities, for example, a choice of many paths, a person cannot, because of his temporality, choose all of them, but must walk one at a time. In addition, the selection of one involves the rejection, at least for the moment, of all the rest. Thus time not only makes the future open, but also is the inherent limit of temporal beings.

Heidegger not only recognized the limits of human freedom; he also acknowledged the common human condition, which sometimes neglects to take hold of the future. At times people forget that they have the choice of constructing their world and therefore weaken their essential forward drive. This happens inevitably while they attend to the distracting cares of everyday life and to the things and people that surround them. Running after this thing and that, they live in a world darkened by their forgetfulness of who they are and of what being is. One example of this is found in the commonsense way of using clocks and calendars. The ordinary way of characterizing time lies in an endless sequence of "nows" that pass away. The natural justification for this treatment of time is the need for a public rubric coordinating common efforts in order to bring the shared possibilities of the community into reality.[17] Though such an interpretation of time is understandable and useful, it must be remembered that it causes us to forget time's character as a durational spread that is primarily focused on the future.[18] "The only time one knows is public time," says Heidegger, "which has been leveled off and which belongs to everyone--and that means to nobody."[19] This interpretation of time forgets to avail itself of the distinction between things and persons and covers up distinctions of value and significance.[20]

Heidegger, who prized authenticity, pointed out the shortcomings of this kind of interpretation of time that spawns "averageness." He therefore invoked the human dimension of time, which prizes individual differences and insisted that without it the genuineness of the self is scattered. If he were writing today, Heidegger would no doubt recognize this scatteredness as even more pronounced. Public time with its stress on the immediate moment, compartmentalized into a three-minute news spot or a thirty-second television commercial, offering an instant technological solution, supports the contemporary image of "the public," reduced to its least common denominator and measured in statistical

averages.   For years, Heidegger, a critic of "frenzied technology," lived
the simple life of a peasant on a mountaintop in Germany's Black Forest.

Death: A View from the Mountaintop

Because of Heidegger's direct and intimate alliance of time, death
and the self, he focused on the highly personal character of death.
Human beings, he claimed, are related to their future as always holding
out the possibility of being no more. Yet death is most often treated in
an abstract way as "all men are mortal" or seen as happening to those
others about whom we read in the headlines. But death must also be
anticipated by the individual who reads these words. Heidegger believed
that a person can be authentic or take charge of his own possibilities
only if he can recognize his own temporal limits. One can unify his
past, present and future if he can live in a manner that recognizes his
debt to the past, his own present capacity for limited choice and his
limited future, that is, if he can recognize his mortal nature.
Temporality, and hence mortality, were for Heidegger man's characteristic
mode of being. Though *Being and Time* did not have death as its central
theme, it explored human temporal existence and focused on death as one
feature of man in which he is powerless over possibilities of the future.
As time was a mystery to Augustine, death was a mystery for Heidegger
because as a mystery, it could not be simply solved. Thus Heidegger
called death an "open wound." The very thought of death can either be
forgotten or denied, or, instead, awareness of the possibility of dying
can force a person to take another path, that is, to transcend his own
ordinary boundaries.

Heidegger believed that anticipation of the experience of death
could afford a privileged place, a kind of mountaintop view, because in
the diminishments of time, in the losses that come with aging, and in the
experience of the very process of time passing, there is a human tendency
to *"dread,"*[21] which pushes a person to see time for what it is in a
subjective sense:

> But just as he who flees in the face of death is pursued by it even
> as he evades it, and just as in turning away from it, he must see
> it, nonetheless even the innocuous infinite series of "nows"' which
> simply runs its course, imposes itself 'on' the human person in a
> remarkably enigmatical way.[22]

Dying, for Heidegger, was not an event that took place once at the
point that is the end of life. One must distinguish between death and
dying. Dying is what determines and embraces the totality of human
experience. A recognition of the reality of time and mortality can offer
a chance for a definitive breakthrough in one's life. Awareness of dying
can serve to pull life together and make possible what Heidegger calls
"authentic living." As a person looks at life and anticipates its
ending, he realizes, according to Heidegger, that life in its entirety is
life facing dying. Awareness of dying lifts one out of scurrying self-
forgetfulness to a larger vision of himself and others. Dread alone
brings with it a kind of freedom, transforming the bleak "nows" of time
into the essential possibilities of being itself. In Heidegger's own
words: "We are set free from illusions . . . in passionate, self-assured,

anxious freedom to death."[23]   Yet Heidegger believed that there was a
difficulty in a person accepting his own dying and understanding it as
something experienced.   He gave an example of this point. Neighbors and
friends, he said, often try to convince a dying person that he will
surely escape death.   They attempt to console him, "tranquilizing him
into everydayness."   Thus, they forbid the dying persons from having the
"courage of anxiety in the face of death."[24]

People often treat death as a social inconvenience. Talk about
death is considered tactless.   The public is always on guard against
awareness of the potential of dying in order to protect itself.   It may
be that in the death of others, one can first experience what is closest
to one's own death.   In seeing someone else die, the persons around can
come to grasp better the difference between life and not-being-there-any-
more.   Millions of war survivors vicariously experienced dying in the
deaths of loved ones.

Like many thinkers of his day Heidegger, in confronting the human
person's experience of dying, did not allow himself to seek refuge in
teleological or theological schemes.   For him, questions about afterlife,
for example, did not arise, God, Heidegger believed, was simply too heavy
for his philosophy.   In spite of this fact, Heidegger's influence has
been strongly felt in the field of theology as seen in the writings of
Rudolf Bultman (1884-1976) and Paul Tillich (1886-1965). Many of his
insights have also affected psychologists such as Ludwig Binswanger (1881-
1966) and Abraham Maslow (1908-1970).   Terms such as "dread," "anxiety,"
or "authenticity," were later made popular by Sartre's writings, which
brought a peak of popularity to existentialism in the 1950s, especially
in Europe.   Regardless of the fact that this peak passed, Heidegger's
thought has maintained itself and has continued to attract attention both
in Europe and America.   Charles Sherover notes that, as with Kant,
whether one agrees with him or not, one must come to terms with
Heidegger's analysis of human temporality: "We can no longer detour
around him. . . . Whether it [this account] is to be accepted, corrected
or repudiated, it would seem that, because of its extensive reach and
foundational nature, it provides the ground from which our discussions
must henceforth proceed."[25]   Heidegger's prominent theme--one must learn
to experience dying as a dimension of authentic living--stands on its own
and has had a profound influence.   This was the theme picked up by the
extentialists who insisted that one must concern oneself with death in
order to live well, and this did counteract in some way the twentieth-
century taboo on the subject of death.   It also brought into focus,
within the philosophical arena, the human experience of time and choice
in explicit relationship to aging and dying.

WHITEHEAD: CREATIVITY AND THE PASSAGE OF NATURE

In the late 1920s, while Heidegger, still in his thirties, was
writing *Being and Time*, Alfred North Whitehead, a man in his sixties, was
producing one of his major works, *Process and Reality*.   He had already
retired from the University of London and moved to America.   Three of
Whitehead's most significant contributions were written after his
retirement, but then, Whitehead never really retired.   At sixty-three he
became professor of philosophy at Harvard University and at seventy-six,

as professor emeritus, he continued to write and discuss ideas with
students, colleagues and friends. In 1945, at eighty-four, he received
the highest honor the British crown bestows on a man of learning, the
Order of Merit.

Whitehead's works laid the foundation for process philosophy and a
new cosmology that would profoundly affect philosophical ideas on time.
His background in science and his experience with mathematics and physics
had long caused Whitehead to question the Newtonian view of the universe,
which he believed continued to misinform the modern mind as it had the
mind of the seventeenth century. To Whitehead, feelings of anxiety and
displacement in the modern world were the legacy of this image of the
universe as a vast machine, "soundless, scentless and colorless," as it
rushed on its way "endlessly and meaninglessly."[26] The new picture that
quantum physics projected was of a world of creativity and change.
Therefore, to a philosopher like Whitehead, for whom the beauty and value
of life were so important, it made sense to conceive of the natural world
not as a machiné but as a society whose members were in process. He
maintained that nature's central principles were obscured by the methods
of classical physics that proceeds from the microscopic or atomic level
of nature, that is, from parts to the general laws of nature. Classical
physics, he argued, reduces the whole to the sum of its parts. He
enjoyed quoting his favorite poet, Wordsworth, who had insisted that the
important facts of nature elude scientific method. Working from the
lower levels to the higher, it is hard to account for free will,
creativity and anything else but determinism and predictability. If
scientists and thinkers work in the other direction, beginning with human
experience, Whitehead believed, a universe of novelty and interdependence
that is in a constant process of transformation is readily disclosed.

It is the unique privilege of the human person, through philosophy,
Whitehead insisted, to focus on the whole and recapture the totality out
of temporal experience. Hence it is not only possible but necessary to
synthesize science and the arts, religion and physics within a coherent
global view that is equipped to tell the whole, ongoing story of the
human experience of the world. Whitehead was not a narrow specialist; he
was well informed in many fields and sensitive to the entire spectrum of
human culture. He found it impossible to accept scientific materialism
and did not believe physical nature or life could be understood unless
they were fused together. One of his major interests was in attempting
to reconcile science and the humanities. Whitehead's wife, Evelyn
Willoughby Wade, had a profound effect on his interest in morals and
aesthetics. She believed that great art and literature best expressed the
essential values of life in a world that her husband (like Heraclitus)
described as "never the same twice."[27] The very spirit of process
thought supported the conviction that no absolute view of the world would
ever be acceptable. Whitehead put this strongly: "How shallow, puny and
imperfect our efforts to sound the depths in the nature of things. In
philosophical discussion, the merest hint of dogmatic certainty . . . is
an exhibition of folly."[28] Philosophical understanding enlightens us as
to a portion of experience, but there is no privileged comprehension of a
final scheme that describes nature as a whole. "The proper test" of a
successful philosophical system, Whitehead said, "is not finality, but
progress."[29]

Reviewing the history of philosophy in *Science and the Modern World*, Whitehead argued that one of the most dangerous of all mentalities in Western thought had developed in the sixteenth century with the rise of modern science. It was the Renaissance discovery of Newtonian time. This phenomenon, he insisted, was not so much a change in conceptual definitions as a general shift in the fundamental tone of thought among intellectuals.   It   was   an   alteration   in   basic   metaphysical presuppositions.   The shift took the form of a passionate interest in detailed and irreducible facts coupled with an equally avid devotion to the search for the timeless laws of nature.[30] For the classical and contemporary scientist as well, Whitehead pointed out, physical laws of nature became the decrees of fate, the solemn and remorseless workings of the way things are. This absolutist view, accompanied and supported by linear Newtonian time, buttressed the conviction that future events were totally predictable.   A firm conviction followed: by examining past causes, determined effects could be foreseen with absolute certainty. Once established,   this dictum became the force behind scientific research.   As a result, Westerners, Whitehead argued, had come to trust that it was surely possible, at least at some future time, to unlock all the secrets of nature.   His philosophy stands as a challenge to the assumptions behind these views.

Whitehead found especially irksome the unwillingness of science to admit philosophy's role in the investigation of the nature of reality. This dismissal, he charged, was grounded in the solid conviction that science, exclusively, dealt with absolute facts and thereby revealed objective laws of the real world of nature, while philosophy was associated with the sphere of the mind and intuition. He pointed out the origin of this bifurcation in concepts of time and duration in Descartes' system of absolutes, which caused science to take charge of material nature, seen as reality, while philosophy was relegated to cogitating. Refusing to accept this traditional mind-body split, Whitehead argued that human experience was incorporated in the very nature of reality as a whole, a reality which he described as a universe of creativity and interdependence.   It was the task of philosophy, he believed, to provide a coherent and consistent description of this dynamic process.

At the heart of Whitehead's unique approach was a basic opposition to both the Newtonian scheme of classical physics and the continuation of the ancient dream that a gods'-eye view, knowledge of the fixed and absolute laws of nature, was within the power of mortal man. Whitehead reversed the standard approach to reality, leaving behind the reductionist dogma, which began with facts excluding the observer and which proceeded from those facts to certitudes and general laws. Whitehead believed that human time is incorporated into reality as a whole because temporal experience and the general principles of the universe are irrevocably tied together.   "Speculative philosophy," he said, "is the endeavor to frame a coherent and necessary system of general ideas in terms of which every element of our experience can be interpreted."[31]

Whitehead therefore selected the metaphor of an organism, a unified living system in which the parts are functionally related to the whole, both giving and receiving support from the whole. For Whitehead, everything in reality, except God, the immanent "urge" toward creativity,

was not only interrelated with, but occasioned or caused by, other
events. The basis of this concept was the principle of relativity:
nothing can be conceived in abstraction from the system as a whole.
Whitehead had shown great interest in Albert Einstein's theory of
relativity but felt it needed radical revisions. Therefore, in 1922, he
published his own theory, *The Principle of Relativity*. (For experimental
reasons, physicists preferred Einstein's version.)

Whitehead argued that the Newtonian concept of time was no longer
satisfactory for interpreting the world because it placed a limit on
nature by stressing the immediate present as the only field for creative
activity. Such a system with all its exactitude, he said, "has all the
completeness of thought of the Middle Ages, which had a complete answer
for everything, be it in heaven or in hell or in nature. There is a
trimness about it, with its instantaneous present, its vanished past, its
non-existent future and its inert matter."[32] Whitehead insisted that
this compartmentalized and abstract interpretation of time is found
neither in human experience nor in nature. In Whitehead, as in Heidegger
there are echoes of Augustine. One can only experience duration in the
form of temporal "breadths" and there is no present shared by everyone:
"What we perceive as present is the vivid fringe of memory tinged with
anticipation."[33] Therefore, in place of the neat reality of classical
physics, Whitehead offered a theory that admitted of greater ultimate
mystery. Hence it is not, in the fixed instant of present reality, but in
the very "passage" of nature itself in alliance with the "passage" of
mind that reality is brought about. For Whitehead, it is not in an
absolute knowledge or a totally predictable future, but in the whole
temporal process of birth, aging and death that the highest levels of
creative advancement can be realized.

The Life-Death Paradox

Whitehead saw all things that come to be as perpetually perishing.
He saw nature as a passage in which the "successors sum up their
predecessors."[34] For Whitehead, this passage is not into nothingness,
and perpetual perishing is not death because the principle of universal
relativity forces us to focus not on the individual components, but the
whole, which is an enduring society. One generation of events bears
within it the next. Therefore, it has sense of worth beyond itself, and
this sense of worth is immediately enjoyed as an overpowering element in
individual attainment. Whatever sorrow and pain is brought about by the
passage of time is transformed into "an element of triumph."[35] This is
part of the ultimate paradox at the heart of creative reality for
Whitehead, a paradox that, while unfathomable and inexplicable, still
urges us to further understanding: "Thus the universe is to be conceived
as attaining the active self-expression of its own variety of opposites .
. . its own freedom and its own necessity, its multiplicity and unity,
its imperfection and perfection. All the opposites are elements in the
nature of things and are incorrigibly there."[36] It is not in cracking
the paradox, but in accepting it, Whitehead said, that transformation
comes about. It is not in fathoming nature completely, but in admitting
the limitations and restrictions of human experience that freedom is to
be furthered. This is seen particularly when we ponder the puzzle of
time. As Whitehead expressed this, "It is impossible to meditate on time

and the mysteries of the creative passage of nature without overwhelming emotion at the limitations of human intelligence."[37]

REDISCOVERING TIME IN QUANTUM PHYSICS

Since Whitehead's process model of temporal reality was constructed in the first half of this century in the context of advances in quantum physics and since a call for a rediscovery of time is coming today from that quarter, it is appropriate to turn to some of the main principles of quantum physics related to time and anti-absolutist models of philosophy. Ilya Prigogine, who won the Nobel Prize in 1977 for his far-reaching theory explaining self-organizing systems (which appear to give unification to the sciences of chemistry, biology and physics), comments in his recent book, *Order out of Chaos*, that the new conception of time in science "gives a new content to the speculations of Whitehead and Heidegger."[38] A summary of the general direction, still relatively new, of the changes taking place in that area is necessary to establish the basis of a process model of aging and dying. Prigogine sums up the general shift in this way: "We are in a period of scientific revolution-- one in which the very position and meaning of the scientific approach are undergoing reappraisal--a period not unlike the birth of the scientific approach in ancient Greece or of its renaissance in the time of Galileo."[39]

When Max Karl Planck (1858-1947) released his new formula in 1901, the quantum age was launched. Quantum physics soon revealed certain limitations and inconsistencies in the Newtonian mechanical picture of matter and motion. The first inconsistency originated from the mechanistic view of the motion of a body as a continuous trajectory of changing positions, matter flowing from one point to another in linear fashion. On the subatomic level, matter behaved in a different way. Electrons appeared to jump from one place to another in what was called a quantum leap, seeming not to pass through the space in between. This phenomenon was discovered by the Danish physicist Niels Bohr (1885-1962), who later was an important advisor on the atomic bomb project. In science, when a phenomenon appears that does not fit with the existing model, it may be judged as simply a misreading of data. "It didn't happen!" because "It is impossible!" Or, if the phenomenon continues to occur, it may be taken as a sign that the model needs revision. In this case, a revision in the concepts of matter and motion were required.

A second problem was generated from the classical view of the methods of research. In science it has been customarily thought, almost indisputably, that objective observation is not only possible but necessary. It was seen as a superior method of gaining scientific knowledge. The neutral observer was thus the key in understanding the facts or the absolute truth about physical matters. But the quantum physicist has come to admit that what one observes seems to depend on the instrument used in the experiment. A person seeing the world through rose-colored glasses sees a rose-colored world. The glasses filter the evidence and color the facts just as the instrument used structures the findings, and, in that sense, disturbs the results. Though scientists believe that they should work with as much objectivity as possible, they can no longer count on a passive observer separated from the instrument.

A third inconsistency originated from the acceptance of classical categories of the laws of nature and the facts. In the past it was assumed that man could eventually come to the end of an exhaustible set of nature's secrets, since the universe was seen as a whole and the whole was seen as the sum of its parts. Therefore, given enough time, total control of nature by means of science was possible. Ever since the sixteenth and seventeenth centuries the optimistic hope was nurtured that through the formulation of the scientific method, with its attendant concepts of absolute time, all ignorance, inconsistency and mystery would eventually be wiped out. It was assumed that this would be done by putting together the pieces of the giant puzzle of nature thereby revealing a determined and totally predictable future course. The inconsistency appeared when quantum physicists disclosed their conviction that the order of nature involves more than an objective and predictable world. The very concept of an atom, they thought, may reveal as much about the observer's way of seeing as it does about the observed.

This brings up the most foundational disagreement between the Newtonian model and the quantum model. The basic definition of change in classical physics involves reversibility. It necessitates a spatial metaphor, the purpose of which is to explain the "room" in which things change. One author calls this the invention of "philosopher's space."[40] Not only does the classical model tell how things change as cause leads to effect, but it is responsible to account for the reverse: effect is traced to cause. As with Aristotle's concept of eternal cyclical movement, the thesis of reversibility in Newton's physics is a logical, not a physical thesis. John Lucas says: "Reversibility is like homogeneity, a stipulation that we impose on a science of things. It reveals a further facet of our concept of 'thinginess.' Things are thought of as manipulable, subject to our wills. 'Glory to Man in the Highest,' sang Swinburne, 'for He is the master of things.'"[41] Whitehead insisted that a minute or an hour is not part of the actual experience of time. These categories are imposed artificially because they prove useful, but it is often forgotten that *they were created by model-makers*. Reversible time is not part of our experience of the world. Lucas puts it this way: "Change is different from time. Not even the gods can make the past not have happened. They cannot *cancel* past events."[42] In the classical scheme, reversibility is strictly an event that takes place in the mind, the world is seen as a conglomeration of things that can be manipulated, as can mathematical formulas. The "thing-world," aimless and lacking in direction, is a timeless world in the sense that the "out there" is cut off from the "in here" although manipulable by us (or by the God in whom Newton believed so firmly). But without us or God the world is a meaningless or aimless thing from which we get the feeling of being lost in a directionless machine of push and pull rules. According to Lucas: "Man having made himself the master of things, cannot complain against them that they . . . are indifferent to values. For that is just how we wanted them to be."[43]

But with the reinsertion of time into the model and the acceptance of many different concepts of time, a new sense of responsibility is abroad that ties model-making to the acceptance of model limits. The classical model has lost its sense of the forward, ongoing duration of time common to our experience. If it is a problem that the universe is abstract and dull or lifeless and devoid of value through the lens of

Newtonianism, then perhaps the solution can be found in a model revision.

Erwin Schrödinger (1887-1961), a physicist who is known for posing philosophical questions about the role of consciousness in the evolution of life, referred in his essay *What is Life*? to the "principle of objectification" or the "hypothesis of the real world" as a simplification we accept in everyday life for of practical reasons. But the fact that we habitually exclude ourselves from the world creates, he believed, unsolvable problems. He claimed we construct, by our own imagination, the concept of objectivity: "We step back into the part of an onlooker, who does not belong to the world, which by this very procedure becomes an objective world."[44] Our dream of freedom through objectivity has cost us a very dear price, according to Schrödinger. The world we created by our wish for such neutrality is a "colorless, cold, mute place." Instead of freedom we find ourselves behind the bars of Cartesian dualism searching for the "illusive place" where mind acts on matter and matter acts on mind.[45] In this way time itself as well as mind is lost to the world because in order to eliminate imagination and get to the facts, the scientist imagines he can take up a gods'-eye view somewhere outside the world. Ironically, all this takes place, Schrodinger mused, without his even knowing it, that is, it is assumed unconsciously. Schrödinger insisted that physicists and other thinkers must come to terms with the limits of their capacity to understand and to conceptualize nature.

Classical physics harbored certain hidden philosophical biases and thus matter came to be defined as reducible to particles which were pictured as localized, that is, occupying a well-defined region of space. But in the experiments of quantum physicists, an electron, for example, when "observed" by means of one instrument appeared as a particle or tiny spot, but through another instrument it appeared as a wave, spread over wider regions of space, or in many locations at the same instant. Schrödinger's special wave theory described an electron in still another way, as an invisible rope which widened as it spread in time. In this case the electron behaved like both a particle and a wave. In 1920 Werner Heisenberg recognized, in his Uncertainty Principle, that such conceptions were, in fact, several versions of the same thing. The scientist's observation by means of different instruments was responsible for different results and the presence of an observer, as a kind of instrument, was disruptive. The observer, in that sense, changed the results. What is more basic, quantum physicists came to agree, is that there is no way to have observerless observation, no way to catch nature in her act. Simultaneously philosophers like Whitehead and Heidegger were coming to see that there was no conceptual system that was assumptionless.

There will always be, Heisenberg concluded, indeterminacy or uncertainty on the electron level. Predictions must depend on statistical of probabilistic descriptions at least on the atomic level. Norwood R. Hanson, philosopher of science, put it this way: "The impossibility of visualizing ultimate matter is an essential feature of atomic explanation."[46] Without a clear way to visualize the ultimate unit of matter, we are left with mathematical laws only and no other way of conceptualizing what exactly is the substance of matter. Motion of individual particles was eliminated in favor of averages. This

statistical averaging washes out details. Ability to speak about
subatomic particles at all means speaking in general--another filter!
What the quantum physicist found was that all instruments, including
human perception and thoughts, have intrinsic limits. In other words,
there were no completely objective data available to either to the
philosopher's mind or the scientist's eye. What is more, some scientists
came to think that acceptance of this apparent limitation may even prove
to be a decided advantage because it might free the scientific mind to
realize higher levels of creative advancement. A new image of reality
might be conceived, the root metaphor of which would embrace temporal
evolution and reinsert human time into the model. Knowledge itself might
be redefined as a form of evolution in conceptual systems.

Nevertheless, these discoveries seemed to some to lead to a
paradoxical bind. The realization that absolute reality seemed to be
unavailable because of the mind's need to package reality or construct
hypotheses or because of the scientist's need for instruments that
disturb the results of experiments, seemed to lead to the shocking
conclusion that in some way the mind or the instruments created reality.
In *Ways of Worldmaking*, the philosopher Nelson Goodman, emeritus from
Harvard University, states it this way: "If worlds are as much made as
found, so also knowing is as much remaking as reporting. All the
processes of worldmaking . . . enter into knowing. Discovering laws
involves drafting them. Regarding patterns is very much a matter of
inventing and imposing them. Comprehension and creation go together."[47]

Further shocking questions arose: Are these quantum physicists
falling into the solipsist trap of subjectivity? If there are no totally
objective criteria for discerning truth among rival hypotheses, does it
mean that bias is allowed free sway? What about the longstanding belief
in the progress of science? Is that a myth, too? Clearly, neither
Whitehead nor physicists such as Heisenberg or Schrödinger took such a
solipsistic position, claiming reality is a product of the mind. The
source of confusion is found when one compares the classical model of
reality with the process model. In the classical model the world was
seen as what is "out there." The process model does not separate the
observer and his world, the "out there" from the "in here," the object
from the subject.

The question "Does the mind create reality?" asked within the
classical model of physics translates to the query: "Can the mind create
the world 'out there'?" Barring magic, the answer must be "No!" But the
same question asked within Whiteheadian categories assumes that the world
"out there" and "in here" are *one* world. This concept is related to the
laboratory situation where the observer is part of the equipment, because
the results tell about the observer as well as the observed.

With the findings of quantum physics the world is the same as it was
before, but the way it is symbolized is different. In post-classical
physics the mind is no longer seen as constructing symbols that mirror
the world as a map is used to reflect the terrain. *The scientist is the
mirror.* As the maker of theories he is forced to admit that there are
philosophical assumptions behind scientific concepts. Thus the world is
seen as an open system in which the scientist is co-creator.
Transformation is built into the model, change comes to be the principle

of principles. In this model, human understanding of the way the world
works is indefinitely open to revision. The admission that there is no
final certitude not only allows for change, but also helps bring it
about.

In the quantum physicist's version of the world the aim of science
is still to be as objective as possible. But unlike a mere calculus, it
recognizes the ethical parameters of its projects. Scientists, in using
one model or another, especially where the matter touches on the lives of
human beings and societies and especially where science has so much to
say about matters of life and death, must choose in accord with
philosophical priorities. Though the roles of scientist and philosopher
are distinct, they are not incompatible. The two can work hand in hand
questioning hidden assumptions behind conceptual systems and examining
the impact of selected categories on the lives of human beings and
societies in general. As the scientist's curiosity about the world of
nature blends with the philosopher's questions about the use of symbolic
systems, a new alliance of strength can come into being. C.P. Snow
said: "Curiosity about the natural world and the use of symbol systems of
thought are two of the most precious and most specifically human of all
human qualities."[48]

PEPPER: A METAMODEL

One more view must be considered before a proposal is made that might
provide a fresh perspective to society's way of viewing aging and dying.
It comes from Stephen C. Pepper (1891-1970), the philosopher whose ideas
were previously outlined.

At Harvard University Pepper was influenced by his teacher, Ralph
Barton Perry (1876-1957), who was a student of William James. He later
joined the philosophy department at the University of California, at
Berkeley. His intellectual maturing process, with its changes in beliefs
and values, took place in a period when crises and violent changes were
sweeping the world. Active competition and conflict between political
ideals reflected the conflict between the "dogmatisms" Pepper had finally
abandoned. He opposed the movement of logical positivism that was so
appealing in the 1920s and 1930s because of his belief that the issues
involved in the justification of human values could not be met by
mathematical and statistical methods. He called this "method running
away with the issues," or "methodolatry."[49] He had even decided that
pragmatism was just one more theory, no better or worse than the others.
Pepper's drive for the truth directed him toward finding a reliable
method rather than a creed. This method, which involved a new attitude
and approach to philosophical systems, is described in his *World
Hypotheses*, which was published in 1942. What Pepper produced in this
study was not a new model but a metamodel, a theory of theory-making.
Pepper argued that the key to the construction of a world hypothesis was
some area of "common sense fact" in terms of which all other areas of
fact were interpreted. This root metaphor arose, not usually from one
person's imagination and experience, but from a whole social context,
just as an image arises piecemeal out of the practical concerns of a
people. A root metaphor, for Pepper, was a basic analogy that gave a
world hypothesis its unique style. When Pepper first published *World

Hypotheses, he described what he considered four equally adequate world hypotheses in the history of philosophy: "formism," for example in Plato and Aristotle; "mechanism," as in Descartes and the Cartesians; "organicism," as in Hegel and Whitehead, and "contextualism," as in American pragmatism. Each stemmed, he pointed out, from a different root metaphor that generated a set of categories.

World Hypotheses was subtitled *A Study in Evidence*, attesting to Pepper's empirical tendencies. The criteria for judging adequacy of a world hypothesis, Pepper claimed, were its scope and precision. An adequate world hypothesis is one that all the facts will corroborate. It was, therefore, a hypothesis of unlimited scope. In addition, adequacy could be judged by a theory's precision, if it exactly fitted the facts or, if it conformed to life situations describing experience accurately. Pepper argued that there was no one system of categories that would satisfy the two criteria of scope and precision completely. Each world hypothesis, in spite of its tendency to preserve its own integrity and not mix with the others, could still tolerantly embrace the others. In other words, Pepper claimed--and this gives his system of thought its unique style--that though each world hypothesis had its own autonomy, its own logic and rational clarity, nevertheless, there is a "reasonable ecclecticism in practice" that is always allowable.

Both Whitehead and Pepper incorporated time as the matrix of their philosophical systems, in quite different ways. Whitehead produced a metaphysics in that he aimed at an *ultimate* explanation of the whole form and content of reality. In contrast, Pepper refused to accept the possibility of *any* ultimate explanatory theory. He argued that no system of thought would prove ultimately adequate because one is never completely outside the web of his own descriptions.

In *World Hypotheses* Pepper's epistemology provided for several adequate philosophical models, whereas Whitehead sought only one. Twenty-four years after *World Hypotheses* was written, Pepper, at age seventy-four, published *Concept and Quality* (1966) in which he proposed a fifth world hypothesis called selectivism with the root metaphor of a purposive act. In this new effort Pepper insisted he was not trying to be a contextualist but was offering a radical revision of contextualism.

It is almost impossible for a convinced model-maker to believe that his theory is not the ultimate one, although Pepper himself made no such claim. He merely presents the evidence that his theory is one of a number of equally adequate theories.[50] Pepper argued against what he called the "myth of the given," claiming there is no certain evidence of any kind, or if there is, we do not have access to it. But Pepper was no skeptic either; he admitted that knowledge involves beliefs. Though these beliefs often fail to be ultimately adequate, Pepper accepted them as at least a starting point of knowledge, as an item of evidence. Thus, his root metaphor theory involved the philosophical imagination as well as logical powers and empirical proof. It is abundantly clear from the outset that Pepper's attempt to act "as if" he could stand outside any system of thought was itself the metaphor of his root metaphor theory. The "as if" can only be maintained if the user of the metaphor consciously remembers it is not the literal truth. The only reason for root metaphors in the first place is to lend explanatory power to a system as a whole. It was

Pepper's belief that the human mind does have the capacity to maintain this kind of distance, keeping itself from mistaking theory for literal truth. Constant recollection of the theory's origin in metaphor places the central focus on the evolutionary nature of philosophy and in this way knowledge is humanized.[51]

Pepper and the Problem of Time

Pepper's key to his pluralistic view was that he maintained a paradoxical "as if" position, whereby one can practically (though not theoretically) step outside one's own philosophical theory, to a metamodel, a philosophy of philosophies. From such a hypothetical position Pepper in 1934 wrote a short paper, "The Orders of Time."[52] In it he gave his view that there is no single concept of "real time" as Newton had said but many equally valid and useful concepts of time carrying out the distinct and important purposes of their users. One such concept, Pepper pointed out, is the familiar one of external time. Men have constructed calendars and clocks that function as universal standards whereby they can keep appointments and measure change objectively. However, time as an internal construct is just as real in experience. This Pepper referred to as the "human sense of time" because it is revelatory of a human way of dealing with the world. It helps people to carry out their intentions and reminds them that they are model-makers.

Pepper and Whitehead agree that the basic metaphor of both systems is the temporal event. But, Pepper condemned Whitehead's belief in the possibility of one general system of metaphysics. This, he claimed, was tantamount to a concealed absolutism. Pepper considered his metamodel of many equally adequate world hypotheses as the most human kind of philosophy because not only is nature full of surprises, but there is no end to the creativity of the human mind.

Certain themes emerge from the thought and work of the scientists and philosophers discussed in this chapter. One theme is a broad recognition of the limits of some generally accepted philosophical models. This recognition brought with it an awareness not only of the inherent limits of human knowledge in the face of time's passage, but also of the potential for new patterns of human thought and behavior, patterns that may already be woven into the fabric of the future. Another theme is that in accepting the temporal dimensions of human experience, the limits of time, the life-death paradox, a new sort of freedom may be found. Like Goethe's Faust, who anticipated the existentalist *angst* of the twentieth century, Western culture may realize that the ultimate enemy of progress is a fear of admitting the limits placed on humankind by time, aging and dying.

Heidegger's recapitulation of Augustine's discovery of the internal character of time brought into focus the human capacity for the unification of past, present and future. His approach threw an important light on the connection between the self, time, aging and dying. For Heidegger, facing one's own death was essential to authentic living. In keeping with this, Whitehead, with his metaphor of organism, conceived of nature as process in which creative advance involved the passage of

nature as a whole. This passage included perpetual perishing of all
things. Death as well as life played an important role in the evolving
scheme. For Whitehead, nature was not something apart from human
experience. Like the quantum physicists Whitehead saw that it was
impossible to separate the observer from the observed. Perhaps even more
than the philosophers of this century it was the quantum physicists who
played the key role in breaking the images of the past and preparing the
way for a new approach that would unify the scientific and philosophical
theories. Their discoveries overturned the conception of a clockwork
universe and pointed to time as a key for understanding the mysteries of
nature. The reevaluation of time by both physicists and philosophers has
lead to a new model that considers the limits of the machine metaphor and
favors a more human approach. Finally, Pepper's pluralistic insight acts
as a capstone that draws together the entire picture. His belief that
there are many equally adequate models and that an eclectic approach on
the practical level may best serve philosophers' purposes is a position
that will be examined further in order to explore the possibilities of a
new image of aging and dying. Such images in the last half of this
century are intimately connected with media, medical advances and the
technologies of destruction, each of which is unique in the history of
mankind.

STEPPING THROUGH
THE LOOKING GLASS

Look! There is tomorrow. Take it with Charity
lest it destroy you.

                                Francis Bacon

The first recorded images of the human imagination were inscribed on the
walls of caves, some thirty thousand years ago, in such places as Lascaux
and Altamira. Included among the paintings of animal forms and magic
dancers were imprints of the human hand, something that this bipedal
creature with opposing thumbs was beginning to recognize as significant.
It was this hand that, along with an invisible universe of ideas and
dreams, would shape the destiny of humankind. This hand some twenty-five
thousand years later would inscribe the letters of an alphabet on clay
tablets, translating the sounds that had been transmitted for millennia
by oral cultures into the visual images of the written word. It was this
hand that in a shorter period, two thousand years, would make the
printing press spread the word to multitudes, and then, in less than five
hundred years this same hand would tap out a message on keys of the
telegraph: "Attention universe."[1] The time lapse between new image-
making technologies had decreased dramatically. Samuel F.B. Morse died
little more than a century ago. Today in this electronic age, which he
introduced, the changing images of millions of people are shaped by
signals transmitted by satellites into their living rooms. Whitehead
said:

> From the age of Plato in the fifth century B.C. to the end of the
> last century the assumption was that each generation would live amid
> the conditions that governed the lives of its fathers and would
> transmit those conditions to mould with equal force, the lives of
> its children. We are living in the first period of human history for
> which this assumption is false.[2]

Today is an age of new images and artifacts. The hand of man has created
an undreamed of world, a world of hopes and fears that stagger the
imagination. The average life span is extended, as Descartes had believed
possible, with the elimination of many devastating infectious diseases.

With artificial organs, transplants, life-prolonging technologies, genetic engineering and a possible cure for cancer there is hope for postponing death even longer. Yet, today we are haunted by another image, an image that is both terrible and terrifying. It is the very real possibility of a nuclear holocaust. Now the hand that through the centuries shaped our destiny is on the "button," and the entire human experiment could end in megadeath.

A culture's image of reality is found in the way it structures experiences of the world. Yet the image it shapes is not the world. The semanticist Alfred Korzybski (1879-1950) reminds us that a word, image or concept is a symbol and not the thing itself. "Whatever you say a thing is, it isn't."[3] The world is not a clockwork universe, though Western culture pictured it that way. The universe itself does not construct metaphors nor do electrons constitute theories. Physicists and philosophers are the symbol-makers. Cultures formulate images, metaphors and models that provide a specific social, political and ideological context, within which certain attitudes, assumptions and expectations are implicit. Some models have proven better than others in carrying out their users' purposes. A model, though it represents reality, is not a simple mirror of reality; it functions in two ways. It liberates its users by giving them a consistent handle or perspective on the world. At the same time it sets limits on the user by proposing one perspective, rather than another, just as a person approaching a fork in the road limits his future by selecting one road and rejecting the other. The first step in selecting one's own images, metaphors and models consists of breaking out of cultural entrenchment by attempting to view, with sympathetic understanding, images, metaphors and models other than one's own.

A review of some of the major model shifts seen so far in Western civilization is necessary in order to set the stage for a consideration of aging and dying in contemporary American society. In focusing on the present, attention will be given to three factors that have a dynamic impact on today's attitudes: the *media*, an important force in shaping the images of society; *medicine*, a social institution that deals intimately with aging and dying; and *megadeath*, the widespread fear of nuclear holocaust, an image which has affected attitudes and expectations toward both aging and dying. Finally, a pluralistic view of time, which emerged late in this century, will be considered as an alternative that may foster a new and more creative approach to aging and dying.

MODELS OF THE PAST: AN OVERVIEW

The Ancient Greeks: Fate Is in Control

In ancient Greece, belief in the absolute power of the gods was coupled with a deep conviction of human helplessness and lack of control. Homer's myths polarized the heavens and the earth, foreshadowing the dualistic model that later pervaded Western tradition. The immortal gods, who were "larger than life," stood in stark contrast to humans, who were creatures of time caught inextricably in the cyclical course of nature, wherein fate would once and for all spell out their destiny. Nevertheless, from the heart of this image of human vulnerability, a fundamental paradox arose. It was the ever-burning desire to resist the long arm of fate, to share in some way the power of the gods. This was hubris, and the punishments described by the ancients, ironically touched the core of human temporal finitude. They were the loss of youth, perpetual old age, painful corruption and living death. Poets spun out the myths of fate's iron grip on mortals in a self-fulfulling prophesy that left blessed hope lying dormant in a psyche that was a nebulous and fleeting appendage to the physical body.

The Golden Age of Greece: Control Through Understanding

With the first stirrings of philosophy, a shift in images gradually began to take place. Old categories were reinterpreted, and fate's grip on the imagination gradually weakened. Time came to be linked, not with the violent, fickle and unpredictable whims of the gods, but with the stability and order of the cosmos as a whole. The human person was redefined as a rational being, part of the general order of nature. Hope sprang forth this time in a new spirit of questioning as philosophers, using the Socratic dialectic, searched for a grasp on why things are the way they are. The ancient and recurrent dream was born that people might somehow exchange views, coming to question and reason together. Thus, the seminal Greek ideal of control by understanding was developed.

Taking a giant philosophical step to bridge the radical opposition of the earth and the heavens, which proved so threatening to mortals, Plato offered new categories of time and the eternal forms. He insisted that time had a dignity of its own. Time, he said, mirrored eternity. In a pure strain of absolutist conviction, Plato defined philosophy as the greatest gift to man wherein the gods supplied sight to humans.[4] Paradoxically, the peace of mind Plato's ideas gave in the face of fleeting time came at the price of a passive acceptance of the way things are. It was crystal clear, according to his system, that humans do not determine the future course of events. Plato taught his followers to practice death daily by escaping to the world of eternal forms and thus to transcend the harsh reality of the things of time. He softened the stark pessimism of Greek tradition when, like the consoling nurse of old age, he sweetened the cup of life by promising that a gods'-eye view of reality was possible. But, for most people of Plato's day, the background chorus continued the ancient chant, reminding mortals of the old model. Though through philosophy they might understand everything, in the end they would control nothing.

Aristotle, like Plato, believed in the possibility of a gods'-eye view, but it was Aristotle's empiricist commitment that placed him outside what he saw as Plato's highly intellectual and idealistic vision of reality. Abandoning his first urge to investigate time as internally perceived, Aristotle settled, at least in the "Physics," for the definition of time as a simple linear measuring or counting of external change. This model influenced Western thinking for two thousand years. At the same time, true to his heritage, Aristotle related his physical sense of time to a teleological system of formal causes not subject to human control, but somehow comprehensible to human understanding. In the final analysis, Aristotle's thesis was a logical one, not a physical one as Newton's later would be. In spite of all his new ideas, the old Greek pessimism never died. Aristotle held a deep conviction about the destructive role of time. For him the diminishments of old age and dread death were absolutes, and the fear of time's ravages would have to be assuaged by pure rational courage in bold acceptance of the limits of things bodily and in stark faith in the eternal course of indestructible nature. Aristotle counted on the vision of the absolute to tranquilize the fear of aging and dying.

Control Through Faith: The Jewish and Christian Models

A second, and older, root of Western images of time, aging and dying was that of the ancient Hebrews. It was in the context of religious faith that the Jewish and later the Christian models of reality were produced. Time was seen as the first gift of God within which creation was brought into being and history began. The dynamics of the Jewish covenant encompassed a God who guided the destiny of the people of Israel and the Jews as builders of history. God had committed to them dominion over the world. However, in the final analysis, the model called for ultimate control of the world by God and never entirely by his people, who lived with a paradoxical sense of conditioned freedom. No gods'-eye view was possible for humans in this plan. Rather, the foundation of faith and trust in God was so strong in the Jewish vision of reality that it was believed that the question of afterlife was not for humans to consider and should be left entirely to the action of God. In stark contrast to the nagging pessimism of the Greeks, this view of reality called for a deep-seated optimism and a sense of creativity because of its emphasis on the root metaphor of life, *le chaim*. Aging and dying were always seen within the context of a creator-God who was good. Long life was taken as a reward and an opportunity for the worthy who were to continue the action of God's creation. Instead of dread death which bestowed discontinuity, dying to the Jews was a realistic part of the natural way of creation, a means of passing life on to future generations.

Though early Christians shared most of the foundational premises of the Jewish model of time, aging and dying, the Christian anticipation of resurrection eventually altered their view of afterlife. As the Judeo-Christian and Greek models converged in the Middle Ages, and formed the basis of Western intellectual culture, Christians gradually became more familiar with the Greek intellectual metaphor of the systematic order of the universe. Christian theologians came to interpret the creator of the lawful and orderly universe as standing outside of time. This interpretation again polarized time and eternity, earth and heaven.

In the light of the Christian dogma of resurrection, the concept of the person was refined and extended. A person was viewed as a unique individual with an immortal soul. By the Middle Ages a strictly stratified and carefully honed set of categories regarding judgment, reward and punishment was prominent in Christian theology and in the imagination of the people. Problematic paradoxes, however, appeared because of the merging of two such disparate views of time: the Greek model, which believed in control by understanding, and the Judeo-Christian model that was founded on control by faith. The historically oriented image of human destiny, so imbedded in Judaism, gave way to the old opposition of heaven and earth of the Greeks. This new dualism was

buttressed by the Pauline image of the warfare between this world and the
next and supported by the powerful imagery of Augustine's two cities and
the Boethian definition of God as timeless. The eternity of God now
stood in opposition to the things of time, which were mere reflections,
or symbols of divine eternal glory. Time was again uncoupled from and
subordinated to eternity. Otherworldly realities were of a first order,
and things temporal of a secondary or derivitive order, associated with
appearances and even illusion. Thus, blessed hope could be found, not in
this world, but in things eternal. Time, as opportunity, faded into
Father Time, the old man with the sickle, who devoured youth and brought
decay and death where life had been. A dread of the transitoriness of
time reverberated in popular art forms. The drive to choose between the
things of time or those of eternal salvation shifted and a mood of grim
despair developed, clouding the possibility of human beings attaining
eternal rewards.

The Enlightenment: Control Through Progress

The absolutism, that so dominated the imagination of the people of
Ancient Greece and the Middle Ages, lived on in the Cartesian dream of an
active hands-on control of nature by means of mathematical physics,
experimentation and medicine. The new methodology, along with the
technology of the scientific age, was interpreted as revealing the true
and objective state of nature. The world, it was believed, could be
analyzed and controlled by dissecting it and understanding its workings,
part by part, based on the assumption that the whole was the sum of its
parts. All need for wonder was to be eliminated within this model since
a new basis for certitude was now recognized in the self. Individual
intuition of a self-evident reality replaced the old reliance on
authority as the ground on which fundamental laws of nature would be
uncovered.This unbounded confidence supplied the energy of the
Enlightenment enthusiasts as they set out to track down the absolute,
simple laws of the universe, by means of which they would solve the
practical problems of life, illness, aging and dying. The key to all
this creative ferment lay in the secularized interpretation of time,
which culminated in Newton's definition of absolute time. This was a
definition of objective time, devoid of human experience. Descartes'
attempt to preserve the spiritual reality of the soul was, for all
practical purposes, aborted from science and much of modern philosophical
thinking under the lens of the mechanistic metaphor. Aging and dying were
soon viewed as flaws that must be corrected. A new view of the future as
totally predictable harbored promises of control over life, aging and
even death itself. The new science of gerontology accepted as its first
premise the need for active therapeutic intervention for the preservation
of health and life extension, even to hundreds of years.

Without many educated people realizing it, the priorities of the new
model had spawned the brand of dualism wherein the automatic, clockwork
universe of objective reality had become uncoupled from the inner world
of the subjective self. Western science became locked into the inflexible
material model of clock time and physical aging. This model remains
today, to a large degree, with its mandate for controlling the ravages of
time by defeating the clock, by mastering physical aging, extending youth
and prolonging life to its maximum quantitative extent. The dichotomy

of the self and the world out there brought about the emergence of what is commonly referred to as the two cultures. Science was on one side, representing the objectively observed world or reality, and the humanities on the other, representing internal self-consciousness and subjectivity associated with the imagination. This bifurcation fostered the same kind of scientific treatment for human beings as for physical objects and raised to a critical level the need for a reconsideration of the nature of time.

Kant's Call for Control by Science and the Self

Immanuel Kant attempted to solve this problem by undertaking a dual commitment: the defense of the Newtonian model of time and the defense of moral choice and human autonomy. This commitment led to his unique reinterpretation of time as the internal structure of the mind acting as a synthesizer of data. Kant saw the advantage of maintaining science's prized metaphor for time as atomized points on a line, and believed it to be compatible with his new category of the transcendental self, which he viewed as a common character in all human beings. In proposing a self that transcends objective data but at the same time acts as synthesizer of this data, Kant was reacting to David Hume's denial of the existence of self. This denial was based on the fact that there were no objective data to support its existence. Kant's two commitments would, in the end, further polarize the two cultures for in science the deterministic mechanism of the old model was preserved while moral indeterminism in human behavior was advocated not on logical, but moral grounds. This finally resulted in a re-enthronement of the absolutist dream. Personal freedom was submerged in the anonymity of Kant's categorical imperative, the universal sense of moral obligation, which he believed to be binding on all human beings. On the other hand, science was radicalized as theoretically objective. In both cases certitude was salvaged. The nagging threat of the transitoriness of time was muffled, this time in the cloak of moral certitude about the future life that must exist, according to Kant, since we all experience the need for "infinite spiritual progress."[5]

One novel upshot indelibly marked the philosophical heritage of Kant. In spite of the fact that he was still under the influence of the Newtonian model, Kant's linking of time and the self caused a ferment that served to reposition time at the center of philosophical discussion in the late nineteenth and early twentieth centuries. Thus the human person, as a creative temporal agent, unique and priceless, was distinguished from passive objects that can be duplicated and priced. Further, Kant's vehement rejection of what he saw as the mechanistic confusion between human persons and objects would ring in the ears of existentialists and process philosophers alike. A person, he proclaimed, is always an "I," and the future for human persons could never be predicted in the same way as the future of objects. The transcendental self, involving temporal activity, implied that a person was to be interpreted as more than the sum of the parts of a body. Here Kant laid down the groundwork upon which the rediscovery of time and the reformulation of a philosophy of aging and dying were to be built.

Voices of the Twentieth Century: Control by Accepting the Limits of Time

Heidegger constructed his model partly on a Kantian foundation. The freshly cut jewel of time now had a new setting, the strength of which lay not in an escape from change or the cold measurement of time, but in the paradoxical acceptance of its limits. Heidegger was able finally to renounce the Newtonian categories that separated past and future from the present. With this the self and time entered a new alliance. Descartes' rethinking of the self that emerged from the Judeo-Christian model of the Middle Ages was again rethought by Heidegger, who recognized the self as a dynamic force that gives unity to past, present and future. The concept of the temporally bound person as selector of possibilities, whose limits were also seen as a kind of freedom, challenged the concept of average time and interpreted aging and dying in a new creative way. Heidegger saw dying and living as inseparable. He viewed attempts to deny, trivialize, or extinguish this reality as inauthentic. In this insight lay the potential source for a re-evaluation of the twentieth-century taboo of aging and dying.

In the meantime, Whitehead had cast another setting for the many-faceted jewel, suggesting, like Heidegger, that instead of avoiding or eliminating the life-death paradox, freedom would follow in accepting it. Whitehead and Heidegger, as well as the quantum physicists, all rejected the deterministic reversibility of Newtonian time, which spoke more of logic than of life. The metaphor of organism, a dynamic world of creativity and change, was what attracted Whitehead. Nature as a whole, together with mind, both perpetually perishing, were no shame in his view. Within Whitehead's process model freedom was enlarged and redefined in terms of interdependent societies that endure through time. With the growing rediscovery of human time, aging and dying were a more acceptable part of the game of life.

At the same time, the reductionist model of objective science continued to thrive. Within the context of a new pluralistic contextualism, both models were acceptable, since it holds that the explanation of reality admits of more than one valid formulation. What used to be a scandal in the history of philosophy, that philosophers do not agree, turned out to be the source of its richness.

WHERE ARE WE NOW?: MEDIA, MEDICINE AND MEGADEATH

Generations have passed since philosophers like Heidegger, Whitehead and Pepper first proposed a radical re-evaluation of the concept of Newtonian time in terms of a process model. Their ideas, however, are just beginning to have a ripple effect in some quarters. Today, many professionals in the fields of gerontology and the social sciences are questioning the social desirability and moral relevance of chronological age as a criterion, particularly in dealing with issues that touch on quality of life.[6] Yet, many people, including policymakers, still measure aging in simple quantitative terms, though this produces an image of older people that is "distorted, tending to be negative and possibly damaging."[7] Younger people in particular stereotype the aged and exaggerate their isolation and problems.[8] Many see the elderly as rigid, unproductive, sexless and prone to senility.[9] Frequently, instead of seeing the later years of life as a unique period of growth and personal experience, aging and dying are coupled together.[10] Institutions that care for the elderly and the dying are aware of inadequacies in communication skills and are concerned about better training for their personnel.[11] The media have played a large role in shaping our images of aging and dying. These subjects have often been either ignored or presented in a negative manner. However, some changes are beginning to take place.

The Media: Aging

The closer to our own times we are, the more difficult it is to evaluate the shifting images that may show the direction of the metaphors and models of the future. For the most part though there is a strongly negative connotation associated with growing old, it is countered by a new hope of doing something about it. A book that became popular in the early 1980s and strongly represents this kind of view is *Life Extension: A Practical Scientific Approach* by Durk Pearson and Sandy Shaw. It opens with a statement by Bernard Strehler, a gerontologist: "I hate death." With 850 pages it remained on the best-seller list of *The New York Times* for thirty-six months. The authors describe the book as a cohesive clearinghouse of information for both physicians and the general public, concerned primarily with the molecular biochemical pathology that underlies the major human disorders associated with growing old and the effects of various nutrients, behavior modification and environmental control. Chapter titles like "Aging Isn't Beautiful" describe old age as "an unpleasant and unattractive affliction." With the help of this book and others like it the reading public is promised that proper planning can be started for a future with a longer life and a greatly extended period of youth.[12]

Another type of book is *Pathfinders*, by Gail Sheehy, author of *Passages* which describes "the predictable crises" of adult life. In *Pathfinders* she tells how "The people who enjoy the highest sense of well being in life are likely to be the older ones."[13] This book begins with that part of the life cycle where *Passages* left off, "true middle age into the eighties." The author describes "pathfinding" as a process whereby ordinary people are capable of "seeking and risking uncommon solutions to common life crises."[14] Describing many portraits of successful aging, she says, "Insofar as we are prepared to accept our humanness and struggle with it, we are all incipient pathfinders."[15] The positive image of every person's ability to negotiate the hardships of life is the ideal projected in this book. The claim is made that "doctors, psychoanalysts and social scientists who have represented aging as synonymous with loss have drawn their conclusions from a severely limited group."[16] Common myths about negative traits of those growing old are listed. A survey is quoted that shows people with the highest sense of well-being saying that they become more spontaneous and better survivors as they age.[17] If we examine these and other popular sources of information about aging, whether the image they project is negative or partly hopeful, it becomes evident that the approach in our society is increasingly becoming solution-oriented, partly because of the emergence of a new population of older Americans. Since 1900 the percentage of

Americans sixty-five and older has tripled and the old are getting older. In 1983 the seventy-five to eighty-four age group (8.5 million) was eleven times larger and the eighty-five and over group was twenty times larger than in 1900. By the year 2030, older persons (sixty-five plus) will amount to two and one-half times their number in 1980. The only age group to experience significant growth in the next century will be those past the age of fifty-five.[18]

Today's elderly are the first in human history to survive in large numbers to old age, and there are few norms to guide them or models to follow.   The   media have presented few role models to demonstrate successful aging, for they have been fixated with youth, a fixation that reached its peak in the middle of this century when the baby-boom generation provided American industry with 76 million young consumers. Advertising   campaigns   spawned by this unprecedented growth in population were geared to the young. Newspapers, magazines, radio and television were saturated with images that appealed to the young and proclaimed youth as a virtue. But being young had already become an American imperative long before the baby-boom generation provided Madison Avenue and the media with a massive resource for exploitation. Since the early days of film, youthful actors and actresses dominated the Hollywood scene and film writers acclaimed the glories of youth. In 1950 the aging movie actress Gloria Swanson was quoted in *Harper's Magazine*: "All they [producers] care about is the ghastly American worship of youth. That is why there is no place for the mature actress on the screen today."[19] America's worship of youth and the film industry's determination to capture a market has continued to the present. Today, teenage ticket buyers are the backbone of the motion picture profit structure. In 1983 almost 70 percent of all moviegoers were between the ages of twelve and twenty-nine. In the same year a movie made for young people *Return of the Jedi*, grossed $45 million. For the film industry, perpetuating the image of youth has been profitable.

Motion pictures were the first of the audiovisual mass media to dominate the American imagination. In 1946 movies attained their highest level of popular appeal. Three-fourths of the American public able to attend movies was attending weekly.[20] However, by the late 1950s a new entertainment medium had entranced the nation. Home television caused a dramatic slump in box office receipts as it began to replace films as the most influential form of media. Its messages, both subtle and blatant, continue the proclamation of youth. Like technologies of the past that have profoundly affected human perception, television may alter people's image of time and influence the way they view the world. When writing was invented and literacy developed, the concept of linear time (which was foreign to oral societies) began to emerge. Like a line on a page, things were expected to have a beginning, a middle and an end and follow in sequence like the letters in a word. The invention of the clock, with revolving hands and succeeding hours, further reinforced the concept of orderly sequence. Like today's digital clock, which represents instantaneous time change, minute by minute, television brings an all-at-onceness to the lives of people. In newspapers, readers are informed about events that have already happened, but television's on-the-spot news cameras bring events into the viewer's living room *as* they happen.   It conveys simultaneity in a multitude of visual impressions focusing on the present, thus cutting the viewer off from the past. Like the digital clock that no longer presents a twelve-hour face, television breaks down into instantaneous clips, the continuum that in the past gave coherence, stability and continuity to the world. As media critic Lori Breslow noted, "Television's ability to spread instantaneous information creates a sense of time that is constantly now-oriented. A craving for now . . . for the drama of the present does not allow time for reflection or analysis. Reflection and analysis require a sense of the past and how one relates to it."[21] The immediacy orientation of television tends to abolish a sense of the past. A heavy television viewer lives in an electronic bubble of time in which all things are in the present. Sometimes inexperienced young people come to expect instantaneous solutions to their problems, just like those given in the compressed time of a television commercial. There are those who no longer appear to be interested in the past. History, they believe, is out of date and irrelevant.

In addition to altering perceptions of time, television not only reflects popular cultural trends but also has the power to impose values. In the early 1930s it was first realized that public relations and advertising could wield great power over public opinion. Today the "tube" may turn the screws on public consciousness, shaping perceptions and influencing thinking, judgment and actions on issues of social significance. Every evening 90 million Americans watch television. Each year the average American views 2,300 hours of television. A child entering kindergarten has already viewed eight thousand hours of television, including eight major acts of violence an hour often, directed at women and the elderly. How does this new image-making technology influence our attitude toward aging? A study by the Anenberg School of Communications found that, although people over the age of forty-five comprise approximately one-third of the U.S. population, only 5 percent of the characters in weekend daytime programming are in this age group, and less than 1 percent of all television characters are sixty-five or older. Researchers contend that on television the symbolic annihilation of older people begins at forty-five.[22]

Saturated with images absorbed from television, many have come to accept distortions about aging and myths regarding the elderly. One study showed that aging in prime-time drama is associated not only with increasing failure and unhappiness but also evil. Only 40 percent of older males and fewer females are portrayed as happy, successful and good.[23] Another study showed that older people presented on television are frequently portrayed as lonely, ineffectual and obstinate. A Harris study showed that 65 percent of viewers under the age of sixty-five agreed with this image and believed that loneliness was a major problem for the elderly. Yet the elderly themselves disagreed. Only 13 percent of those over sixty-five found loneliness a major problem.[24] Television has had an enormous impact, not only on perceptions of the aged but, to an extent, on their self-perception as well.

The media, especially television, are the main form of leisure activity. Radio and television provide an invaluable service to many elderly in America, 7.9 million of whom live alone. They are sometimes cut off from intimate daily contacts and lack involvement with the outside world. Television can bring people into their lives and provide an illusion of living in a populated world rather than in the isolation of an empty room. The social construction of reality whereby interacting individuals create a world that makes sense is not as easy for the elderly. As isolated members of society, some of the elderly may find it problematic to test the validity of the media messages they receive. Like many other viewers, they often believe the stereotypes that influence the behavior of those who are not yet self-directed pathfinders.

Magazines and newspapers, like television do not present a positive picture of older people. Negative assumptions about aging can be found in advertising and even filter into news copy. Magazines that flatter youth are profitable, and advertisements abound with the quick fix to help you look younger everyday, erase wrinkles, or, wipe out gray. The superficial image projected is that these signs of age must be eradicated along with grimy sinks, and ring-around-the-collar. The stereotypical view is that old people make poor copy, for they remind the public that aging brings role loss, predictable crisis and death.[25]

But if, for purposes of profit, the images projected by the media are to appeal to the largest audience of consumers, then some changes may be in store. The baby boomers will be past fifty by the end of this century, and the ever-increasing average age of the population may bring an end to television's neglect of the over-forty-five age group. Some industries are already gearing their profit picture toward the growing senior citizen market. The "Pepsi Generation" commercials of the 1960s were, by the 1980s the "Pepsi Spirit" commercials portraying three generations, and Clairol's anthem for its "Silk and Silver" hair coloring changed to "Free, Gray and Fifty-one." As the "Me Generation" creeps into middle age and the pendulum swings away from large youth statistics, more entertainment may be developed that will better suit the middle aged and elderly. Already, aging and the accompanying adjustments, once treated as humorous, are being treated more honestly by writers in a way not before acceptable. It appears that aging is increasingly becoming a viable subject for prime-time shows and films.

In the second half of this century the elderly have become a more prominent segment of the population. Lobbying groups and national organizations, such as the American Association of Retired Persons (with a membership of 17 million) have raised their voices, and this call for recognition has increased society's awareness of the rights and needs of older citizens. In the past two decades geriatrics and gerontology have grown as fields of research. An increasing number of universities are instituting programs of study in gerontology, and some medical schools offer geriatrics as a specialty. Process-oriented theories and progress in the field of developmental psychology have opened new conceptions of aging, interpreting it as a stage of growth toward greater well-being. Because the number of older people in our society is growing, industry's need for consumers and the politician's need for votes may require a substantial shift in the image the media projects. An initial breakdown in myths and stereotypes and eventually a change in the image of the elderly could bring about a change in society's attitudes, assumptions and expectations regarding aging.

The Media and Dying

The image of dying went through a dramatic shift in the second half of the twentieth century. Until 1950, serious presentation of death and dying in the media and society's discussion of the topic in general was considered taboo, but in the late 1960s this taboo appeared to be weakening, and by the 1970s the market was flooded with literature on the subject. New organizations, such as the Thanatology Foundation and the Center for Death Education and Research at the University of Minnesota, encouraged research and publications, and many colleges and universities, and even some high schools across the country, introduced courses on death and dying. In some school systems, such as New York City Public Schools, the subject of death was introduced into elementary education, and in Boston, an entire museum is devoted to the education of children in death and dying. The media, too, turned attention to this once-taboo subject. Movies such as the award-winning *Brian's Song*, which dealt with a football player dying of cancer, were produced. Television dramas dealing with the lives of cancer patients were aired, and talk shows devoted an increasing amount of time to topics such as grief work. A spate of Broadway plays that dealt with various aspects of death and dying were well received. Paradoxically, American society seems to have had the need to confront as well as conceal death. This need expressed itself in the late 1960s when millions of people found themselves attracted to a book *On Death and Dying*, by Elisabeth Kübler-Ross. There are many reasons why the need to confront death more forthrightly and honestly welled up in society at that time. Perhaps the writings of existentialist authors, such as Sartre and Camus, laid the groundwork. The growing nuclear threat, was undoubtedly a contributing factor, as was the war in Vietnam, the first televised war. Nightly newscasts disclosed the latest body counts, bringing death and destruction into living rooms in vivid color. Whatever the reason for the new attitude, society moved in the direction of addressing some of these issues. Newspaper articles appeared almost daily, discussing the ethics and legal considerations surrounding life-prolongation technologies and practices.

Simultaneously, increased numbers of elderly and an army of survivors of the new technologies of medicine began to raise their voices in the media with the demand for a revised model of aging and dying. These survivors were not necessarily crying out for longer life. In fact, newspapers still tell stories of elderly persons who speak out about their dread of being kept alive beyond their time, perhaps on machines that merely prevent their worn out bodies from dying. Even though the race toward increased life prolongation is still on, more and more is being said about dying with dignity and with a definition of "dignity" that fits within the priorities of the person whose life is in question. The legitimacy of Living Wills, (some of which request the withdrawal of life-support systems when there is no longer any hope for survival) is being recognized by some states. But many physicians feel uncomfortable honoring them, and they are still a topic of open debate especially in the media.

Medicine

Social institutions are deeply impregnated with metaphors that are simply taken for granted; the more a metaphorical system is used, the more its users become convinced that they are dealing with true descriptions of the way the world really is. The same feedback pattern can be detected in society's attitude toward aging and dying. Not only are these attitudes reflected in its medical institutions, but those institutions undoubtedly have helped to determine them. For most medical professionals, the challenge of medicine lies in finding cures and treating curable diseases. Naturally, doctors want positive results. They want their patients to get well. As a result, geriatrics, which is a relatively new field in medicine, has not attracted many physicians. Perhaps this is because medical students frequently view aging as an incurable and fatal disease. Physicians may consider the death of a patient as failure. A doctor working with the elderly would, then, have to expect many failures. The question of why medicine has come to look on something as natural and inevitable as death as failure, and on aging, as a disease to be cured instead of a process intrinsic to all life forms, may be explained by investigating the model out of which medicine operates.

The roots of modern medicine can be traced directly to Descartes' machine metaphor for the body. In 1855 Rudolph Virchow (1821-1902) the father of cellular pathology, called on all investigators of nature to be united by a general mechanistic interpretation of life. Cell activity, he claimed, could not be other than mechanical. The mechanistic model of medicine proved extremely successful, particularly in the nineteenth and twentieth centuries, when extraordinary progress was made in pathology, histology and pharmacology. In 1910 the Flexner Report, which critically evaluated medical education in the United States, recommended that all medical schools prepare students in basic science and research. This research was extremely important for medical advances. It led to the development and production of various vaccines and antibiotics, which eliminated many infectious diseases. Once-feared killers, such as tuberculosis, pneumonia and typhoid fever were all but wiped out. Great strides have been made in the development of artificial organs and the design of heart-lung machines. Such technological advances, which make it possible to maintain body functions artifically almost indefinitely, have led to a reconsideration of the definition of death itself. The clinical definition, requiring cessation of heartbeat and breathing, is today replaced by a neurological definition requiring a flat electroencephalogram for twenty-four hours. This has made it easier to obtain functioning organs for transplant, though the need for such organs is still much greater than their availability. One factor involved in bringing pressure for redefining death was the need to "harvest" organs. This is important to consider, for it reveals that the nature and function of a definition is not value free and that biomedical progress is forcing us to reshape our values.

The old ethics and moralities were not developed in the context of the kinds of problems we face today. Technological advances have made life-prolongation one of the most difficult social issues of our time. We can now save many more lives, but at great cost and the difficulty in treating everyone fairly is becoming more apparent with each technical success. There are competing values in biomedicine and competing values necessitate a choice of priorities. Agonizing decisions are being forced on, not only the medical community, but individuals, families and the general public. What should take precedence: procedures for a few critical patients with the hope of increasing the population of patients saved in the future, or should the bulk of resources be directed toward general education and preventive medicine that would touch the lives of more people? Are there other options? Doctors, courts and families of patients are begging for guidance. There is a need for new standards and procedures to guide the decision-making process. In response to problems of this kind, a flurry of ethics committees have been set up in hospitals. Such committees have been referred to as "God Committees," since the decisions they must frequently make may involve the life or death of a patient. In the 1960s and early 1970s these committees had to decide which patients would and which would not receive kidney dialysis. In 1972 the U.S. Congress passed an act that allowed public funds to be used for dialysis, under the assumption that adequate resources existed to take care of everyone who could be saved and that costs could be contained. But costs have escalated and this has become a major concern. New government regulations now limit how much can be spent through Medicare for a given disease. In the past, aggressive treatment was always favored, but as the twentieth century moves into its last decade, federal restrictions on funds have halted this trend. Since 40 percent of all medical costs occur in the last six months to a year of a patient's life, cost containment will have a great impact on the elderly in the population.

Today there are approximately 1.5 million terminal patients living with the knowledge that they are dying. There are few families that have not personally experienced, or at least known of a friend or colleague who has experienced, this crisis in their lives. Support groups of cancer patients working, talking, sharing with other cancer patients, and family support groups that meet to discuss their problems, have sprung up all over the country. It is likely that this large population of people personally experiencing death has had a great deal to do with society's change in attitude toward confronting death openly. It was a population that first came into being during the 1960s when the physicians' policy on telling terminal patients their prognosis began to change. In the late 1970s, a study showed that 97 percent of all physicians interviewed indicated a preference for informing patients of a terminal diagnosis. The same study, conducted almost twenty years earlier, found 90 percent of the physicians interviewed preferred not to tell terminally ill patients their diagnoses.[26] The physicians' new preference was influenced by a legal responsibility to inform a patient of his condition and by the growing movement for patients' rights. It was also the result of research that had made the course of many illnesses statistically predictable. In the second half of this century detailed and carefully charted protocols and prognoses became common for diseases such as cancer. Cures were being developed, and patients were given the opportunity to participate as subjects in research. Informed consent, however, required the patient to know his prognosis.

The focus of the mechanistic model of medicine, with its basic orientation toward physiochemical reductionism and experimentation, was on the *cure* of disease and its *control*. What the model tends to de-emphasize is the personal side of illness. Psychosocial concerns have traditionally been of low priority in medical education. Doctors, taught to focus on the disease, are not unconcerned about the person they treat, they merely consider the social and psychological aspects of the illness beyond their area of expertise. This may be so, even to the point where preoccupation with disease-cure may obscure the importance of patient care. This becomes a critical problem in situations that occur almost daily in which medical professionals must deal with socially and psychologically vulnerable patients such as the chronically ill or dying. Another difficulty of modern medicine has been in integrating clinical observations with the statistical approach which tends toward "abstract medicine" in which the major concern appears to be the physiochemical condition that deviates from the norm. As a physician quoted by Dr. George Engel put it, "We must concentrate on real diseases and not get lost in the psychosocial underbrush."[27] One of the tenets of the traditional medical model is summed up by Horacio Fabrega, who points out: "In biomedicine, disease signifies an abstract thing or condition that is, generally speaking, independent of social behavior."[28] Yet social behavior appears to be related to many of today's major diseases, particularly those thought to be connected with stress. Traditional medicine, insofar as it has been reluctant to address this relationship, has not dealt with the psychosocial aspects of disease management, including doctor/patient communication which is critically important in dealing with the elderly as well as in caring for patients who are terminally ill.

This neglect is one factor that led to what some observers have cited as a crisis in medicine. By the late seventies in a lead article in *Science*, "The Need for a New Medical Model," Dr. George Engle, a noted medical educator, was arguing that the traditional biomedical model, with its reductionist approach to disease and its adherence to the doctrine of mind-body dualism, was no longer adequate for the scientific tasks and social responsibilities of medicine.[29] He proposed, instead, a nondualistic "biopsychosocial" model that would address itself to the patient as well as the disease, recognizing that the physician's responsibility for his decisions and actions on the patient's behalf involves the social and psychological as well as the biological element. Such a model, requiring a new philosophical basis has not yet emerged. However, in many quarters the limits of the old model are being recognized, and as a result medicine has begun to expand its horizons. There is a growing awareness of the need, not only for behavioral change, but for a new way of seeing the issues. This was evidenced in the early 1980s in medical education. An increasing number of medical schools began to introduce courses in behavioral sciences, interpersonal communication, medical ethics and death and dying.[30] Today "frontline doctors are paying increasing attention to psychosocial factors."[31]

In the past, the sources that funded research recognized mainly surgical and pharmaceutical solutions to medical problems. Today some interest is being shown in the long-neglected area of preventive medicine: mobilizing the body's own defenses against disease. Diet, exercise and relaxation techniques are being integrated into patient treatment by some medical centers such as the Mark Taper Center for Health Enhancement at UCLA's Health Sciences Center. But, American medicine as a whole remains dubious about preventive medicine. The traditional approach, with its main emphasis on disease research and its dependence on statistical results from the laboratory, seems to prevail. There is still a heavy dependence on the Cartesian metaphor, which treats the body as a machine to be fixed. The public generally turns to the medical establishment only when illness strikes and depends on doctors for treatment or cure. Preventive medicine's emphasis is on the body as a self-healing organism. One important factor it emphasizes is proper health habits long before the onset of illness. Formal courses in preventive medicine are not yet offered by most medical schools, but there is a growing awareness that such new areas are not a repudiation of traditional medicine. Though there is at present a period of strain as the two models attempt to adjust to one another, it must be recognized that if the contextualist thesis is taken seriously, it is not necessary to give up one in favor of the other. The mechanistic model of biomedicine can remain intact, while the new parameters of preventive medicine and the model of psychosocial care can be incorporated. As long as the users of the models take each seriously, integration is possible, at least on a practical level. An educated public and a reeducated medical community hold the key to success.

Megadeath

What is megadeath? It is death on a large scale. For a person living in the fourteenth century, it was the plague that wiped out a large portion of the human race. For an African living in the 1980s it was famine in which millions perished. It could involve a chemical plant disaster or a nuclear meltdown affecting large numbers of people. On a still larger scale, megadeath could take the form of nuclear disaster, bringing death to entire societies. But consider the difference between the megadeaths possible today and the plague that struck in the fourteenth century. The plague was thought by some to be the work of the devil or a punishment sent from God. Some more educated people of the time knew that such things had nothing to do with its cause. They also knew they had no idea how to stem its course. All were helpless in the face of disaster. This is not so today. Megadeaths, if not of our own making, are at least largely controllable by our actions. The question is, will our actions be adequate and appropriate, and will they be on time? It has been said that we have not inherited the earth from our ancestors, we have borrowed it from our children.

The concept of megadeath, which has most deeply influenced our culture in the second half of this century, grew out of a fear of ultimate holocaust in the form of ecological disaster or nuclear war. This fear was brought to the forefront of public consciousness in the 1960s by books such as Rachael Carson's *Silent Spring* and in the mid 1980s by television films such as *The Day After*. The nation became aware of the possibility of nuclear destruction during the Cold War (as evidenced by the bomb shelter fad of the 1950s), but not until the late 1960s and early 1970s did it become aware of the possibility of destruction through ecological disaster. Walter Cronkite focused the nation's attention on the ecological threat with a segment of his nightly newscast, "Can the Earth be Saved?" Many biologists warned that the thin life-sustaining skin of this planet was threatened by an unprecedented discharge of toxic waste into the water and air. They pointed out that some of these wastes could have catastrophic effects. Freon from aerosol cans, for example, rises into the atmosphere, threatening the protective layer of ozone that deflects dangerous ultraviolet rays. Wholesale destruction of forests (greenbelts are being replaced with asphalt) endangers the life-giving supply of oxygen and the increase of carbon dioxide from automobiles and factories can bring about large-scale climatic changes by warming the earth's atmosphere. This could result in the melting of the polar icecaps and drowning of coastal cities as well as a rearrangement of desertsand agricultural lands. But ecological shifts such as these occur slowly, and in an age of immediacy, the voices of ecological prophets dimmed. As the years passed and events such as teach-ins and earth-days subsided, subconscious if not conscious concerns regarding ultimate disaster came to focus on nuclear holocaust.

Since the 1950's world tensions made the threat of nuclear disaster grow. This was a demon that would not go away. Today we are haunted by the image of ultimate demise in a blast of untold megatons followed by a nuclear winter that could destroy the last survivors. Politics is unpredictable, and even the most optimistic cannot discount the possibility of a human mistake or an uncalculated computer error that could result in megadeath. In the late Middle Ages, with the development of the concept of the self as separate from the community, death became a personal concern. Today the death of the human race by nuclear disaster has become a collective concern even though it is an image that affects each of us personally. At eighty years of age the novelist Graham Greene reflected the feelings of some elderly people when he suggested that the big advantage of being old today is that "You are more likely . . . to beat out encountering your end in a nuclear war."[32]

The young, too, are affected. In this media-saturated world, children cannot be shielded from images of nuclear disaster. It is difficult to protect or prepare them for an uncertain future. In the shadow of megadeath, aging and dying have taken on new dimensions. They are no longer the same as they were a half century ago. Some young people fear that they will not be able to grow old. Studies show that many grade school and high school students, particularly those from middle- and upper-class families, expect a nuclear war in their lifetime.[33] Such expectations of ultimate destruction, whether conscious or unconscious, undoubtedly affect one's orientation toward time. With "the bomb" at hand it was not only television that caused young people of the 1960s to be known as the "Now Generation." With a question mark hanging over their future, concerns for immediate pleasures became paramount. By the 1980s, the right to a youth free from fear and concern for the future seems no longer to be the legacy of childhood. We are reminded of Hesiod, the ancient Greek poet, who predicted in "Myth of Ages" that the time would come in which infants would be born old and childhood would not exist. The hope that remains is that philosophical and ethical decisions will be made regarding the future that will restore confidence where it has begun to erode.

Toward a New Image of Aging and Dying

The cultural shelves of this century are cluttered with biases inherited from the past. By sifting through these perceptions, it is possible to discard cherished but unsuitable concepts, while retaining and reformulating valuable ones. This is a formidable task, however, because biases are subtle, due to society's general lack of awareness of

them. However, by the consciousness-raising process of reviewing and re-
evaluating models, it is possible to see alternative points of view
sympathetically.   The point of departure here is the contextualist
hypothesis associated with Stephen Pepper.   Intellectual sympathy with
the contextualist model does not necessitate the overthrow of other
models but asks for the recognition that there is no one correct model,
but many adequate ones. Nor is there one way of interpreting aging or one
way of seeing dying. On the contrary, the contextualist view necessitates
accepting the validity of many world hypotheses and different concepts of
time.   At the heart of this model is the acknowledgment that a hypothesis
or model cannot disclose the actual structure of reality. A theory of
time does not merely mirror time. For example, clocks and calendars do
not necessarily reflect the world as it really is. They are only
instruments that give one perspective, artificially dividing time as if
it were linear. Different models disclose or illuminate different aspects
of reality, and each model has its advantages and disadvantages which
need constant re-examination.

The concept of time in the Newtonian model, for example, has many
disadvantages, not the least of which is that it makes no distinction
between time for persons and time for things. Its emphasis on
chronological time sets up artificial categories and standards,
dictating, for example, a uniform retirement age or an age at which an
older person is eligible for residence in a leisure village. The
physical basis of Newtonian time tends to eliminate individual
differences in favor of statistical averages and fixed standards. By
doing so it satisfies demands for certitude and provides absolute
definitions that favor institutional solutions, but it also tends to
describe processes in frozen or static categories. This is dangerous,
especially where human life and growth are concerned. Nevertheless, the
Newtonian model of time has some distinct advantages because of its bias
toward statistical methods and its tendency to standardize. It has had
paramount success in the biological sciences as in the study of cell
pathology, etiology and diagnostic techniques.

Without an objective, physical model that deals with time under the
spatial metaphor of a line that can be divided and measured according to
homogeneous standards, we would be without the basis for the unmatched
medical and technological advances we have today. The reductionistic
model of time has been accepted, then, for the benefits it affords, but
its limitations must be consciously recognized. In circumstances within
which disadvantages outweigh advantages, alternative models can be
employed.

At a conference on Cell Pathologies in Aging, Lewis Thomas recently
recommended that his audience of pathologists read three books. Each was
a biography written by an elderly person telling what the experience of
aging is like. After the reading, which was meant to raise the experts'
consciousness of the elderly person's point of view, Thomas advised the
scientists to return to their laboratories and take up their reductionist
methods again because their contribution is important to old people's
lives. But he cautioned them not to forget the experiences they had read
about.[34] Here we have advice to his colleagues by one of the leaders of
contemporary medicine, that more than one model is needed if we are to
retain the ability to keep a broad perspective on the experience of

aging.

The idea of accepting a contextualistic view requires retention of the *as if* quality when viewing the metaphors at the root of every model. This *as if* function will help the model user to keep a distance, a sense of detachment from the absolutist urge to settle for a single model as a "true" description of "the way things are." The *user* would tend not to *be used by* the model as long as it is remembered, as Schrodinger prescribed, that one's world hypotheses must be taken with a big grain of salt.

The view that there are many adequate world hypotheses has its complications. In one sense, different models can be seen as incommensurable in that rational clarity dictates that it is a mistake to mix metaphors; that is, logic disallows exchanging categories between models in midstream. Nevertheless, a reasonable eclecticism, as in Pepper, can be defended. The classical mechanical definition of time can be useful in the laboratory as well as in keeping our appointment books. Here its numerical exactitude, objectivity and the carefully drawn divisions, standards and connections between specific and predictable causes and effects are a distinct advantage. But where the human person is involved, a more value-laden model is required, a model that will consider the individual's experience of time. Such a model is essential in the care of the elderly or in managing the psychosocial aspects of treatment for the terminally ill.

The Use and Misuse of Models of Aging

A prime instance of the shift in the model of aging that has taken place in the twentieth century can be found in the field of gerontology itself. Gerontologists who research the psychology of learning and memory have long constructed their hypotheses on the grounds of assumptions about whether cognitive development during adulthood is characterized by growth, stability, or decline. The interesting element here is that serious distinctions have been raised, not so much about the usual matters, such as interpretation of the data on either side of the debate, but about the philosophical models on which they are based. Model shifts in the history of basic research on adult learning and memory have been traced by David Hultsch.[35] He pointed out three models in the history of gerontology: the *associative model*, based on a mechanistic metaphor, which dominated research on aging until the 1950s; the *information-processing model*, based on the metaphor of organism, which became prominent in the 1960s and lasted until the late 1970s and 1980s; and a new approach, the *contextualistic model*, which uses a temporal event as its basic metaphor, recently appearing in some quarters, especially developmental psychology. Because each of the three is derived from a unique metaphor and therefore has different priorities, all these models have intrinsic disagreements. They each use different basic definitions and criteria for acceptable evidence. They even disagree on what is successful aging.

The unique aspect of the contextualist approach, however, is that it relieves the tension found in the others, which claim exclusive correctness for their views. Within the contextualistic approach the advantages and disadvantages of each model can be evaluated. Thus it is a broad metamodel of pluralism, an approach that has been called "multi-synchronicity," which corresponds with "the many-world hypothesis" that Pepper first used.[36]

The Mechanistic Associative Model

The term "ageism," coined by Robert Butler, refers to stereotyping people on the basis of age. It often identifies old people as unhappy, sick and approaching death. The roots of" ageism" are deep in our culture beginning with the ancient fear of old age seen as a loss of prized youth, hence a march toward dread death. In fact, Western philosophy traditionally wove a strong thread of negativity around the emerging science of gerontology.[37] This has been generally recognized as part of the history of gerontology as well as geriatrics and of general research in the social sciences.[38]

The associative model used an analytic methodology in keeping with its Cartesian-based scientific roots. Within this model, behavior was viewed as response to external stimulation. Development was seen as continuous, predictable, and due to causes that could be studied and verified. Stress was placed on quantitative measurements and statistical similarities. Both mental and physical changes were seen as primarily biologically based. Age-segmented periods, such as adolescence, middle age and old age, with carefully specified beginning and cutoff points, were characteristic of this model. Submerged within this perception were assumptions about what constituted growth and development. In general the associative model viewed growing old as a continuous and inexorable deterioration, both mentally and physically. Research in learning and memory has long assumed the model of regression, which usually pictured cognitive and intellectual functions reaching a peak in early adulthood, remaining on a gently downward sloping plateau until late middle age, and then declining at a faster rate until death. Only recently has this hypothesis been challenged. Gerontologists are beginning to realize that age-biased assumptions have prevented the elderly from receiving a fair evaluation in the fields of medicine, psychology and physiology as well as the social sciences. One of the most pivotal of these assumptions was the absolutist belief that one system, one way of seeing the world and of treating the elderly as a group, was valid.

Evidence of model bias can be gleaned from the earliest history of the field of gerontology. The first modern gerontologist, officially recognized in the tradition, was a Belgian named Lambert Quetelet (1796-1874).[39] In 1835 he published *On the Nature of Man and the Development of His Faculties*. The basic concept Quetelet used was that of average man. He listed averages and extremes of various characteristics by measuring and developing a curve of normal distributions. His contribution of a mathematical and statistical model set up the earliest methodology for the new field of gerontology. Out of this model was developed the "Gaussian curve," which was thought to represent a model revolution overturning the static stages projected by the Aristotelian model of aging. Karl Gauss (1777-1855) and others introduced the concept that traits had degrees and were not applicable to the elderly across the board. These early pioneers were convinced that the "scientific approach," using measurement, careful observation and statistical averages was the way to a new era in age theory. Their work leaped ahead by controlling the facts in a scientific way.

At the turn of the century Sir Francis Galton (1822-1911), George R. Minot (1885-1950), and others refined and extended the earlier model, studying the problems of age, longevity, and prolongation, and related aging to dying.[40] The popular American image had long since shifted from viewing aging as bearing the natural fruits of a life cycle, leading to wisdom and insight. Old age came to be separated into a distinct period of life characterized by negative features such as weakness, obsolescence and dependency. The twentieth century inherited a gerontological model of aging that focused on the physical and mental *limits* of the elderly and was coming to view aging itself as a social problem. A notable exception to this attitude appeared in the work of G. Stanley Hall (1846-1924) in *Senescence: The Second Half of Life*, his last creative work at the age of eighty.[41]   While his colleagues studied deterioration in old age and sought the secrets of longevity, Hall's selected area of focus was the psychology of aging and its social significance. Hall defined aging differently from his predecessors. In his model it was not viewed as a period of decline and decay; he saw it as a stage of development and consolidation of accomplishment. He claimed, "There is a certain maturity of judgment about men, things, causes and life generally that nothing in the world but years can bring, a real wisdom that only age can teach."[42] Hall had constructed the concept of "adolescence" and compared it to old age as a unique period in a person's development that has its "own feelings and physiology, and requires its own regimen."[43] Whereas others studied aging from an objective and physical point of view, Hall reflected on psychological factors, studying the fears old people might have of dying. He found that, though others assumed that the elderly dreaded death, the elders themselves did not necessarily grow more fearful as they grew older. Current research verifies this, indicating that the young fear death more, whereas the elderly are more wary of the circumstances in which they may die. The brand of dread that elders have today is fear of excessive and painful prolongation and lingering death.

The Information Processing Model

In the early 1960s a model-shift took place. Research in learning and memory took an alternative approach, basing aging theory on the metaphor of a living organism, which aligned it with process philosophy. The new approach was called the *information processing model*. The essential difference between the mechanistic and process based models is the part played by the subject in activities involving learning or remembering. Unlike the associative approach, the information- processing model treated the individual as a whole person within a context, emphasizing qualitative as well as quantitative changes. Its methodology dealt not so much with automatic stimulus-response mechanisms, as with voluntary transformation, such as active processing of information by the aging individual. Within this model, the concept of development is interpreted not as continuous but discontinuous, according to modifications made by the individuals themselves. For example, acquisition of knowledge and potential for recall included factors such as the way a person organized material which transformed it into a form the person could remember. Therefore, a person's development could not be predicted in advance by external circumstances alone because unpredictable changes were assumed to be possible in the future.

Formerly, many gerontologists and researchers believed that cognitive growth did not continue into adulthood, but leveled off or reached a plateau after childhood and adolescence.[44] The information-processing model helped explode this and other myths. Though it was clear that the time it takes to learn something new is often longer for old people, studies showed that most older individuals can learn new things about as well as younger persons, if they are given enough time and the instructions are clear to them. Both the associative and this newer model focused on progressive deterioration due to aging, but the organistic or information processing model included modifiability.

In this model, however, modifications are toward a particular end, that is, change is judged to be successful or unsuccessful by being measured against an idealized state, a single plateau of perfect development, an end state that is ideal. In this model, the time of optimal functioning is preceded by immaturity on the one side and infirmity on the other. This calls to mind Aristotle's concept of the prime of life, the perfect point or mean between extremes.

The organismic model also tends to build into itself the concept of stages. For example, Erik H. Erikson, who built on Freud's ideas, was one of the first theorists to conceive of the notion of stages of adult emotional development in *Identity: Youth and Crisis*. In eight sequential steps he defined the crises or challenges of each stage. Recent research has retained and developed this way of dividing human growth.[45] In the *Seasons of a Man's Life*, Daniel Levinson elaborated on the stages of adult development.[46] Gail Sheehy popularized Levinson's ideas in *Passages* and applied them to women. The concept of the normal crises of life, due to passage through the stages of aging, became popular in the 1970s as had the concepts of stages of normal grief in Elisabeth Kubler-Ross's *On Death and Dying*. But the assumption hidden at the heart of the model was that there were certain acceptable or proper norms tied to each stage. Correct grieving and normal development were standardized as implicit categories in this framework of thought. The organismic model operates that way as was seen in the analysis of Whitehead's process model of philosophy.

But more recently researchers began questioning some of these assumptions, asking whether all people develop in patterned and standardized ways. What were the disguised expectations, some inquired, in the expected mid-life crisis? Must everyone fit into the system so neatly? Margaret Huyck and William Hoyer, for example, think these stages "become identified as a kind of achievement ladder, with individuals . . . to be coached and evaluated in terms of their progress."[47] Users of this model are cautioned that age norms ought not to be set up as standards. They are meant merely for purposes of orientation and interpretation. If they become institutionalized as rules or absolute norms, they are being misused. When this happens, individuals who are different from the norm, for whatever reason, are in danger of being measured and pronounced as abnormal or as failures. This notion of being out of sync is dubbed as being "off-time" by Victoria Secunda in her book *By Youth Possessed* in which she examines the cultural expectations of age-related behavior.[48] Implicitly criticizing the process or organismic model with its progression of growth stages, she says: "There are many reasons why people are 'off-time,' due to some innate biological or intellectual clock, or because of their upbringing or because of outside events that alter for a time . . . their capacity to remain in the normative mainstream. Such people are often described as 'early' or 'late bloomers.'"[49] Individual differences tend to be blurred where categories of the model include normative requirements.

The Contextualistic Model

The contextualistic model is different from the other two because it is a major revision of the traditional theoretical and metatheoretical assumptions, not only about learning and memory theory, but also about aging itself. Contextualism accepts some of the basic ideas of the organismic model. Both emphasize qualitative, not merely quantitative, change as an impetus to growth and development within which the persons themselves play a pivotal part. The basic difference is that the contextualist does not project an ideal end state or stages toward which the person ought to be measured. The organismic model offers a process approach, qualitatively different stages of development, but eventually homogenizes development into a single monistic adult form as a kind of end or goal. The contextualistic model, on the other hand, because it is based on the metaphor of an open-ended event, makes no universal claims and offers no fixed theories of behavior, believing they are revisable indefinitely. Instead, it suggests general norms relative to cultural contexts and empirical findings and calls for ongoing reexamination and revision of theories, taking into account the historical and ideological context. To the contextualist, knowledge and model construction must be sensitive to the subject's particular circumstances and abilities. This interaction model has been deemed more satisfactory by some psychologists and gerontologists because of its accent on individual differences, however, it has its disadvantages as well. Its assumption of open-endedness makes it necessary to deal with constant change and revision. Research is more complex within this model and is not so compatible with statistical averaging. Nevertheless, these disadvantages are balanced by the heuristic posture of the contextualist who is open to using other models.

Many people think the aged are a homogeneous lot, set in their ways, often irritable and unhappy, mostly lonely and even senile. Erdman Palmore, who presents some of the most comprehensive and up-to-date research compiled on elderly Americans, discusses these myths. He thinks these descriptions are largely cultural in origin resulting less from the way the elderly really are than from people's images of the way they are.[50] The problem is that frequently, public policy is built on those stereotypical views.[51] Palmore presents extensive and reliable data to show that old people are not "pretty much all alike" but, if anything, are more varied than younger age groups. "There are . . . as many individual differences between old people as there are at any age level; they are . . . happy and sad, healthy and sick, of high and low intelligence. . . . In fact some evidence indicates that as people age,

they   tend   to   become   less   alike   and   more   heterogeneous   in   many
dimensions."[52]

Overall   decline   in performance   is less likely to appear in findings
when   a   healthy   population   with   a   positive outlook   is used.   Research
shows   that   the   adaptation   and   continuance of the model of progressive
regression   with   age has been due mainly to a nonrepresentative data base
which   was   most   often   gathered   from   depressed,   ill   and   unhealthy
subjects.[53]

The   contextualist   approach   is   aimed   not   so   much at arriving at
statistical   averages   and objective facts, rather it takes into account a
subject's   experience   and the evolution of his knowledge over a period of
time.   The   mechanistic   model,   so   pervasive   in medicine and science in
general   with   its   objectivity   and   standard clock time, its bias toward
quantitative   prolongation   of   life,   and   its   concern for the defeat of
disease   through   surgical   and   pharmaceutical   methodologies,   has
unquestionable   merits.   But   there seems to be a growing recognition that
there   are dissatisfactions with the shortcomings of this model.   There is
a   gradual   shift in the education of medical and gerontological personnel
toward   greater   emphasis   on   the   broad context of a patient's concerns,
emphasizing   care as well as cure and concern with quality of life as well
as   quantity.   The   public   is   calling for the medical profession to give
more   attention   to   communication   with patients.   However, an awareness
that   there   is   no either-or choice between models is also appearing both
in   professional literature and public consciousness. For example, doctors
cannot   be   urged   to abandon professional objectivity or take on the role
of   psychologist.   There   is   instead   a new recognition of the need for a
pluralistic   approach   to models of health care.   The mechanistic approach
might   dominate   where   technical procedures are complex and exacting, for
example   during surgery. A patient-oriented model might be stressed during
recovery.   The   melding   of   varied perspectives requires a sensitivity to
goals and priorities according to the context.

Models of Dying: Models of Life Extension

There   are   many   models   currently   operative within the fields that
consider   both   dying   and   life   extension.   Some experts think the human
life   span   has   a   natural   cap   of   about 115 years.   They urge that the
irreversible   arrow   of   time, ending with inevitable death, which is part
of   the   human   condition, be simply accepted.   Sigmund Freud (1856-1939),
for   example,   often quoted Bernard Shaw's warning, "Don't try to live for
ever,   you will not succeed."[54]   Freud speculated that there are two basic
instincts: one   in   the   service of life and one in the service of death.
The   death   instinct,   the   goal of which is return to the constancy of an
inanimate   state,   assures   that   no   particular   living thing can survive
forever.   Life,   for   him   was   nothing but a roundabout way to inevitable
death,   Atropos, the inexorable. But Freud pointed out that, paradoxically,
the   necessity   of   dying   remains   hidden. The natural tendency is to put
death   aside   and ignore it or disguise it, reducing it to a chance event,
not   a   universal   and   necessary one.   As   a result, individuals imagine
"Nothing   can   happen   to *me*!"   Freud argues that therein we are paralyzed:
"Life   is   impoverished"   by   this   illusion of immortality, "it loses in
interest,   when   the   highest stake in the game of living, life itself, may

not be risked."[55]

Recalling Shakespeare's line, "Thou owest Nature a death," Freud admitted that inevitably the reality of death forces its way into our lives.[56] When it is acknowledged with resignation as the termination of life, Freud hypothesized, finite life recovers its significance. This acceptance of death he, like Heidegger, saw as a task of life. If you want to endure life, he claimed, be prepared for death.[57] Freud's physician and friend, Max Schur, author of *Freud, Living and Dying*, followed every stage of Freud's painful and protracted terminal illness, and compared Freud's death to that of Faust, who died only after having achieved in a vision his ultimate goal. Freud, Schur claims, died having overcome his fear of death, without a trace of self-pity, as far as is humanly possible.[58]

Modern writers in the area of death and dying have been deeply affected by Freud's ideas. Ernest Becker's central thesis in the *Denial of Death* was that the fundamental driving force of life is the avoidance of death through impossible heroics, ultimately forms of self-deception.[59] Though Becker believed that one cannot escape human temporal finitude, or eliminate the terror it brings, he insisted that one can face it without pretense and thus use the anxiety that springs from acceptance as the wellspring of creativity. He argues that the symbolic spirit that seeks rebirth in building metaphors and creating models of meaning and value knows it is making an impossible effort against certain death, yet seeks therein the courage to renounce dread. Becker said: "It doesn't matter whether the cultural hero-system is frankly magical, religious and primitive or secular, scientific and civilized. . . . The hope and belief is that the things that man creates in society are of lasting worth and meaning, that they outlive or outshine death and decay."[60] He was diagnosed, unexpectedly, in the final stages of cancer soon after the publication of *Denial of Death*. In an interview shortly before he died he reiterated his hope: "Truth is a value, an ultimate value and false hope is a great snare." He claimed, "I think the truth (of our human condition) is something we can get to. It will have some meaning. It is this passion for truth that has kept me going."[61]

The belief that human development is at its highest point when there is an acceptance of death amounts to a new reconciliation with the human limits of time. If Heidegger is correct, this view could provide unique freedom to choose in terms of those limits. But it involves a revolutionary change in attitude from defeating the clock to accepting consciously and dealing with the process of living-dying as it unfolds. James Carse believes, "If we . . . deny our mortality we will only have locked ourselves into an airless spiritual trap. By denying death we will have denied life."[62]

Acceptance of mortality and acceptance of aging go hand in hand. But the concept and practice of life extension have a long history. Robert Parker and H. Gerjuoy in discussing the current state of the art classify three approaches. The first is the *meliorist* school of thought, which is bent on improving quality of life more than extending the length of life, except as a secondary effect. The belief is that the improved life situation would indirectly end up extending the life span because those who live in satisfactory circumstances have been shown to have lower incidence of stress-related diseases.[63]

The second approach, called the *immortalist* view, argues that death can be defeated by a greater concentration on research directed to preventing aging altogether by controlling degenerative diseases. The proponents of this school of thought, like the authors of *Life Extension*, are concerned with diet, nucleic acid therapy and hormonal approaches to better health. They argue that within the current medical model, recent advances have served primarily to sustain life at the last stages of degenerative disease. This strategy, they say, is not only impractical but costs the patient a great deal of suffering. The sicker the patient, the slimmer the chances for success, if success is thought of in terms of more time.[64] If we could counteract or reverse the aging process itself, the immortalist argument insists, decline of physical and mental functioning with advancing years and the occurrence of degenerative diseases would diminish.

A third alternative, called the *incrementalist* approach to life extension, aims at extinguishing not aging itself, but all disease. Its proponents believe that step-by-step research, within the current medical model, has brought great benefits to general health. With continued research, they say, incremental advances will eventually give us a population of older people who are effectively younger. Emil Freireich, a professor of medicine and leading medical researcher, argues this way:

> Why should we put borders on what we expect from life? Why should anyone in good conscience, who knows what I know, who stands in the posture of being able to create as I have had the privilege to do . . . imagine that death is part of life? My mind is open to the possibility . . . that humans may live forever. . . . I don't know of any causes of death other than disease. If that's the case, and, if we can understand disease and manipulate it, then I think one of the options that people must consider for themselves is the possibility of life forever.[65]

This is the Cartesian dream as it appears in the last quarter of the twentieth century. It is a dream of immortality that has been around for a long time, and it still exists today, not so much in the womb of philosophy or theology, but in the cool glass test tubes of the scientific laboratory. However, if it is true that by anticipating possibilities we bring them about, we must be prepared to live in the world we have created. Even if science could foresee the defeat of the clock, the philosophical questions about priorities and the concerns about ultimate values, the "why's," will not go away.

Intentional Futures

In the last decades of the twentieth century Western society is standing at the point where two worlds meet. One world is governed by the mechanistic model; the other offers an alternative in the form of a contextualistic approach. It may remind us, analogically, of the conquistador discovering the Hopi. The Spanish army represented the age in which the model of modern science was beginning to emerge. The contextualistic model may recall some aspects of the Hopi view of time, aging and dying. The Hopi believed that the future was already present and being shaped by their intentions. Since the future was coming about because of the cumulative past, they valued and accepted the quality of life of the elderly and believed that dying was part of the cycle of life. We know also that the Hopi were unable to recognize the advantages of the Western European model, nor could they see the limits of their own.

The conquistadors as well were trapped in their own world view. When metaphors and models that help shape thinking and behavior are taken for granted, they become largely invisible and are accepted as the truth. Other models, therefore, must be rejected. But once we understand how images and root metaphors develop into models, we have the keys to many world hypotheses in our pockets and it is possible to open untold doors to the future.

The Western roots of present-day attitudes toward time, aging and dying reach deep into the past, but today we are at the point where a conscious shift in thinking appears to be necessary. Earlier in the course of human history, creative minds asked the question: "What is it possible for us to do?" Today, as the vast range of possible achievements seems almost unlimited, the question is shifting to: "What do we desire to do?" If we can do almost anything, what should it be? The answer, of course, will depend on our values and priorities. These will have been shaped by images of time and the dominant metaphors and models held by society. Though we cannot change the stubborn past, the history of models as it has taken place, what can be brought into being, in the light of our experience and understanding of the past, is a future wherein consciously selected priorities will help determine the models used by science and the humanities alike. By becoming aware of the part we play in choosing our own metaphors and models, we can move beyond the limits of the past. In recognizing that we ourselves are the mirror of time, we will have stepped through the looking glass. If human knowledge and human experiences are considered cumulative, creative emergence might just be possible and our futures may become intentional.

NOTES

CHAPTER 1

1. Arthur P. Miller, Jr., "Hopis: 'The Peaceful Ones' Confront the 20th Century," in *Vanishing Peoples of Earth* (Washington, D.C.: National Geographic Society, 1971), p. 184.

2. Michel Philibert, "Phenomenological Approaches to Images of Aging," in *Philosophical Foundations of Gerontology*, ed. Patrick M. McKee (New York: Human Sciences Press, 1982), p. 321.

3. Alfonso Ortiz, "Ritual Drama and the Pueblo World View," in *New Perspectives on the Pueblos*, ed. A. Ortiz (Albuquerque, New Mexico: University of New Mexico Press, 1972), pp. 136–37.

4. Mary Douglas, *Purity and Danger: An Analysis of Concepts of Pollution and Taboo* (London: Routledge and Kegan Paul, 1966), pp. 89–90.

5. Stephen C. Pepper, *World Hypotheses* (Berkeley, California: University of California Press, 1942), pp. 46–47.

6. Philibert, "Images of Aging," p. 321.

7. Pedro de Castaneda, "The Narrative of the Expedition of Coronado," in *Spanish Explorers in the Southern United States, 1528-1543*, ed. F. W. Hodge (New York: Barnes and Noble, 1907), pp. 306–7.

8. Ibid., p. 300.

9. Don Talayesva, *Sun Chief: The Autobiography of a Hopi Indian*, ed. Leo Simmons (New Haven, Connecticut: Yale University Press, 1942), pp. 376–77.

10. Patricia Broder, *Hopi Painting* (New York: Brandywine Press, 1978), p. 7. "Until the end of the nineteenth century all Hopi paintings were part of religious ceremonies. Indeed the paintings themselves were a form of visual prayer and always . . . a communal occupation . . . the artist, as a contributor to the tribal welfare, was rewarded with inner peace and a sense of well-being." The painting entitled "Emergence" fits into that Hopi tradition, exhibiting as it does the central myth of the origin of the Hopi people.

11. Fig. 1 is Dawakema-Milland Lomakema's 1974 acrylic painting *Emergence* in the Hopi Cultural Center Museum, Second Mesa, Arizona. Artist's permission granted. Fig. 2 Pieter Brueghel's engraving, "The Triumph of Time," in the Metropolitan Museum of Art, New York, New York, Harris Brisbane Dick Fund, 1939. (39.94.7)

12. Harold Courlander, *The Fourth World of the Hopis* (New York: Crown Publishers, 1971), pp. 28–29.

13. V. Scully, *Pueblo: Mountain, Village and Dance* (New York: Viking Press, 1972), p. 339.

14. Ortiz, "Ritual Drama, " p. 145.

15. Benjamin L. Whorf, *Language, Thought and Reality*, ed. J. Carroll (Cambridge, Massachusetts: M.I.T. Press, 1956), p. 143.

16. Frank Waters, *Pumpkin Seed Point* (Chicago: Sage Books, 1969), p. 107. Waters explains that in his experience the Hopi never asked a person's chronological age because they felt it was unwise to count the years as the white men did. See also Alex M. Stephen, *Hopi Journal*, ed. Elsie C. Parson (New York: A.M.S. Press, 1936), p. 598.

17. Whorf, *Language, Thought and Reality*, pp. 143–59.

18. It is interesting to note that in the legend of the first Hopis, when they emerged onto the earth, they found it dark and sunless. Therefore, they determined to create a sun and a moon such as they had in the underworld. They did this and threw them up into the sky. In short, they had some part in bringing forth what they thought of as the source of life. In their prayers and other practices this sense of bringing the future about was very much a part of their folk philosophy.

19. James Snyder, "Jan Mostaert's West Indies Landscape," in *First Images of America: The Impact of the New World on the Old*, 2 vols. (Berkeley, California: University of California Press, 1976), 1: 497.

20. Talayesva, *Sun Chief*, pp. 58–59.

21. Ibid., pp. 85–86.

22. Ibid., p. 381.

23. Ricardo J. Quinones, *The Renaissance Discovery of Time* (Cambridge, Massachusetts: Harvard University Press, 1972), p. 3.

24. Edwin Panofsky, *Studies in Iconology: Humanistic Themes in the Art of the Renaissance* (New York: Oxford University Press, 1939,(rev. 1967), p. 82.

25. Ibid., p. 92. Antiquity's basic image of time has represented the Greek *kairos*, a crucial "choice point" in human or world development, as Opportunity, a young figure winged on shoulders and heels, carrying a scale representing balance and a wheel of fortune symbolizing chance, and decked in a forelock by which he could be grasped. The youth, who represented plentitude and power, now accompanied by the Renaissance addition of the hourglass, introduces the new consciousness that time is fleeting.

26. The rushing chariot and the theme of "Triumph" can be associated particularly with the Italian lyric poet and scholar, the fountainhead of Renaissance humanism, Francesco Petrarch (1304–1374), whose writings and entire consciousness were preoccupied by the need to reckon with the pressure of time.

27. The term "clock" comes from "clocca" meaning "bell." The first clocks were aural, not visual devices. They had no face and hands.

28. Panofsky, *Studies in Iconology*, p. 82. By the sixteenth and seventeenth centuries, "the mirror became an attribute of time . . . and inversely the figure of Time was used to draw a curtain from a mirror to reveal the gradual decay of health and beauty . . . and the mirror finally became a typical symbol of transience equally frequent in art and literature."

29. Brueghel combines two ideas here: the northern Italian figure of death mounted on a horse and trampling men underfoot, based on the Apocalypse, and the northern European symbol of the Dance of Death commonly depicted by artists such as Holbein.

30. The "Gaetulian bull" is a poetic expression for an African elephant and refers to all things strange and exotic.

31. This approach to time would be formalized in the seventeenth century in the work of Descartes and Newton.

32. Stephen C. Pepper "Philosophy and Metaphor," *Journal of Philosophy*, 25 (March 1928), p. 130.

33. Stephen C. Pepper, "Metaphor in Philosophy," *Dictionary of the History of Ideas*, ed. Philip P. Wiener (New York: Charles Scribner's Sons, 1973), p. 196.

34. Susanne K. Langer, *Philosophy in a New Key* (Cambridge, Massachusetts: Harvard University Press, 1942), p. 140.

35. Colin Turbayne, *The Myth of Metaphor* (Columbia, South Carolina: University of South Carolina Press, 1970), p. 18.

36. In one scene from his autobiography, *The Sun Chief*, Don Talayesva described how, as a young boy going through his initiation rites, he came to realize that the Kachina gods represented in the ritual dance were his own relatives. They took off their masks, and he knew

them all. The crisis of belief that followed was not long lasting. Don's empirical evidence was soon overridden by confidence in the traditional belief that the gods were present once the masks were donned.

37. Pepper, "Metaphor in Philosophy," p. 199.

38. Erwin Schrodinger, *What is Life? and Mind and Matter* (Cambridge, England: At the University Press, 1967), p. 172.

39. Turbayne, *Myth of Metaphor*, p. xiv.

40. Ibid.

41. Pepper, "Metaphor in Philosophy," p. 199.

42. Anonymous poem heard as part of a lecture by Neil Postman from the Media Ecology Program at New York University.

43. Michael Polanyi, *Study of Man: Lindsay Memorial Lectures* (Chicago, Illinois: University of Chicago Press, 1958), p. 15.

44. Pepper, *World Hypotheses*, p. 149.

CHAPTER 2

1. Jacob Bronowski, *The Ascent of Man* (Boston: Little Brown & Company, 1973), p. 180. The assumption was that the mind can comprehend the universal scheme of things, not as it seems, but as it *is*.

2. Homer, *The Iliad of Homer*, trans. Alexander Pope (New York: D. Appleton and Company, 1899), p. 465-67. All quotations from Homer are from this translation.

3. Stephen Mason, *A History of the Sciences* (New York: Collier Books, 1952), p. 38.

4. Ernst Cassirer, *Language and Myth* (New York: Harper Brothers, 1946), p. 74.

5. Julian Jaynes, *The Origin of Consciousness in the Breakdown of the Bicameral Mind* (Boston: Houghton Mifflin, 1977), pp. 68-9.

6. Homer, *The Iliad*, p. 467.

7. Ibid., pp. 1-2.

8. "Technikos" comes from "techne" meaning an art or artifice.

9. Hesiod, *Works and Days* in *Hesiod: The Homeric Hymns and Homerica*, trans. Hugh G. Evelyn-White (London: William Heinemann, 1964), p. 9.

10. This is reminiscent of the book about childhood in today's electronic age by Neil Postman, *The Disappearance of Childhood* (New York: Delacorte, 1982).

11. Hesiod, "Works and Days" in *An Introduction to Early Greek Philosophy* by John Robinson (Boston: Houghton Mifflin, 1968), p. 19.

12. Ibid., p. 16.

13. Eric Havelock, *Origins of Western Literacy* (Toronto: Havelock Institute for Studies in Education, 1976), p. 46.

14. Kathleen Freeman, trans., *Ancilla to the Pre-Socratic Philosophers: A Complete Translation of the Fragments in Diels,* Fragmente der Vorsokratiker (Cambridge, Massachusetts: Harvard University Press, 1966), Fragment 91, p. 31.

15. Ibid., Fragment 30, p. 26.

16. Ibid., Fragment 67, p. 29.

17. Ibid., Fragment 20, p. 26.

18. Ibid., Fragment 23, p. 26.

19. Ibid., Fragment 88, p. 30.

20. Ibid., Fragment 52, p. 28.

21. Plato, *The Collected Dialogues of Plato*, ed. Edith Hamilton and Huntington Cairns (New York: Random House, Bollingen Series 71, Pantheon Books, 1966), Timaeus 37d. All quotes from Plato are from this text. Used by permission of Oxford University Press.

22. Plato noted mirrors also have the quality of deception. They are bright surfaces in which right appears as left and left as right (Tim. 46b). Plato's suspicion of artists arose from the fact that they carried a mirror, fooling people about reality by showing only images and not the truth (Rep. 596e).

23. Plato, "Timaeus," 47b.

24. Ibid.

25. Plato, "Phaedrus," 246b.

26. Plato, "Republic," VII, 518d.

27. Cecil M. Bowra, *The Greek Experience* (New York: The World Publishing Company, 1957), p. 112, quoting Diel's *Fragments* 2.55.

28. Ibid.

29. Plato, "Republic," VII, 518d.

30. Ibid., VII, 540a-b.

31. Ibid., VII, 519c.

32. Ibid., VII, 540c.

33. Ibid., I, 329.

34. Ibid, 330d.

35. Ibid., 330e.

36. Patrick McKee, ed., *Philosophical Foundations of Gerontology* (New York: Human Sciences Press, 1982), p. 187.

37. Homer, *The Iliad*, p. 9.

38. Plato, "Laws," V, 730d.

39. Plato, "Republic," III, 406a-e.

40. Aristotle, *The Basic Works of Aristotle*, ed. Richard McKeon (New York: Random House, 1966), "Nicomachean Ethics," III, 6:1115a,25. All quotes from Aristotle, excepting "On Longevity and Brevity of Life," are from this text. Used by permission of Oxford University Press.

41. Plato, "Laws," II, 666b.

42. Ibid., IV, 717b-c.

43. For further explanation see Maria Haynes, "The Supposedly Golden Age of the Aged in Ancient Greece," *Gerontologist* 2 (June 1962): 93-98.

44. Plato, "Phaedo," 80e-81a.

45. A. E. Taylor, *Plato: The Man and His Work* (New York: Meridian Press, 1956), note 179.

46. Plato, "Phaedo," 67e.

47. Plato, "Apology," 29a.

48. Ibid., 41a.

49. Plato, "Phaedrus," 248-249.

50. Ibid., 248e-249.

51. Ibid., 250c.

52. Aristotle, "On Longevity and Brevity of Life," in *The Works of Aristotle Translated into English, III*, trans. J. L. Beare, ed. W. D. Ross (Oxford, England: Clarendon Press, 1931) V, 466a 15-20 *Parva Naturalia*.

53. Ibid., V, 466a, 20.

54. Aristotle, "Rhetoric," II, 13, 1390b, 15.

55. Aristotle, "On the Senses," 448b, 25-30.

56. Hans Georg Gadamer, "Western Views of the Inner Experience of Time and the Limits of Thought," in *Time and Philosophies*, ed. Paul Ricoeur, et. al. (Paris: UNESCO Press, 1977), p. 42.

57. Ibid.

58. "Form" is considered by Aristotle as the "whatness" of a thing, the properties we think of when we ask "what" a substance is.

59. Aristotle, "Nicomachean Ethics," I, 7, 1098a, 10-15.

60. Ibid., 20.

61. Aristotle did not mean by this that men have free will. He simply meant that man is accountable for the habits he develops. Good habits are rational choices, bad habits the result of disharmony between reason and desire and result from failure of the individual and, to some degree, from circumstances he could not control.

62. Aristotle, "Physics," 221, 2b.

63. Euripides, "Medea," in *Ten Greek Plays*, trans. Gilbert Murray, ed. L. Cooper (New

York: Oxford University Press, 1936), p. 326.

64. Aristotle, "Rhetoric," II, 12-16.

65. Aristotle, "De Generationes Animalium," trans. Arthur Platt, in *The Works of Aristotle Translated into English*, ed. W. D. Ross and J. A. Smith (Oxford, England: Clarendon Press, 1908-1952), 745a.

66. Bessie E. Richardson, *Old Age Among the Ancient Greeks* (New York: Greenwood Press, 1969), passim.

67. Jacques Choron, *Death and Western Thought* (New York: Collier Books, 1963), p. 45 quoting the Todd translation of Xenephon's *Socrates' Defense to the Jury*.

68. Aristotle, "Rhetoric," I, 5, 136b, 15-30.

69. Ibid., 1, 5, 1361b,5.

70. Richardson, *Old Age*, p. 35.

71. Aristotle, "On the Soul," I, 4, 408a, 30.

72. Aristotle, "Metaphysics," 1070a, 25.

73. Some scholars believe Aristotle meant that there was only one intellect functioning in two ways. Others interpret active reason as a lasting entity, in effect, God thinking in man. However, Aristotle said the distinction between active and passive reason arises *within* the soul.

74. Aristotle, "On the Soul," III, 5, 430a, 20.

75. Aristotle, "Nicomachean Ethics," I, 7, 1098a, 10-15.

76. Ibid., X, 7, 1178a, 5-10. Italics by Aristotle.

77. Ibid., X, 7, 1178a, 1.

78. Ibid., X, 1115a, 11.

CHAPTER 3

All Biblical quotations from *Holy Bible*, Revised Standard Version, 2nd Edition (New York: Thomas Nelson, 1971).

1. Some scholars consider this to indicate that God has set a limit of one hundred years on human longevity. This is interesting in that physicians studying long-lived people of Soviet Georgia, in spite of exaggerated claims by some, have not been able to document any person who has lived beyond 115 years.

2. Instead of "B.C." and "A.D." modern Jewish scholars use "B.C.E." (Before the Common Era) and "C.E." (Common Era).

3. Thorleif Boman, *Hebrew Thought Compared with Greek*, trans. J. Moreau (Philadelphia: Westminster Press, 1966), p. 131.

4. Many authors describe Hebrew time as linear in the sense of historical, but this metaphor can deceive, allowing too much emphasis on perfect, regular succession. The metaphor of a pulse ties Hebrew time to memories and expectations, which are more selective and interpretative.

5. Boman calls this "psychological" time. Caution must be exercised lest the term be confused with the personal, subjective time as used later by the existentialists. In Jewish thought time of human experience refers to the experience of the People of Israel, not of individuals as such.

6. S.G.F. Brandon, *The Judgment of the Dead* (New York: Charles Scribner's Sons, 1967), p. 74.

7. "Time and the Destiny of Man," in *Voices of Time*, ed. Julius T. Fraser (New York: George Braziller, 1966), p. 148.

8. Andre Neher, "The View of Time and History in Jewish Culture," in *Cultures and Time*, ed. L. Gardet et al. (Paris: UNESCO Press, 1976), p. 149.

9. James Mullenburg, "The Biblical View of Time," *Harvard Theological Review* 56, 4 (October 1961): 231.

10. Ibid., p. 236.

11. Actually the coming together of the Jews into one people under one God was a long and arduous process.

12. Neher, "The View of time," p. 154

13. James Carse, *Death and Existence: A Conceptual History of Human Mortality* (New York: John Wiley and Sons, 1980), p. 196.

14. Judah Goldin, ed. and trans., *The Living Talmud* (New York: New American Library, 1957), p. 8.

15. Ibid., p. 51. See also Carse, *Death and Existence*, p. 188.

16. Samuel Spector, "Old Age and the Sages," *International Journal of Aging and Human Development* 4 (1973): 199–209.

17. Carse, *Death and Existence*, p. 182.

18. Hans Wolff, *Anthropology of the Old Testament* (Philadelphia: Fortress Press, 1974), p. 99.

19. Brandon, *Judgment of the Dead*, p. 57.

20. Harold Knight, *The Hebrew Prophetic Consciousness* (London: Lutterworth Press, 1947), p. 125.

21. Roy Eckart, "Death in the Judaic and Christian Traditions," *Soul Research* 39: 3 (Autumn 1972): 492.

22. "Fly away" here implies most likely that life leaves and the person is dead, not that he continues to live somewhere else.

23. Brandon, *Judgment of the Dead*, p. 57.

24. Here is another example of vague definition. Whether death is final or whether some part of the person may go to Sheol is not made clear.

25. Carse, *Death and Existence*, p. 179.

26. Ibid., p. 178.

27. Wolff, *Anthropology of the Old Testament*, p. 115.

28. Brandon, *Judgment of the Dead*, p. 75.

29. Goldin, *The Living Talmud*, p. 146.

30. Eckart, "Death in the Judaic and Christian Traditions," p. 504.

31. Brandon, *Judgment of the Dead*, p. 66.

32. Carse, *Death and Existence*, p. 221.

33. Brandon, *Judgment of the Dead*, p. 153.

34. Ibid., p. 152.

35. Eckart, "Death in the Judaic and Christian Traditions," p. 514.

36. Brandon, *Judgment of the Dead*, p. 172.

37. Ibid., p. 173.

38. Evister Zerubaval, *Hidden Rhythms* (Chicago: University of Chicago Press, 1981), p. 98.

39. Ibid., p. 74, quoting Joshua Manoach, "The People of Israel: the People of Time," in *Calendar for 6000 Years*, ed. A. A. Akavia (Jerusalem: Mossad Harav Kook,1976), p. xx, xix.

40. The state of the person between death and general resurrection was not clear. Even for the early fathers of the Church, the Second Coming was seen as not long distant, and therefore, the waiting period was viewed as not very long in duration. Everyone was content to leave the nature of the waiting state vague.

41. Long life is never mentioned as a reward for a good life in Christian scripture except where it quotes the Old Testament.

CHAPTER 4

1. Boethius, *Consolation of Philosophy*, trans. W. V. Cooper (New York: Random House, 1943), p. 115.

2. Ibid., p. 112.

3. Max Muller and Alois Halder, "Person" in *Sacramentum Mundi*, 6 vols., ed. Karl Rahner (New York: Herder and Herder, 1970), 5: 404.

4. Judaism conceived of the person as a social being while Christianity emphasized humans

as personal beings. This notion ought to be seen in perspective, however. Early Christian communities emphasized a common life, a general resurrection and a general judgment.

5. Muller and Halder, "Person," p. 404.

6. St. Augustine, *The City of God*, trans. Marcus Dods (New York: Random House, 1950), p. 460.

7. Ibid., p. 677.

8. Ibid., pp. 258-60.

9. Ibid., pp. 428-29.

10. Ibid., p. 424.

11. Ibid., p. 708.

12. Ibid., p. 709

13. James Carse, *Death and Existence* (New York: John Wiley and Sons, 1980) p. 243.

14. T.S.R. Boase, *Death in the Middle Ages* (New York: McGraw-Hill, 1972), p. 46.

15. Augustine, *City of God*, p. 623.

16. Boase, *Death in the Middle Ages*, p. 21.

17. St. Thomas Aquinas, "Summa Theologica," in *Basic Writings of St. Thomas Aquinas*, 6 vols., ed. and annotated Anton C. Pegis (New York: Random House, 1944), 6:704.

18. Ibid.

19. Ibid.

20. Ibid., p. 868.

21. St. Thomas Aquinas, "Summa Contra Gentiles," in *On the Truth of the Catholic Faith*, Book 4, *Salvation*, trans. Charles J. O'Neil (Garden City, New York: Image Books, Doubleday and Company, 1956), p. 299.

22. T. Spencer, *Death and Elizabethan Tragedy* (New York: Pageant Books, 1960), p. 3.

23. Philippe Aries, *The Hour of Our Death*, trans. Helen Weaver (New York: Alfred A. Knopf, 1981), p. 96. "In the Middle Ages the world lived in the shadow of the Church, but this does not mean a total and unquestioning acceptance of Christian dogma."

24. Aquinas, "Summa Theologica," 2a-2ae, Quest. XI, Art. iii.   Ancient Roman law was the root of Papal Canon Law, which gave the Roman Church the title *Societas Perfecta*: a state in its own right, with powers of legislation and the sanction of punishment, even the death penalty, for heretics.

25. Robert Kastenbaum and Ruth Aisenberg, *The Psychology of Death* (New York: Springer-Verlag, 1976), p. 200, and Boase, *Death in the Middle Ages*, pp. 15-16.

26. J. Huizinga, *The Waning of the Middle Ages* (New York: Doubleday, 1963), p. 144.

27. Jacques Choron, *Death and Western Thought* (New York: Collier Books,1963), p. 93.

28. Philippe Aries, *Western Attitudes Toward Death*, trans. P. Ranum (Baltimore, Maryland: Johns Hopkins University Press, 1974), pp. 51-52.

29. Carla Gottlieb, "Modern Art and Death," in *The Meaning of Death*, ed. Herman Feifel (New York: McGraw-Hill, 1959), pp. 171-72.

30. Boase, *Death in the Middle Ages*, p. 31, and Choron, *Death and Western Thought*, p. 91.

31. Aries, *Western Attitudes Toward Death*, p. 34.

32. Ibid., p. 38.

33. An example of this can be seen in *The Triumph of Death* by L. Costa (ca. 1490) fresco, S. Giacomo Maggiore, Bentivoglio Chapel, Bologna.

34. Gottlieb, "Modern Art and Death," p. 172.

35. Brandon, *Judgment of the Dead*, p. 209.

36. Gerald Gruman, "A History of Ideas about Prolongation of Life," *Transactions of the American Philosophical Society* 56, 9(1966): 18.

37. C. H. Haskins, *Renaissance of the Twelfth Century* (Cambridge: Massachusetts: Harvard University Press, 1927), p. viii.

38. George Coffman, "Old Age from Horace to Chaucer," *Speculum* 9, 3 (July 1934): 254.

39. Ibid., pp. 244-45.

40. Skakespeare's theme of the "Seven Ages of Man" is mounted in stained glass windows above his tomb in Collegiate Church of the Holy Trinity, Stratford-upon-Avon, England.

41. Erwin Panofsky, *Studies in Ideology* (New York: Oxford University Press, 1939), p. 92.

42.   John Cohen, "Subjective Time," in *Voices of Time*, ed. Julius Fraser (New York:George Braziller, 1966), pp. 274–75.

43.   Panofsky, *Studies in Ideology*, p. 92.

44.   Cohen, "Subjective Time," p. 275.

45.   J. Hendricks, and C.D.   Hendricks, *Aging in Mass Society: Myths and Realities*, (Boston: Little, Brown & Company, 1981), p. 35; also see L. I. Dublin, *Factbook of Man*, 2d ed. (New York: Macmillan, 1965), p. 394.

46.   Robert Kastenbaum, "Historical Perspectives on Care," in   *Modern Perspectives in the Psychiatry of Old Age*, ed. John G. Howells   (New York: Brunner–Mazel, 1975), p. 433.

47.   Hendricks and Hendricks,   *Aging in Mass Society*, p. 36.

48.   Roger Bacon, *Roger Bacon's Letter Concerning the Marvelous Power of Art and of Nature and Concerning the Nullity of Magic* (Easton, Pennsylvania: A.M.S. Press, 1923), pp. 35–37.

49.   Roger Bacon, *Opus Majus*, trans. Robert Burke (Philadelphia: University of Pennsylvania Press, 1928), p. 618.

50.   Ibid.

51.   Gruman, "Ideas About Prolongation of Life," p. 65.

52.   R. Bacon, *Letter Concerning Power of Art*, p. 36.

53.   K. Sterns and T. Cassirer,   "Gerontological Treatise of the Renaissance," *American Journal of Psychiatry* 102 (1946): 771.

54.   Ibid., p. 772.

55.   St. Augustine, *Confessions and Enchiridion*, ed. and trans. Albert C. Outler (Philadelphia: Westminister Press, 1955), p. 9:1.

56.   This sounds as if Paleotti was echoing Plato, but Plato seems not to have had an influence on Paleotti.

57.   Luigi Cornaro,   *Discourses on the Sober Life*, Discourse 61 in *The Art of Living Long*, ed. William F. Butler (Milwaukee, Wisconsin: W. F. Butler, 1913), pp. 37–113.

58.   Ibid., Discourse 80.

59.   Ibid., Discourse 59.

60.   Ibid., Discourse 65.

61.   Ibid., Discourse 106.

62.   Ibid., Discourse 85.

63.   Ibid., Discourse 58.

64.   Ibid., Discourse 113.

65.   Choron, *Western Attitudes Toward Death*, p. 96.

66.   Ibid., p. 93.

CHAPTER 5

1.   Leon Roth, Commentary in René Descartes' *Discourse on Method*, ed. and trans. Leon Roth (Oxford, England: Clarendon Press, 1937), p. 7.

2.   René Descartes, *Meditations*, trans. Laurence J. Lafleur (Indianapolis, Indiana: Bobbs–Merrill, 1960), p. xvii.

3.   Ibid., "Third Meditation," pp. 107–8.

4.   René Descartes, *Treatise on Man*, trans. Thomas S. Hall (Cambridge, Massachusetts: Harvard University Press, 1972), p. 4. Hall notes that "Automata" were familiar to Descartes especially in sixteenth–century garden fountains containing intricate figures that produced the illusion of self–instigated movement.

5.   Descartes, "Rules for Guidance of Our Native Powers" in *Descartes' Philosophical Writings*, trans. Norman Kemp Smith (New York: Random House, 1958), Rule III, p. 9.

6.   Descartes, *Discourse*, Part 5, p. 41.

7.   Descartes, "Search for Truth," in Smith, *Descartes' Writings*, p. 300.

8.   Joan Boyle and James Morriss,   "Philosophical Roots of the Current Medical Crisis," *Metaphilosophy* 3 and 4 (July and October 1981): 296.

9.   Colin Turbayne, *Myth of Metaphor* (Columbia, South Carolina: University of South

Carolina Press, 1970) p. 69.

10. Boyle and Morriss, "Philosophical Roots," p. 296.

11. René Dubos, *Man Adapting* (New Haven, Connecticut: Yale University Press, 1965), p. 33.

12. G. Sebba, "Time and the Modern Self: Descartes, Rousseau, Beckett," in *The Study of Time*, 5 vols., ed. J. T. Fraser, C>F> Haber and G H Müller, (New York: Springer-Verlag, 1972), 1:453. This is the true Cartesian circle, because it claims that thought and extension, mind and body, exhaust reality by first assuming these categories and defining them as the first principles understood by intuition alone.

13. Descartes, *Discourse*, Part 5, p. 44.

14. Descartes, "The Passions of the Soul" in Smith, *Descartes' Writings*, Articles 5 and 6, pp. 267–68.

15. Descartes, *Descartes par lui-meme*, ed. Samuel S. DeSacy (Paris: Editions du Seuil, 1956), p. 126.

16. Edwin Arthur Burtt, *Metaphysical Foundations of Modern Science*. (Garden City, New York: Doubleday, 1954), p. 122.

17. Herbert Butterfield, *Origins of Modern Science: 1300-1800*, Rev. ed. (New York: Free Press, 1957), p. 136.

18. Descartes, *Treatise on Man*, p. 113.

19. Animals dissected alive were thought of by Descartes as unfeeling and thus having no suffering.

20. Turbayne, *The Myth of Metaphor*, p. 69.

21. Descartes, *Treatise on Man*, p. 115.

22. Michael Cakeshott, ed., *Leviathan* (New York: Collier-Macmillan 1962), p. 19.

23. Phillippe Aries, *The Hour of Our Death* (New York: Alfred A. Knopf, 1981), p. 366.

24. Elizabeth Thomson, "The Role of Physicians in the Humane Societies of the Eighteenth Century," *Bulletin of History of Medicine* 37 (1936): 43. Thomson notes that before the eighteenth century it was commonly thought that "a drowning person was beyond help . . . because the idea of recalling a person from death, even if put forward by physicians of distinguished reputation, was greeted with derision and ridicule." Therefore, the suggestion that persons ought to be resuscitated was a very new idea.

25. There is evidence that wealthy individuals had their own private dissecting laboratories. Amateur anatomists displayed the same kind of fascination in the dissection of a cadaver as one would in taking apart a clock to learn how it worked.

26. Burial grounds were always in the churchyard.

27. Burtt, *Metaphysical Foundations*, pp. 123-24.

28. Charles Sherover, *The Human Experience of Time* (New York: New York University Press, 1975), pp. 97–98.

29. Ibid., p. 100.

30. Sir Isaac Newton, *Mathematical Principles of Natural Philosophy and His System of the World*, trans. Andrew Motte (Berkeley, California: University of California Press, 1947), p. 6.

31. C. Benjamin, "Ideas of Time in the History of Philosophy," in *The Voices of Time*, ed. J. T. Fraser (New York: George braziller, 1966), p. 18.

32. Mark C. Taylor, *Kierkegaard's Pseudonymous Authorship* (Princeton, New Jersey: Princeton University Press, 1975), p. 81.

33. J. D. North, "Monasticism and the First Mechanical Clocks," in *The Study of Time II*, eds. J. T. Fraser, F.C. Haber, G.H. Müller, (New York: Springer-Verlag, 1975), p. 381.

34. The year was probably 1288, but the actual inventor or place of invention is not known. The escapement controls the speed and regularity of the balance wheel by the movement of a notched wheel of which one tooth at a time is permitted to escape from the detaining catch.

35. Lewis Mumford, *Technics and Civilization* (New York: Harcourt Brace and World, 1963), p. 15.

36. Lynn Whyte, *Medieval Technology and Social Change* (Oxford, England: Oxford University Press, 1962), p. 124.

37. M. Clagett, ed., *Nicole Oresme and the Medieval Geometry of Qualities and Motions* (Madison, Wisconsin: University of Wisconsin Press, 1968), pp. 6-11.

38. Johannes Kepler, *Gesammelte Werke*, 4 vols., ed. V. von Dyk and M. Caper (Munich, Germany: Beck, 1938), 15:146.

39. George Woodcock, "The Tyranny of the Clock," in *Politics* 3 (1944): 266.

40. Mumford, *Technics and Civilization*, p. 15.

41. Marshall McLuhan, *Understanding Media* (Boston: Signet Books, 1964), p. 135.

42. Jacques Maritain, *The Dream of Descartes* (New York: Philosophical Library, 1944), p. 25.

43. Burtt, *Metaphysical Foundations*, p. 106.

44. Maritain, *The Dream of Descartes*, p. 29.

45. Floyd Matson, *The Broken Image* (New York: George Braziller, 1964), p. 22.

46. Descartes, *The Search for Truth*, p. 299.

47. Descartes, *Discourse*, Part 6, p. 56.

48. Gerald Gruman, "A History of Ideas about the Prolongation of Life," in *Transactions, American Philosophical Society* 56: 9 (1966): 79.

49. Descartes, *Discourse*, Part 3, pp. 20-21.

50. Ibid., Part 6, p. 45.

51. Ibid., p. 46.

52. René Descartes, "The Description of the Human Body," in *Descartes' Works*, 3 vols., trans. Charles Adam and P. Tannery (Paris: Cerf, 1897-1910), 3: 223-24.

53. Descartes, *Discourse*, Part 5, p. 56.

54. Descartes, "Description of the Human Body", 4: 329.

55. Descartes, *Discourse*, Part 1, p. 4.

56. Ibid., Part 6, p. 49.

57. Descartes, "Letter to Constantyn Huyghens, January 25, 1638" in *Descartes' Works*, 3 vols., ed. & trans. Charles Adam and P. Tannery (Paris: Cerf, 1897-1910), 1: 507.

58. Gruman "History of Ideas," p. 79.

59. Jacques Choron, *Death and Western Thought* (New York:Collier Books, 1963), p. 111.

60. Gruman, "History of Ideas," pp. 551-52, and 581-82, quoting Charles Adam, *Vie et Oeuvres de Descartes: Étude Historique*, Paris, 1910.

61. Descartes, *Treatise on Man*, p. xvii. Comments by Thomas Hall.

62. Butterfield, *Origins of Modern Science*, p. 128.

63. Loren Eiseley, *The Man Who Saw Through Time* (New York: Charles Scribner's Sons, 1973), pp. 29, 32.

64. Francis Bacon, *Works*, 15 vols., ed. James Spedding et. al. (Boston: Taggard & Tompson, 1861), 5: 398.

65. F. Bacon, "The Masculine," in *Works of Francis Bacon*, ed. Peter Shaw (London: J. J. & P. Knapton, 1733), p. 146.

66. Leonell C. Strong, "Observations on Gerontology in the Seventeenth Century," *Journal of Gerontology* 7,4 (1952): 618-19, quoting Francis Bacon, "The Differences of Youth and Old Age," trans. William Rawley, in *The History of Life and Death* (London: I. Okes, 1638), p. 172.

67. Ibid.

68. Ibid., p. 619.

69. René Dubos, *The Dreams of Reason* (New York: Columbia University Press, 1961), p. 41. Bacon, though he spent fourteen years in prison after being condemned by religious authorities for his unorthodox views and methods, was not discouraged from further work on scientific projects. Nevertheless, ecclesiastical proscription prevented his works from exerting a greater influence on the thinkers of his day, as well as the ages following him. Full awareness of the power of the experimental method did not reach the public until the nineteenth century.

70. Strong, "Observations on Gerontology," p. 619.

71. Bacon, *Works*, p. 400. Bacon's imaginary Academy of Science, called "Solomon's House," was a place where, through special diet and medicines such as the "Water of Paradise," life was prolonged and disease rapidly controlled.

72. Eiseley, *The Man Who Saw Through Time*, p. 2.

73. Ibid., p. 21.

CHAPTER 6

1. Benjamin Franklin, *Benjamin Franklin*, 10 vols., ed. Albert H. Smyth (New York: Macmillan, 1905-1907), 1: 196.

2. Benjamin Franklin, *Benjamin Franklin*, 10 vols., ed. John Bigelow (New York: G. P. Putnam's Sons, 1887-1888), 1:174-75.

3. Ernest Cassirer, *Philosophy of the Enlightenment* (Boston: Beacon Press, 1955), p. 50, quoting Bernard Fontenelle, *Conversations on the Plurality of Worlds*.

4. Edwin Arther Burtt, *Metaphysical Foundations of Modern Science* (Garden City, New York: Doubleday, 1954), p. 299.

5. Ibid., p. 300.

6. Aram Vartanian, *LaMettrie's L'Homme Machine* (Princeton, New Jersey: Princeton University Press, 1960), Introductory Monograph, p. 1.

7. Joseph Needham, *Science, Religion and Reality* (New York: George Braziller, 1955), p. 236, quoting Julien de LaMettrie, *L'Homme Machine*.

8. Vartanian, *LaMettrie's L'Homme Machine*, Introductory Monograph, p. 58.

9. Lenora Rosenfield, *From Beast-Machine to Man-Machine* (New York: Octagon Books, 1968), p. 146.

10. Burtt, *Metaphysical Foundations*, p. 301.

11. Philippe Aries, *The Hour of Our Death* (New York: Alfred A. Knopf. 1981) p. 322.

12. Jacques Choron, *Death and Western Thought* (New York: Collier Books, 1963), p. 135, quoting LaMettrie.

13. Paul-Henri d'Holbach, *Système de la nature*, ed. Yvon Balaval (Paris: Hildesheim, G. Olms, 1966).

14. Burtt, *Metaphysical Foundations*, p. 301.

15. Choron, *Death and Western Thought*, p. 135.

16. Aries, *Hour of Our Death*, p. 94.

17. Ibid., p. 331.

18. Gruman, "A History of Ideas about the Prolongation of Life," *Transactions of the American Philosophical Society* 56, 9(1966): 75.

19. Gerald Gruman, "An Historical Introduction to Ideas about Euthanasia," *Omega* 4 (1973): 102.

20. William Pepper, *The Medical Side of Benjamin Franklin* (Philadelphia, Pennsylvania: W.J. Campbell, 1911) p. 35.

21. Nathan Goodman, "Restoration of Life by Sun Rays" in *The Ingenious Dr. Franklin: Selected Scientific Letters*

22. Aries, *Hour of Our Death*, p. 403.

23. Ibid., p. 406.

24. *Encyclopédie, ou Dictionnaire Raisonné des Sciences, des Artes et de Métiers*, 1759-1772, S.v. "Morte."

25. Aries, *Hour of Our Death*, p. 351.

26. Ibid., pp. 250-51.

27. Carl L. Becker, *The Heavenly City of the Eighteenth Century Philosophers* (New Haven, Connecticut: Yale University Press, 1932), p. 31.

28. Ibid.

29. A. C. Crombie, *Medieval and Early Modern Science* (Cambridge, Massachusetts: Harvard University Press, 1963), pp. 313-14.

30. The word "psychology" is derived from the Greek word *psyche*.

31. Floyd Matson, *The Broken Image: Man, Science and Society* (New York: George Braziller, 1964), p. 31.

32. David Hume, *A Treatise of Human Nature*, ed. and trans. V. C. Chappell (New York: Modern Library, 1963), p. 172.

33. Ibid., p. 173.

34. Ibid., p. 174.

35. Ibid.

36. Ibid.

37. John Lyons, *The Invention of the Self* (Carbondale, Illinois: Southern Illinois University Press, 1978), p. 22.

38. David Hume, *On My Life* (London: Hunt & Clark, 1826), p. 62.

39. Gruman, "An Historical . . . Euthanasia," p. 102.

40. *Encyclopédie*, S.v. "Morte."

41. Sir John Floyer, *Gerontological Medicine or Galenic Art of Preserving Old Men's Healths* (London: Isted, 1724), p. 124.

42. Joseph Freeman, "The History of Geriatrics," *Annals of Medical History* 10 (July 1938): 329.

43. Christoph Hufeland, *The Art of Prolonging Life* (London: J. Bell, 1797), 1: 175–76.

44. Ibid., p. 193.

45. Ibid., p. 195.

46. Ibid.

47. Ibid., pp. 193–94.

48. Gruman, "An Historical . . . Euthanasia," p. 102.

49. Frederic Zeman, "Life's Later Years," *Journal of Mt. Sinai Hospital* 10 (October 1944): 944.

50. Ibid., p. 951.

51. William Godwin, *Enquiry Concerning Political Justice and Its Influence on Morals and Happiness*, 3 vols., ed. F.E.L. Priestly (Toronto: University of Toronto Press, 1946; Orig. published, 1798).

52. Ibid., p. ix.

53. Ibid., 1: 8.

54. Ibid., 2: 8.

55. Ibid., 1: 4.

56. Ibid., 2: 88.

57. Ibid., 1: 93.

58. Ibid., 1: 89.

59. Ibid., 3: 21.

60. Ibid., 2: 522.

61. Ibid., 2: 526–527.

62. Ibid., 2: 527.

63. Ibid.

64. Gruman, "History of Ideas . . . Prolongation of Life," p. 87.

65. Marquis Marie Jean de Condorcet, *Sketch for a Historical Picture of the Progress of the Human Mind*, trans. June Barraclough, intro. Stuart Hampshire (New York: Library of Ideas, 1955), p. 173.

66. Ibid., p. ix. Condorcet feared he would be arrested for publicly criticizing a new constitution. He was taken into custody in 1794 and found dead in his cell the next day. His death might possibly be attributed to suicide by poison, but that has not been surely established.

67. Ibid., p. 200.

68. J. Salwyn Schapiro, *Condorcet and the Rise of Liberalism* (New York: Octagon Books, 1963), pp. 189–90 and Chapter 10 passim.

69. de Condorcet, *Sketch for a Historical Picture*, intro. Stuart Hampshire, p. ix.

70. Marquis Marie Jean de Condorcet, *Fragments on Atlantic in Antoine-Nicolas de Condorcet, Oeuvres*, 12 vols., eds. A. Condorcet O'Connor and M. F. Arago (Paris: Firmin Didot Frères, 1847-1849), pp. 621-23.

71. Gruman, "An Historical Introduction . . . Euthanasia," p. 102.

72. Condorcet, *Sketch for a Historical Picture*, pp. 201–2.

73. Jean Jacques Rousseau, *Discourse on the Origin of Inequality* (Amsterdam: M. M. Rey, 1755), p. 141.

74. Jean Jacques Rousseau, *The Confessions of Jean Jacques Rousseau*, ed. and trans. W. Conyngham Mallory (New York: Tudor Publishing Company, 1928), p. 374.

75. Ibid., pp. 400–401.

76. Rousseau, *Discourse*, p. 144.

77. Ibid., p. 115.

78. A "juggernaut" was originally a reincarnation of the Hindu god, Vishnu, whose idol, when rolled along in a large cart at the time of religious festivals, it is said, was so exciting to the people that they sprawled themselves under the wheels and were crushed. The word, therefore, applies to anything that exacts blind devotion or terrible sacrifice.

79. Rousseau, *Confessions*, p. 611.

80. G. Sebba, "Time and the Modern Self: Descartes, Rousseau, Beckett," in *The Study of Time*, ed. J.T. Fraser, C.F. Haber, C.H. Müller (New York: Springer–Verlag, 1972), 1: 456.

81. Rousseau, *Confessions*, p. 3.

82. William Wordsworth, "The Tables Turned," stanza 6, lines 21-24 in *The Complete Poetical Works*, ed. Henry Reed (Philadelphia: Porter and Coates, 1851). All citations from Wordsworth's poetry are from this source.

83. Ibid., stanza 8, lines 29-32.

84. Friedrich von Hardenberg, "Spiritual Songs" in George Macdonald "*Exotics*," (London: Strahan and Company, 1876) p.4.

85. Choron, *Death and Western Thought*, p.157.

86. Ibid.

87. Wordsworth, "Sonnet XXIX," lines 1-8, p.212..

88. Wordsworth, "Intimations of Immortality from Recollections of Early Childhood," stanza X, lines 179-90 p.460-62

89. Simone de Beauvoir, *The Coming of Age*, trans. P. O'Brien (New York: Warner Publishing Company, 1973), p. 659.

90. Thomas McFarland, *Romanticism and the Forms of Ruin* (Princeton, New Jersey: Princeton University Press, 1981), p. 159.

91. Wordsworth, "Resolution and Independence," stanza VII, lines 48-49 181.

92. Percy Bysshe Shelley, "The Daeman of the World," Part I, line 1 and "Queen Mab," Part I, line 1 in *The Complete Poetical Works of Shelley*, ed. Thomas Hutchinson (Oxford: At the Clarendon Press, 1904). All citations of Shelley's poetry are from this source.

93. McFarland, *Romanticism and Forms of Ruin*, p. 15.

94. John Keats,"Why Did I Laugh Tonight?" line 13-14 in *The Poems of John Keats*, ed. Ernest Rhys (London: J. M. Dent and Company, 1906). All citations of Keats poetry are from this source except note 96.

95. Keats, "Ode to a Nightingale," stanza VI, lines 5-8.

96. Keats, *Poetical Works* Vol. 1: "Ben Nevis" lines 9 and 7.

97. David Luke, "How Is It That You Live and What Is It That You Do?" in *Aging and The Elderly*, ed. Stuart Spicker, k. Woodward, D. Van Tassel (New York: Humanities Press, 1978), pp. 231-32.

98. Keats, "On Death," stanzas I and II, lines 1-8.

CHAPTER 7

1. Morse Peckham, *Beyond the Tragic Vision* (New York: George Braziller, 1962), p. 92.

2. Richard Friedenthal, *Goethe: His Life and Times* (Cleveland, Ohio: World Publishing Company, 1965), p. 64.

3. Gerald Gruman," An Historical Introduction to Ideas about Euthansia," Omega 4(1973): 105.

4. Peckham, *Beyond the Tragic Vision*, p. 128.

5. Lester Crocker, *Jean Jacques Rousseau: The Prophetic Voice*, 2 vols. (New York: Macmillan, 1973), 2: 149.

6. Sherover, *The Human Experience of Time* (New York: New York University Press, 1975), p.119.

7. Charles Sherover, *Heidegger, Kant and Time* (Bloomington, Indiana: Indiana University

Press, 1971), p. 4.

8. Immanuel Kant, *Critique of Pure Reason*, trans. Norman K. Smith (New York: St. Martin's Press, 1929), p. 607.

9. Ibid., p. 606.

10. Ibid., p. 22.

11. Plato," Theatetus," 193e.

12. Aristotle," On the Soul" II, 412a, 5–10.

13. John Locke, *An Essay Concerning Human Understanding*, ed. J.J.W. Yolton (New York: J. M. Dent, 1961), p. II.i.2.

14. Kant, *Critique of Pure Reason*, p. 22.

15. Ibid., p. 34.

16. Ibid., p. 80.

17. Sherover, *Heidegger, Kant and Time*, p. 15. Sherover notes that the term "transcendental" has no connection with the term "transcendent" although they both share the implication of "going beyond the immediately given."

18. Kant used the notion of *antinomies* to show inconclusiveness. An antinomy is an unavoidable contradiction or a paradox to pure reason.

19. Kant, *Critique of Pure Reason*, p. 20.

20. Immanuel Kant, *Critique of Practical Reason*, trans. Lewis W. Beck (New York: Bobbs Merrill, 1956), p. 148.

21. Kant, *Critique of Pure Reason*, p. 650.

22. Ibid.

23. Ibid., p. 652.

24. Kant, *Critique of Practical Reason*, p. 127.

25. Ibid.

26. Immanuel Kant, *Foundations of the Metaphysics of Morals*, trans. Lewis W. Beck (New York: Bobbs Merrill, 1959), pp. 18 and 47.

27. Immanuel Kant, *Lecture on Ethics*, trans. L. Infield (New York: Harper Torchbooks, 1963), pp. 148–49.

28. This important distinction between persons and things is taken up later by Martin Heidegger and the existentialists.

29. Kant, *Foundations*, p. 54.

30. Ibid.

31. See Antonio Cua, "Dignity of Persons and Styles of Life," *Proceedings of American Catholic Philosophical Association*, 45 (1971): 120–29.

32. Kant, *Foundations*, p. 54.

33. Kant, *Critique of Pure Reason*, p. 128.

34. Ibid., p. 340.

35. Ibid.

Chapter 8

1. Arthur O'Shaughnessy, "Ode," in *Poems of Arthur O'Shaughnessy*, ed. William A. Percy (New Haven, Connecticut: Yale University Press, 1923), p. 39, stanza 3, lines 23–24. Reprinted with permission of Leroy P. Percy.

2. The period was named after Victoria, the queen of the United Kingdom for more than sixty-three years, the longest in English history. She was born in 1819, crowned in 1838, and died in 1901. The Victorian era is known for advances in science, art and literature, both in England and America.

3. Jerome Buckley, *The Triumph of Time* (Cambridge, Massachusetts: Belknap Press of Harvard University Press, 1966), p. 136.

4. John Morley, *Death, Heaven and the Victorians* (Pittsburgh, Pennsylvania: University of Pittsburgh Press, 1971), p. 11.

5. By "life," Shelley meant "time." In this sense, "The Triumph of Life" referred to the

defeat of man by his fate as a temporal creature.

6. Percy Bysshe Shelley, "The Triumph of Life," stanza 50 and 53, lines 149, 153–154, 159–60 in *The Complete Works of Shelley*, ed.Thomas Hutchinson (Oxford: At the Clarendon Press, 1904).

7. Ibid., p. 511, lines 165-167.

8. O'Shaughnessy, "Ode," stanza 1, lines 7–8.

9. Jerome Buckley, "The Four Faces of Victorian Time," in *Aspects of Time*, ed. C. A. Patrides (Buffalo, New York: University of Toronto Press, 1976), p. 57.

10. Blaise Pascal, *Pensées*, trans. W. F. Trotter (New York: Random House, 1941), p. 75.

11. Buckley, "The Four Faces," p. 57.

12. Ibid., p. 60.

13. Harvey Green, "The Problem of Time in Nineteenth Century America," in *A Time to Mourn: Expressions of Grief in Nineteenth Century America*, ed. Martha Pike and Janice G. Armstrong (Stony Brook, New York: The Museums at Stony Brook, 1980), p. 38.

14. Shelley, "The Triumph of Life,"last stanza, last line.

15. Martin Tropp, *Mary Shelley's Monster* (Boston: Houghton Mifflin, 1976), p. 52.

16. Ibid., p. 65.

17. Ibid., p. 53.

18. In the popular mind the name "Frankenstein" is usually associated with the monster, however, in the original work the monster was nameless and the mad young scientist was Victor Frankenstein.

19. Tropp, *Mary Shelley's Monster*, p. 19.

20. At the end of the book the monster does not die. The last scene depicts the monster as jumping overboard, vowing to immolate itself at the North Pole, and it is soon lost in the distance.

21. Tropp, *Mary Shelley's Monster*, p. 63.

22. Ibid., p. 66.

23. W. Andrew Achenbaum, *Old Age in the New Land: The American Experience Since 1790* (Baltimore, Maryland: Johns Hopkins University Press, 1978), p. 25.

24. Ibid., p. 10.

25. Thomas Bailey, *Records of Longevity* (London: Darton & Company, 1857), pp. 4–5.

26. James Hinton, *The Mystery of Pain: A Book for the Sorrowful* (London: K. Paul, Trench, 1866), chapter 5.

27. Emily Dickinson, "574" in *The Complete Poems of Emily Dickinson*, ed. Thomas H. Johnson (Boston: Little, Brown & Co., 1960), pp. 279–80, stanza 1, lines 1–4, stanza 7, lines 25–28. All citations from E. Dickinson are from this source.

28. Albert Barnes, *The Peaceful Death of the Righteous* (Philadelphia: Henry B. Ashmead, 1858), p. 6.

29. Thomas Cole, "The Ideology of Old Age and Death in American History," *American Quarterly* 31 (Summer 1979): 230–31.

30. Emily Dickinson, "1346", p. 582, stanza 1, lines 1–4, stanza 3, lines 9–12.

31. John Reed, *Victorian Conventions* (Athens, Ohio: Ohio University Press, 1975), pp. 19–20.

32. Cole, "Ideology of Old Age and Death," p. 231.

33. Achenbaum, *Old Age in New Land*, p. 45.

34. Carl Snyder, "The Quest for Prolonged Youth," *Living Age* 251, 10 (November 1906): 323.

35. William James, *Principles of Psychology* (New York: Henry Holt & Company, 1892), p. 328.

36. Cole, "Ideology of Old Age and Death," p. 230.

37. Achenbaum, *Old Age in New Land*, p. 54.

38. Ibid., 54.

39. W. Andrew Achenbaum, "The Obsolescence of Old Age in America, 1865-1914," *Journal of Social History* 8,1 (Fall 1974): 57.

40. David Fisher, *Growing Old in America* (New York: Oxford University Press, 1977), p. 157.

41. Daniel W. Howe, ed., *Victorian America* (Philadelphia: University of Pennsylvania Press, 1976), p. 3.

42. John Morley, *Death, Heaven and the Victorians*, (Pittsburg,Pennsylivania: University of Pittsburg Press, 1971), p.11.

43. Lawrence Taylor, "Symbolic Death: An Anthropological View of Mourning Ritual in the Nineteenth Century," in *A Time to Mourn*, ed. Martha Pike and Janice G. Armstrong, (Stony Brook, New York: Museums at Stony Brook, 1980), p. 39.

44. David Stannard, "Where All Our Steps are Tending," in *A Time to Mourn*, p. 19.

45. Robert Kastenbaum and Ruth Aisenberg, *The Psychology of Death* (New York: Springer-Verlag, 1972), p. 193.

46. Stannard, "Where All Steps Tending," pp. 19-20.

47. Charles O. Jackson, "Death Shall Have No Dominion: The Passing of the World of the Dead in America," in *Death and Dying: A View from Many Cultures*, ed. Richard Kalish (Farmingdale, New York: Baywood Publishing Company, 1980), p. 48.

48. Morley, *Death, Heaven and Victorians*, p. 14.

49. Reed, *Victorian Conventions*, p. 156.

50. David Stannard, ed., *Death in America* (Philadelphia: University of Pennsylvania Press, 1975), p. 41.

51. Reed, *Victorian Conventions*. p. 171.

52. Buckley, "The Four Faces," p. 64.

53. Philippe Aries, *The Hour of Our Death* (New York: Alfred A.Knopf, 1981), p. 571.

54. Timothy Dwight, *Travels in New England and New York* (Cambridge, Massachusetts: Belnap Press, 1969), p. 360.

55. William Cullen Bryant, "The Burial Place," in *The Poetical Works of William Cullen Bryant*, ed. Henry C. Sturges (New York: A.M.S., 1969), pp. 34-35.

56. Edwin M. Betts, *Thomas Jefferson's Garden Book* (Philadelphia: American Philological Society, 1944), pp. 25-27.

57. Stanley French, "The Cemetery as Cultural Institution," in *Death in America*, ed. Stannard, p. 74.

58. H.F. Gould, "A Voice from Mt. Auburn," in *Mourner's Gift* ed. Mary A. Patrick (New York: Van Nostrand and Dwight, 1837), p. 29.

59. Wilson Flagg, *Mount Auburn: Its Scenes, Its Beauties and Its Lessons* (Boston: James Munroe, 1860), p. 37.

60. Pike and Armstrong, "The Cemetery and the Funeral," in *A Time to Mourn*, p. 50.

61. Morley, *Death, Heaven and Victorians*, p. 11.

62. Stannard, "Where All Our Steps are Tending," p. 28.

63. Jackson, "Death Shall Have No Dominion," p. 53.

64. Ibid., pp. 53, 54.

CHAPTER 9

1. John Cruickshank, *Albert Camus and the Literature of Revolt* (London: Oxford University Press, 1960), p. 3.

2. St. Augustine, *Confessions of St. Augustine*, trans. Rex Warner (New York: New American Library of World Literature, Mentor-Omega Books, 1963), pp. xi, 27.

3. Ibid., p. 25.

4. Ibid., p. 26.

5. Ibid., p. 20.

6. Ibid.

7. Ibid., p. 14.

8. Hans Georg Gadamer, "Western Views of the Inner Experience of Time and the Limits of Thought," in *Time and Philosophies*, ed. Paul Ricoeur et. al. (Paris: UNESCO Press, 1977), p. 42.

9. Ibid., p. 27.

10.   Charles Sherover, *Heidegger, Kant and Time* (Bloomington, Indiana: Indiana University Press, 1971), p. xi.

11.   Martin Heidegger, *Being and Time*, trans. John Macquarie and Edward Robinson (New York: Harper and Row, 1962).

12.   Ibid., p. 1.

13.   The method Heidegger invoked in defense of his interpretation of time was the phenomenological mode of inquiry, which sought to search out the basic structures used in organizing experience.

14.   Heidegger, *Being and Time*, p. 41.

15.   Ibid., pp. 392-93.

16.   Charles Sherover, *The Human Experience of Time* (New York: New York University Press, 1975), p. 456.

17.   Heidegger, *Being and Time*, pp. 456, 464.

18.   Ibid., p. 380, and section 65-69, p. 81.

19.   Ibid., p. 477.

20.   Ibid., section 39, p. 81.

21.   Kant had anticipated this note of dread (*angst*), and the existentialists make it one of their central categories. Dread arises from the way humans *are* in this life and from consciousness of their own mortality.

22.   Heidegger, *Being and Time*, pp. 477-78. Quotation marks are the author's.

23.   Ibid., p. 266.

24.   Ibid., p. 598.

25.   Sherover, *Human Experience of Time*, p. 465.

26.   A. N. Whitehead, *Science and the Modern World* (New York: Free Press, 1967), p. 47.

27.   A. N. Whitehead, *Process and Reality* (New York: Free Press, 1929), p. 47.

28.   Ibid., p. 141.

29.   Ibid., pp. 20-21.

30.   Whitehead, *Science and the Modern World*, pp. 3-4.

31.   Ibid., p. 4.

32.   Alfred North Whitehead, "Time," in *Concept of Nature*, ed. A. N. Whitehead (Cambridge, England: Cambridge University Press, 1920), p. 73.

33.   Ibid., pp. 72-73.

34.   Whitehead, *Process and Reality*, pp. 531-32.

35.   Ibid.

36.   Ibid.

37.   Whitehead, "Time," p. 73.

38.   I. Prigogine and Isabelle Stengers, *Order Out of Chaos* (New York: Bantam Books, 1984), p. 310.

39.   David Bohm, *From Being to Becoming* (San Francisco, California: W. H. Freeman & Co., 1980), pp. xii-xiii.

40.   John L. Lucas, *A Treatise on Time and Space* (London: Methuen and Company, 1973), p. 256.

41.   Ibid., p. 257.

42.   Ibid.

43.   Ibid.

44.   Erwin Schrödinger, *What Is Life and Mind and Matter?* (Cambridge, England: Cambridge University Press, 1967), p. 127.

45.   Ibid., p. 128.

46.   Norwood R. Hanson, *Patterns of Discovery* (New York: Dover Books, 1954), p. 385.

47.   Nelson Goodman, *Ways of Worldmaking* (Indianapolis, Indiana: Hackett Publishing Co., 1978), p. 22.

48.   C.P. Snow, *Two Cultures: A Second Look* (New York: New American Library, 1963), p. 62.

49.   Stephen C. Pepper, *World Hypotheses* (Berkeley, California: University of California Press, 1942), p. 4.

50.   Stephen C. Pepper, *Concept and Quality* (LaSalle, Illinois: Open Court, 1966), p. 4.

51. Ibid.

52. Stephen C. Pepper, "The Orders of Time," in *The Problem of Time*, University of California Publications in Philosophy, Vol. 18 (Berkeley, California: University of California Press, 1934).

CHAPTER 10

1. The popular belief is that the first words Samuel F.B. Morse tapped out on the telegraph he invented in 1835 were "What hath God wrought?" However, records indicate that the first words were actually, "Attention universe."

2. Whitehead, *Adventures of Ideas* (New York: Free Press, 1933), pp. 92–93.

3. Alfred Korzybski, *Science and Sanity* (Lakeville, Connecticut: International Non-Aristotelian Library Publishing Company, 1958), p. 90.

4. Plato, "Timaeus," 47 a–c.

5. Immanuel Kant, *Critique of Practical Reason*, trans. Lewis W. Beck (New York: Bobbs-Merrill, 1956), p. 127.

6. W. Andrew Achenbaum, *Old Age in the New Land: The American Experience Since 1790* (Baltimore, Maryland: The Johns Hopkins University Press, 1979), p. 164.

7. Louis Harris and Associates, Inc., *The Myth and Reality of Aging in America* (Washington, D.C.: National Council on Aging, 1975), p. 193.

8. Louis Harris and Associates, Inc. *Aging in the Eighties: An America in Transition* (Washington, D.C.: National Council on Aging, 1975), pp. 8, 13.

9. Richard H. and James A. Davis, *TV's Image of the Elderly: A Practical Guide for Change* (Lexington, Massachusetts: D.C. Heath & Company, 1985), p. 55.

10. Michel Philibert, "Phenomenological Approaches to Images of Aging", in *Philosophical Foundations of Gerontology* ed. Patrick M. McKee (New York: Human Sciences Press,1982), p. 321.

11. Robert Blauner, "Death and Social Structure," in *Aging in America*, ed. Cary Kart and Barbara Manard (Sherman Oaks, California: Alfred Publishing Company, 1976), p. 538.

12. Durk Pearson and Sandy Shaw, *Life Extension* (New York: Warner Books, 1980), p. 82.

13. Gail Sheehy, *Pathfinders* (New York: William Morrow & Co., 1981), p.18–19.

14. Ibid., p. 54.

15. Ibid.

16. Ibid., p. 225.

17. Ibid., pp. 226–27.

18. American Association of Retired Persons and the Administration on Aging, *A Profile of Older Americans* (Washington, D.C.: U.S. Department of Health and Human Services, 1984), p. 2.

19. Sumner Elliott, "The Cracked Lens," *Harper's*, Dec. 1960, p. 81.

20. Robert Sklar, *Movie Made America* (New York: Vantage Books, 1978), p. 269.

21. Lori Breslow, "TV and Our Sense of Time," *Et Cetera*, Spring 1981, p. 88.

22. George Gerbner et al., "Aging with Television: Images on TV Drama and Conceptions of Social Reality," *Journal of Communications* 30 (1980): 37–47.

23. Craig Aronoff, "Old Age in Prime Time," *Journal of Communications* 24, 4 (Autumn 1974): 86–87.

24. Louis Harris and Associates, Inc., *Aging in the Eighties*, p. 12.

25. Davis and Davis, *TV's Image of the Elderly*, p. 54.

26. D. H. Novak, "Changes in Physicians' Attitudes Toward Telling the Cancer Patient," *Journal of the American Medical Association* 241 (March 2, 1979): 900.

27. George Engel, "The Need for a New Medical Model: A Challenge to Biomedicine," *Science* 169 (April 1977): 135.

28. Horacio Fabrega, "The Need for an Ethnomedical Science," *Science* 189 (September, 1975): 969.

29. Engel, "The Need for a New Medical Model," passim.

30. James E. Morriss, "A Descriptive Study of Medical Training in Interpersonal Communication and the Care of Children Who May Die" (Ph.D. dissertation, University of

Michigan, 1981), pp. 16–21.

31. David Gelman et. al., "Patient Heal Thyself," *Newsweek* (March 25, 1985): 25.

32. John Vinocure, "The Soul Searching Continues for Graham Greene," *New York Times Magazine*, March 3, 1985, p. 37.

33. Fox Butterfield, "Experts Disagree on Childrens' Worries About Nuclear War," *New York Times*, October 16, 1984, p. 16.

34. Lewis Thomas, "Cellular Pathology in Aging," Lecture at Brookhaven Laboratory, Brookhaven, New York (February 1985).

35. David Hultsch, "Changing Perspectives on Basic Research in Adult Learning and Memory," *Educational Gerontology* 2 (1977): 367–382.

36. Gisela Labourie-Vief and Michael J. Chandler, "Cognitive Development: Idealism vs. Contextualism" in *Life Span: Developmental Psychology*, 2 vols., ed. Paul Baltes (New York: Academic Press, 1978), 1: 187–209.

37. For a study of this see Cyril P. Svoboda, "Senescence in Western Philosophy," *Educational Gerontology* 2 (1977): 219 35.

38. Robert H. Pollack, "Regression Revisited: Perceptuo-Cognitive Performance in the Aged," in *Toward a Holistic Developmental Psychology*, eds. S. Wapner and B. Kaplan (Hillsdale, New Jersey: Lawrence Erlbaum Associates, Publishers, 1983), pp. 133–42.

39. J. E. Birren, "A Brief History of the Psychology of Aging," *Gerontologist* 1,2 (June 1961): 67–77.

40. George Minot, *The Problems of Age, Growth and Death* (New York: Putnam and Sons, 1908); E. Metchnikoff, *The Prolongation of Life* (New York: Putnam and Sons, 1908); C. M. Child, *Senescence and Rejuvenescence* (Chicago, Illinois: University of Chicago Press, 1915).

41. G. Stanley Hall, *Senescence: The Second Half of Life* (New York: D. Appleton, 1922).

42. Ibid., p. 366.

43. Ibid., p. 100.

44. Arnold Gesell and Frances L. Ilg, *The Infant and the Child in the Culture Today* (New York: Harper, 1943), p. 346.

45. Robert Havighurst, *Developmental Tasks and Education*, 3d ed. (New York: Longman, 1972), p. 42.

46. Daniel Levinson, Charlotte N. Darrow, et al., *The Seasons of Man's Life* (New York: Alfred A. Knopf, 1978).

47. Margaret Huyck and William Hoyer, *Adult Development and Aging* (Belmont, California: Wadsworth Publishing Company, 1982), p. 217.

48. Secunda, *By Youth Possessed*, p. 35.

49. Ibid.

50. Erdman Palmore, *Social Patterns in Normal Aging: Findings from the Duke Longitudinal Study,1953–1981* (Durham, North Carolina: Duke University Press, 1981), p. 108. Erdman Palmore, ed., *Handbook on the Aged in the United States* (Westport, Connecticut: Greenwood Press, 1984), p. xxv.

51. Douglas W. Nelson, "Alternative Images of Old Age as the Basis of Policy," in *Age or Need*, ed. Bernice Neugarten (Beverly Hills, California: Sage Publications, 1982), pp. 131–70.

52. Palmore, *Handbook*, p. xxv.

53. Labouvie-Vief and Chandler, "Cognitive Development," p. 197; Pollack, "Regression Revisited," p. 134.

54. Max Schur, *Freud: Living and Dying* (New York: International Universities Press, Inc., 1972), p. 358.

55. Sigmund Freud, *Gesammelte Werke*, 18 vols., ed. C. Geordnet (London: Imago Publishing Co., 1940), 10: p. 342.

56. Paul Ricoeur, *Freud and Philosophy: An Essay on Interpretation*, trans. Denis Savage (New Haven, Connecticut: Yale University Press, 1970), p. 329.

57. Sigmund Freud, "Thoughts on War and Death," in *Gesammelte Werke*, 10: p. 355.

58. Schur, *Freud, Living and Dying*, p. 358.

59. Ernest Becker, *Denial of Death* (New York: Free Press, Macmillan, 1973), Chapters 2 and 4.

60. Ibid., pp. 218-19.

61. Sam Keen, "A Day of Loving Combat: A Sketch of Ernest Becker," in *Readings in Aging and Death*, ed. S. Zarit (New York: Harper & Row, 1977-1978), p. 304.

62. James Carse, *Death and Existence* (New York: John Wiley and Sons, 1980), p. viii.

63. Robert J. Parker and H. Gerjouy, "Life-Extension: The State of the Art," in *Life-Span: Values and Life Extending Technologies*, ed. Robert Veatch (New York: Harper and Row, 1979), pp. 7-8.

64. Ibid., p. 8.

65. Emil Freireich, M.D., paper delivered at Seventh Annual Euthanasia Conference, New York, December 1974. Printed in *Death and Decisions* by Euthanasia Educational Council, p. 12.

BIBLIOGRAPHY

Achenbaum, W. Andrew. *Old Age in the New Land: The American Experience Since 1790*. Baltimore, Maryland: Johns Hopkins University Press, 1979.

Aries, Philippe. *The Hour of Our Death*, translated by Helen Weaver. New York: Alfred A. Knopf, 1981.

————. *Images of Man and Death*, translated by Janet Lloyd. Cambridge, Massachusetts: Harvard University Press, 1986.

————. *Western Attitudes Toward Death*, translated by P. Ranum. Baltimore: Johns Hopkins University Press, 1974.

Becker, Carl L. *The Heavenly City of the Eighteenth Century Philosophers*. New Haven, Connecticut: Yale University Press, 1932.

Boase, T.S.R. *Death in the Middle Ages*. New York: McGraw-Hill, 1972.

Boman, Thorleif. *Hebrew Thought Compared with Greek*, translated by J. Moreau. Philadelphia: Westminster Press, 1966.

Boyle, Joan, and Morriss, James E. "Philosophical Roots of the Current Medical Crisis." *Metaphilosophy* 3 and 4. (July and October 1981): 284-303.

Brandon, S.G.F. *The Judgment of the Dead*. New York: Charles Scribner's Sons, 1967.

Buckley, Jerome. *The Triumph of Time*. Cambridge, Massachusetts: Belknap Press, 1966.

Butler, Robert. *Why Survive? Being Old in America*. New York: Harper and Row, 1975.

Carse, James. *Death and Existence: A Conceptual History of Human Mortality*. New York: John Wiley and Sons, 1980.

Choron, Jacques. *Death and Western Thought*. New York: Collier Books, 1963.

Death Education: Special Issue on Death in Contemporary America. Vol. 6, no. 2 (Summer 1982):1-213.

Eckart, Roy. "Death in the Judaic and Christian Traditions." *Soul Research* 39: 3 (Autumn 1972): 489-95.

Fisher, David. *Growing Old in America*. New York: Oxford University Press, 1977.

Fraser, Julius T. *Voices of Time*. New York: George Braziller, 1966.

————, Haber, F.C. and Muller G.H., eds. *The Study of Time: Proceedings of Conferences of the International Society for the Study of Time*. vols. 1-3. New York: Springer- Verlag, 1972-1978.

Gadamer, Hans Georg. "Western Views of the Inner Experience of Time and the Limits of Thought." In *Time and Philosophies*, edited by Paul Ricoeur et al. Paris: UNESCO Press, 1977 pp. 38-45.

Gatch, Milton. *Death: Meaning and Morality in Christian Thought and Contemporary Culture*. New York: Seabury Press, 1969.

Goodman, Nelson. *Ways of Worldmaking*. Indianapolis, Indiana: Hackett Publishing Company,

1978.

Gruman, Gerald. "An Historical Introduction to Ideas about Euthanasia." *Omega* 4 (1973): 87-138.

————. "A History of Ideas about the Prolongation of Life." *Transactionsof the* American Philosophical Society 56, 9 (1966): 5-98.

Haynes, Maria. "The Supposedly Golden Age of the Aged in Ancient Greece." *Gerontologist* 2 (June 1962): 93-99.

Huizinga, J. *The Waning of the Middle Ages*. New York: Doubleday, 1963.

Kalish, Richard, ed. *Death and Dying: Views from Many Cultures*. Farmingdale, New York: Baywood Publishing Company, 1980.

Kart, Cary, and Barbara Manard. *Aging in America*. Sherman Oaks, California: Alfred Publishing Company, 1976.

Kastenbaum, Robert, and Aisenberg, Ruth. *The Psychology of Death*. New York: Springer-Verlag, 1976.

Leviton, Dan, and Wendt, William. "Death Education: Toward Individual and Global Well Being." *Death Education* 7 (1983): 369-84.

Louis Harris and Associates, Inc. *The Myth and Reality of Aging in America*. Washington, D.C.: National Council on Aging, 1975.

Lyons, John. *The Invention of the Self*. Carbondale, Illinois: Southern Illinois University Press, 1978.

Morley, John. *Death Heaven and the Victorians*. Pittsburg, Pennsylvania: University of Pittsburg Press, 1971.

McKee, Patrick M., ed. *Philosophical Foundations of Gerontology*. New York: Human Sciences Press, 1982.

Mullenburg, James. "The Biblical View of Time." *Harvard Theological Review* 56: 4 (October 1961): 225-52.

Palmore, Erdman. *Social Patterns in Normal Aging: Findings from the Duke Longitudinal Study 1955-1981*. Durham, North Carolina: Duke University Press, 1981.

Panofsky, Edwin. *Studies in Iconology: Humanistic Themes in the Art of the Renaissance*. New York: Harper and Row, 1939.

Pepper, Stephen C. "Metaphor in Philosophy." In *Dictionary of the History of Ideas*, edited by Philip P. Wiener. New York: Charles Scribner's Sons, 1973, pp. 196-201.

————. "The Orders of Time." In *The Problem of Time*, University of California Publications in Philosophy, Vol. 18. Berkeley, California: University of California Press, 1934.

————. "Philosophy and Metaphor." *Journal of Philosophy* 25 (March 1928): 130-32.

————. *World Hypotheses*. Berkeley, California: University of California Press, 1942.

Pike, Martha, and Armstrong, Janice G., eds. *A Time to Mourn:Expressions of Grief in Nineteenth Century America*. Stony Brook, New York: The Museums at Stony Brook, 1980.

Priestley, J. B. *Man and Time*. Garden City, New York: Doubleday, 1964.

Prigogine, Ilya, and Stengers, Isabelle. *Order Out of Chaos*. New York: Bantam Books, 984.

Quinones, Ricardo J. *The Renaissance Discovery of Time*. Cambridge, Massachusetts: Harvard University Press, 1972.

Reed, John. *Victorian Conventions*. Athens: Ohio University Press, 1975.

Richardson, Bessie E. *Old Age Among the Ancient Greeks*. New York: Greenwood Press, 1969.

Rosenfield, Lenora. *From Beast-Machine to Man-Machine*. New York: Octagon Books, 1968.

Secunda, Victoria. *By Youth Possessed: The Denial of Age in America*. Indianapolis, Indiana: Bobbs-Merrill Company, 1984.

Sherover, Charles. *Heidegger, Kant and Time*. Bloomington, Indiana: Indiana University Press, 1971.

————. *The Human Experience of Time*. New York: New York University Press, 1975.

Spector, Samuel. "Old Age and the Sages." *International Journal of Aging and Human Development* 4 (1973): 199-209.

Spencer, T. *Death and Elizabethan Tragedy*. New York: Pageant Books, 1960.

Spicker, Stuart. *Aging and the Elderly*. Atlantic Highlands, New Jersey: Humanities Press, 1978.

Stannard, David, ed. *Death in America.* Philadelphia: University of Pennsylvania Press, 1975.

Tiso, Francis, ed. *Aging: Spiritual Perspectives.* Lake Worth, Florida: Opera Pia
    International, Sunday Publications, 1982.

Turbayne, Colin. *The Myth of Metaphor.* Columbia, South Carolina: University of South Carolina
    Press, 1970.

Veatch, Robert, ed. *Life Span: Values and Life Extending Technologies.* New York: Harper and
    Row, 1979.

Zerubavel, Evister. *Hidden Rhythms.* Chicago: University of Chicago Press, 1981.

INDEX